An Armada Thr

Three Gre
Three Investigators Stories

Armada

Three Investigators Mysteries availabe in Armada

1 The Secret of Terror Castle
2 The Mystery of the Stuttering Parrot
3 The Mystery of the Whispering Mummy
4 The Mystery of the Green Ghost
5 The Mystery of the Vanishing Treasure
6 The Secret of Skeleton Island
7 The Mystery of the Fiery Eye
8 The Mystery of the Silver Spider
9 The Mystery of the Screaming Clock
10 The Mystery of the Moaning Cave
11 The Mystery of the Talking Skull
12 The Mystery of the Laughing Shadow
13 The Secret of the Crooked Cat
14 The Mystery of the Coughing Dragon
15 The Mystery of the Flaming Footprints
16 The Mystery of the Nervous Lion
17 The Mystery of the Singing Serpent
18 The Mystery of the Shrinking House
19 The Secret of Phantom Lake
20 The Mystery of Monster Mountain
21 The Secret of the Haunted Mirror
22 The Mystery of the Dead Man's Riddle
23 The Mystery of the Invisible Dog
24 The Mystery of Death Trap Mine
25 The Mystery of the Dancing Devil
26 The Mystery of the Headless Horse
27 The Mystery of the Magic Circle
28 The Mystery of the Deadly Double
29 The Mystery of the Sinister Scarecrow
30 The Secret of Shark Reef
31 The Mystery of the Scar-Faced Beggar
32 The Mystery of the Blazing Cliffs
33 The Mystery of the Purple Pirate
34 The Mystery of the Wandering Caveman
35 The Mystery of the Kidnapped Whale
36 The Mystery of the Missing Mermaid
37 The Mystery of the Two-Toed Pigeon
38 The Mystery of the Smashing Glass
39 The Mystery of the Trail of Terror
40 The Mystery of the Rogues' Reunion

The Three Investigators in

The Mystery of the Coughing Dragon
The Mystery of Death Trap Mine
The Mystery of the Magic Circle

Armada

This Armada *Three Investigators Three-in-One* was first published in the U.K. in Armada in 1987 by William Collins Sons & Co. Ltd
8 Grafton Street, London W1X 3LA

Armada is an imprint of the Children's Division, part of the Collins Publishing Group

Published pursuant to agreement with Random House, Inc., New York

Printed in Great Britain by
William Collins Sons & Co. Ltd, Glasgow

1
The Mystery of the Coughing Dragon

Text by Nick West

The Mystery of the Coughing Dragon was
first published in the U.K. in a single volume
in hardback in 1971 by William Collins Sons & Co. Ltd,
First published in Armada in 1974

Contents

	Introduction by Alfred Hitchcock	9
1	Mysterious Beginnings	11
2	Horror from the Sea	18
3	The Test of Terror	29
4	A Surprising Hand	36
5	Trouble Below!	42
6	Trapped!	46
7	A Mysterious Warning	52
8	A Forced Retreat	58
9	Message from a Ghost	67
10	The Death of Seaside	70
11	Terror in the Night	78
12	The Grip of Fear	90
13	Jest of the Joker	96
14	Start of a Dragon Hunt	106
15	Questions and Answers	112
16	Return to Danger	120
17	Mystery of the Old Tunnel	128
18	Caught!	140
19	A Desperate Situation	145
20	Alfred Hitchcock Offers a Hand	154

Introduction by Alfred Hitchcock

THIS INTRODUCTION is solely for the purpose of acquainting latecomers with The Three Investigators. If you have met them before, you are under no obligation to read it.

The Three Investigators are an enterprising firm of youthful detectives, amateurs perhaps, but remarkably effective in achieving their goal, namely, solving mysteries.

By his own admission, Jupiter Jones is the leader-in-residence and the brains of the trio. Pete Crenshaw, the most athletic member, assists on missions that call for his kind of contribution. Bob Andrews is in charge of Records and Research. All together, a lively team.

The boys reside in Rocky Beach, a small town some miles from Hollywood, close to the Pacific Ocean. Their headquarters is a converted mobile home trailer located in the Jones Salvage Yard, which is run by Jupiter's aunt and uncle. The trailer has a small office, a lab, a darkroom and equipment which the boys rebuilt from junk in the yard. It can be entered by certain secret passages that are best negotiated by youthful individuals.

Now that you know all that is needed, I shall remove myself from the premises so that you may get on with the real entertainment.

ALFRED HITCHCOCK

1

Mysterious Beginnings

"I WONDER," Jupiter Jones said one morning, "how we would go about attempting the biggest robbery ever seen in this area."

His two companions reacted with surprise. Bob Andrews dropped the stack of small cards he was feeding into their old printing press. Pete Crenshaw, who was mending an old radio, jerked and saw his screwdriver glance off in an erratic arc.

"What was that you said?" Pete asked, trying to smooth out the jagged scratch he'd made on the wooden back of the radio.

"I said I wonder how we would go about attempting the biggest robbery ever tried in this area," Jupiter repeated. "That is, if we were master criminals."

"While you're wondering," Pete said, "try to find out what happens to us after we get caught. I heard somewhere that crime doesn't pay."

Bob Andrews picked up the scattered cards he had dropped. "I don't think we'd be good at being master criminals. I can't even master putting cards into this printing press."

"It was merely a thought," said Jupiter. "After all, we are investigators. It occurs to me that if we could imagine a well-planned crime, we'd be ahead when it came to solving it. All we need to do is reverse our thinking and assume the anti-social mind of a master-mind criminal."

Pete nodded. "That's a neat idea, Jupe. But first I've got to reverse the thinking of the last owner of this radio. He tried to mend it himself and got the wires all twisted. After that, I'll be willing to play mastermind games with you."

The three boys, who called themselves The Three Investigators, were in Jupiter's workshop section of the Jones Salvage Yard. Secluded here, under a six-foot roof extending from the junk yard's high fence, they worked on repairing junk that Jupiter's Uncle Titus bought. They used part of the profits for pocket money and part for such luxuries as the telephone in their secret headquarters.

Pete finished tightening a screw on the radio and held it up proudly for Jupiter's inspection. "This job ought to be worth at least three dollars to your uncle," he said. "Now he can sell it as a working radio instead of the piece of busted junk it was when it came in here."

Jupiter smiled. "Uncle Titus isn't given to throwing his money about carelessly. I suggest you try it first and see if it works."

Pete shrugged and snapped a small dial. "It works, all right," he said. "Listen."

The radio hummed, spluttered and came to life. An announcer's voice was heard, apparently well into his news broadcast. "Authorities continue to be stumped," he said, "over the mysterious happenings in Seaside. Within the past week, five dogs have been reported missing. The pet owners are puzzled over the disappearance of their animals. . . . Now, for news overseas, we take you to—"

"Turn it off, Pete," Jupiter said.

Pete switched the dial to off. "How about that?" he said. "Five missing dogs. Evidently there's a mad dognapper on the loose."

"I think we've got the master criminal Jupe was talking about," Bob said, grinning. "He's going to steal all the dogs he can and corner the market. Then, when people are willing to meet his price, he'll unload and make a fortune."

Jupiter sat pinching his lower lip, a sign that his mental machinery was moving into high gear. "Odd," he said finally.

"What's odd?" Bob asked. "You mean the number of dogs stolen? Five is a good odd number, all right."

Jupiter shook his head, frowning. "No, I was referring to the dogs reported missing within the week. Usually when pets disappear, it happens at irregular intervals, rather than within the short span of one week."

"Well, it must be like I said," Bob answered. "There's this master criminal loose with this mad plan of getting control of the doggie market. Maybe he intends knocking down the price of hamburger meat, in addition to selling the stolen dogs at a handsome profit."

Jupiter smiled thinly. "Nice try. But it doesn't answer the question. Why five missing dogs in one week? Another question is, why haven't we been contacted to investigate these mysterious disappearances?"

"Perhaps they're not so mysterious," Pete said. "Sometimes dogs roam away from home and it takes them longer to get back. That's my guess."

"I agree with Pete," Bob said. "The report didn't mention the dogs being valuable. Just five missing dogs."

Jupiter nodded slowly and reluctantly. "Perhaps you two are right," he admitted. "It may be just a freak coincidence, much as I dislike making such an assumption."

The other two boys smiled. It was Jupiter's habit of using long words whenever possible, apart from his keen deductive abilities as an investigator, that endeared him to them and made him the acknowledged leader of the three.

"I wonder," said Jupe, "how we can solve the mystery without being asked to by any of the pet owners."

Bob and Pete looked at each other blankly. "What mystery?" Pete demanded. "I thought we agreed it was just a freak happening, not a mystery."

"Perhaps," Jupiter said. "But we are investigators, and Seaside is south of here, not too far away. Apparently our fame as investigators is less than we imagined. We should do something about it."

Bob motioned to the stack of cards he had placed in the old printing press. "That's just what I'm doing, Jupe," he said. "Printing new business cards. A fresh batch."

"A good idea, Bob," Jupiter said. "But I was thinking of something else. We will have to be better known, so that when strange things happen, people will think immediately of The Three Investigators of Rocky Beach, California."

Bob threw up his hands. "Well gosh, Jupe, how do you propose doing that? We can't afford to take a TV commercial or hire sky writers."

"I know," Jupiter said. "I suggest we go immediately to Headquarters and have a meeting to discuss ways and means of getting the name of The Three Investigators known to more people."

He got up immediately without waiting for an answer. Bob and Pete exchanged looks, shrugged and followed.

"What I like about you, Jupe," Pete said, smiling, "is the democratic way you run things. I mean, the way we always take a vote before deciding on anything."

The boys moved a piece of old iron grating hidden by the printing press, uncovering the mouth of a large section of corrugated pipe. They crawled into it, replaced the grating, then went forward on hands and knees about forty feet. The pipe went underground some of the way, then ran between some nondescript iron beams. It opened at the other end directly under the mobile trailer which the boys had converted into Headquarters. When Jupiter's uncle, Titus Jones, found he couldn't sell the old trailer, he had given Jupiter and his friends permission to use it.

The boys pushed a trap-door upwards and scrambled through. Then they were inside a tiny office fitted with a desk, a few chairs, a typewriter, filing cabinet and a telephone. Jupiter had connected a microphone and radio loudspeaker to the telephone, which permitted the boys to listen to any phone conversation together. The remainder of the trailer consisted of a tiny darkroom, a miniature lab and a washroom.

Because the trailer was surrounded by piles of junk outside, it was dark inside. Pete switched on the light over the desk.

At that moment the telephone rang.

The boys looked at one another. Hardly anyone ever phoned them.

After the second ring, Jupiter reached for it, switching on the little radio loudspeaker.

"Jupiter Jones?" asked a woman's voice. "Alfred Hitchcock is calling."

"Wow!" Bob yelled. "Maybe he has another good case for us!" Ever since Mr Hitchcock, the famous film director, had learned of The Three Investigators, he had put them on several cases.

"Hello, young Jones!" It was Mr Hitchcock speaking. "Are you and your friends busy on a case at the moment?"

"No, sir," Jupiter said. "But according to the law of averages we should find something interesting soon."

Mr Hitchcock chuckled.

"Law of averages, indeed!" he said. "If you're not busy, I have something for you. An old film director friend of mine can use some help."

"We'd be glad to try, Mr Hitchcock," Jupiter said. "What is your friend's problem?"

Mr Hitchcock hesitated, as if he were trying to sum up a difficult situation in a few words.

"It appears to be dog trouble," he said finally. "That is to say, he told me on the telephone a little while ago that his dog is missing."

Jupiter's eyes brightened. "Would your friend happen to be a resident of the town of Seaside, Mr Hitchcock?" he asked.

There was a brief silence.

When Mr Hitchcock came on again, he sounded thunderstruck. "He does live in Seaside, for a fact, young Jones. Now how on earth did you deduce that?"

"Merely putting a few odd occurrences together," Jupiter said.

"Remarkable," Mr Hitchcock was saying. "Quite remarkable, really. I'm pleased that you are still alert and not permitting your organization to become stagnant with conceit and boredom."

Jupiter grinned. "Not a chance, Mr Hitchcock. But you said that your friend 'appears' to be having dog trouble. You put stress on the word 'appears,' sir. Was that your intention?"

"As a matter of fact," Mr Hitchcock said, "you have

guessed quite accurately what I was intending to communicate. I don't believe this is an ordinary case, at all. When you think of it, no case that involves a dragon can be considered ordinary. Wouldn't you agree?"

Jupiter cleared his throat. "A dragon?"

"Yes, my boy. My friend's house overlooks the ocean, and there are caves running beneath it. The night that his dog disappeared, my friend insists he saw a rather large dragon emerge from the ocean and enter one of the caves underneath his dwelling."

There was a stunned silence.

"Well, what do you say, my boy? Are you and your companions willing to try to unravel this mystery?"

Jupiter was so excited, he started to stutter. "J-j-just give me your friend's name and address, sir!" he said. "This sounds as if it could be our most exciting case!"

He wrote down the information Mr Hitchcock gave, promised to report all progress, and hung up. He looked at Pete and Bob triumphantly.

"Anything about a dragon living in our times should be investigated. Don't you agree?"

Bob nodded. Pete shrugged.

"You seem to have some reservations, Pete," Jupiter said.

"You made only one mistake," Pete said. "You told Mr Hitchcock it could be our most exciting case."

"Well, yes, I did," Jupiter replied. "Don't you agree?"

"Not entirely," Pete said.

"What would you have said, then?"

"As long as there's a dragon in it," Pete said, "I would have said—this could be our *last* case!"

2

Horror from the Sea

The town of Seaside, where Mr Hitchcock's film director friend lived, was about twenty miles away along the Pacific Coast Highway. Hans, one of the two Bavarian yard helpers, had a collection and delivery to make in the area after lunch. Jupiter got permission from his Aunt Mathilda to be taken along with his friends in the small junk yard truck.

Jupiter's aunt fed them all, and then they hurried out and piled into the front with Hans. Jupiter gave him the address, and they were soon on the smooth Coast Highway travelling south.

"You've had time for a little research, Bob," Jupiter said. "What can you tell us about dragons?"

"A dragon," Bob said, "is a mythical monster, usually represented as a large reptile with wings and claws, breathing out fire and smoke."

"I haven't done any research," Pete interrupted. "But I think Bob left out something important. Dragons are not friendly."

"I would have mentioned that, too," Bob said, "but Jupiter is interested only in facts. Dragons are mythical, which means they aren't real. So if they aren't real, we don't have to worry if they're friendly or not."

"Exactly," Jupiter said. "Dragons are creatures of the legendary past. If there ever were any actual ones, it would seem they've all been eliminated by the due processes of evolution."

"That's fine with me," Pete said. "So, if they've all been eliminated, how come we're on our way down to investigate one?"

"We heard that five dogs have disappeared within the past week in the peaceful town of Seaside," Jupiter said. "And Mr Hitchcock told us that a friend of his lost his dog and saw a dragon near his house. Doesn't that suggest anything to you?"

"It sure does," said Pete. "It suggests I should be back in Rocky Beach surfing on my board instead of coming along with you to catch a dragon."

"If Mr Hitchcock's friend, Henry Allen, engages our services, then it will be a profitable adventure for The Three Investigators," Jupiter said. "Why don't you try to look at it that way?"

"I'm trying, I'm trying," Pete said.

"Whether there is a dragon or not," Jupiter said, "something mysterious is apparently going on. Soon we will have facts to work with. Meanwhile we'll have to approach the matter with an open mind."

They had reached the outskirts of Seaside, and Hans slowed the truck as he searched for the street number Jupiter had given him. They travelled slowly another mile and then Hans stopped. "I think this is your party, Jupe," he said.

All they could see was high hedges and palm trees. If a house was there, it seemed to be hiding.

Pete spotted the small sign on a white letterbox. "H. H. Allen," he read. "This must be the place."

The boys piled out. "This preliminary investigation should take approximately two hours, Hans," Jupe said. "Can you make your collection and delivery and come back for us then?"

"Sure thing, Jupe," the husky Bavarian said. He waved and swung his truck round to head down a steep road that led to the centre of the town.

"Let's take a quick look round first," Jupiter said. "It may help if we're better orientated when we speak to Mr Allen."

Houses were strung out along the high ridge overlooking the Pacific. The neighbourhood had a lonely, deserted air. They boys walked to a piece of vacant ground next to the film director's house and looked down.

"Looks nice and peaceful," Bob said, regarding the beach below them and the sparkling waters.

"Neat rollers," muttered Pete, watching the surf. "Not much, but pretty good three-footers. I guess later at night, when the tide and breakers start coming in, would be the best time for the dragon. He'd have a lot more cover."

Jupiter agreed. "You're right, Pete. If there *is* a dragon." He craned his head to look below. "Mr Hitchcock said there were caves below. But they can't be seen from this angle. Later, after our interview with Mr Allen, we'll go down there and look them over."

Bob looked at the deserted beach far below them. "How do we get down?" he asked.

Pete pointed to some rickety-looking, white, weatherbeaten boards. "Steps going down, Bob. Beats scaling up and down the cliff wall."

Jupiter pointed along the ridge. "There are some other staircases, too. But I don't see many of them. Well, I believe we have the lie of the land. Now let's hear what Mr Allen will tell us."

He led the way back to a gate in the hedge, swung it open, and they all stepped through. Beyond a winding path, they could see a house of faded yellow brick, surrounded by palm trees, bushes and wild flowers. The garden had an air of neglect as did the old house itself, perched almost on the edge of the wind-swept cliff.

Jupiter raised the door knocker and let it fall.

The door opened, and a small plump man stood there. He had large mournful brown eyes, bushy eyebrows, and a fringe of white hair above his tanned and wrinkled face.

"Come in, boys," he said, extending his hand. "I imagine you're the boys my good friend Alfred Hitchcock said might help me. Investigators, are you?"

"Yes, sir," Jupiter said. He whipped out one of The Three Investigators' business cards. "We've solved several cases so far."

The old man looked at the card in his gnarled fingers. It said:

THE THREE INVESTIGATORS

"*We Investigate Anything*"

? ? ?

First Investigator – JUPITER JONES
Second Investigator – PETER CRENSHAW
Records and Research – BOB ANDREWS

"The question marks," Jupiter explained, "are our symbol, our trademark. They stand for questions unanswered, riddles unsolved, mysteries unexplained. We attempt to solve them."

The old man nodded, as if satisfied, and put the card in his pocket. "Come into my study, and we'll talk," he said.

He led them to a large sunny room. The boys gasped as they looked about them. From ceiling to floor, the walls were hung with pictures almost fighting for space. Apart from the many paintings, there were neatly framed autographed photographs of famous film stars and other celebrities.

The large desk was covered with papers and small wooden carvings. The bookcases were crowded, too, with strange artifacts, Pre-Columbian figurines, and small, grotesque African figures. Some of them looked cruel and frightening.

The old man indicated three chairs for them and took the large carved chair behind the desk. "Please sit down, boys, and I'll tell you why I called my old friend Alfred Hitchcock. Perhaps he has already told you that I am a film director?"

"Yes," said Jupiter. "He mentioned that, sir."

The old man smiled. "*Was* would be a better word for it. I haven't done anything for many years. I was a film director years before Alfred became one. And quite famous in my own right, too. While Alfred has made the Hitchcock thriller his own speciality, I had mine, too. Almost in the same vein, but slightly different. Alfred concerns himself with logical mysteries of the real world, but mine went beyond it."

"What do you mean, sir?" Jupiter asked.

"It will explain why I couldn't go to the police or other authorities with my problem. You see, my pictures were bizarre, of the world beyond, of nightmares and fright. They concerned themselves with monsters, werewolves, creatures of strange and hideous natures and violent emotions.

"In short, my speciality, boys, was the horror film!"

Jupiter nodded. "Yes, I remember your name now, sir. I've seen it at film festivals in museums."

"Good," said the old man. "So when I tell you about what I saw coming out of the water the night my dog disappeared, you will know why I hesitated to speak about it. With my reputation and my inability to find work for many years, it would be only natural for stupid people to think I was merely trying to attract attention, gain publicity.

"My work is finished. They saw to that—the powers that be. I have enough money to live quietly. And no worries, no fears—except—"

"Except the dragon now living in the cave below you, sir?" Jupiter suggested.

Mr Allen grimaced. "Yes." He looked carefully at the boys. "I told Alfred I saw it coming out of the sea. But I omitted one fact. You see, I *heard* it, too!"

The room became suddenly quiet.

"You heard the dragon," Jupiter said calmly. "Exactly what did you hear? And where were you at that moment?"

Mr Allen drew out a large coloured handkerchief and mopped his brow. "I was standing on the cliff outside my house looking down at the ocean when I saw it," the old man said. "Perhaps it was an illusion."

"Perhaps," Jupiter said. "Now tell us exactly what you heard. This might be an important lead in the mystery."

"Well, confound it," Mr Allen said. "As far as I know, there aren't any dragons around, and there haven't been for several million years. Of course, I've done pictures about them, using mechanical monsters. In those cases, we used some kind of muffled roar of an engine combined with shrill whistles, blended together to create the effect we were trying to achieve—that of frightening the audience.

"But what I heard last night wasn't anything like

that at all. It was rather a high-pitched rasping sound—almost as if it were breathing with difficulty—or coughing."

"What about the cave under your house?" Jupiter asked. "Is it large enough to contain a dragon, or any creature large enough to be mistaken for one?"

"Yes," the old man said. "There are a series of caves running under this ridge. Extending north and south as well as inland. In the old days, they were used by rum-runners, and before them by smugglers and pirates. There was a landslide some years ago as the cliffs eroded, covering much of what was known then as Haggity's Point. But many of the caves are still under here."

"Hmmmm," Jupiter muttered. "But this is the first time you've ever seen or heard a dragon, and yet you've been living here for years. Is that correct?"

The old man nodded and smiled. "Once is enough. And I might not even have seen this one if I hadn't been out looking for my dog, Red Rover."

The boys exchanged glances, smiling. One of their secret entrances into Headquarters was called Red Gate Rover.

"I guess it's time we discussed your missing dog and the circumstances, sir. Bob, take notes," Jupiter said.

Bob, in charge of Records and Research, took out his pad and pencil.

Mr Allen started, then smiled at this example of the business-like proficiency of The Three Investigators.

"I've been abroad for the past two months," he said. "Even though I am no longer actively working in films, I am still very much interested in them, and their development. As a rule I tour Europe ever year, going to most of the major film festivals in different foreign cities. This year was no different. I went to the festivals in Rome, Venice, Paris, London and Budapest, and also visited old friends.

"As usual, when abroad, I boarded my dog at a local kennel. I returned a week ago, got Red Rover out—he's an Irish setter, by the way—beautiful animal. Friendly, too.

"Red Rover likes to run. As I can't keep up with him, I let him loose at night. Two nights ago he didn't return. Although I've had him three years, I thought he'd picked up new habits and returned to the kennel. I called and he wasn't there. I waited for him to come back and he didn't.

"I was out looking for him—when I saw—*it!*"

"You didn't go down to the beach?" asked Jupe.

The old man shook his head. "No. It was an eerie sensation. I'd spent most of my life making pictures to shock and scare people out of their wits, and now it had happened to me. There's no way I can describe the feelings I had. Panic, first, that this awesome creature might have attacked and devoured my dog. Then the fear that I might be losing my mind. To admit openly that you have seen a dragon takes some doing, believe me!"

"You took no other steps then," pursued Jupiter, "but phoned your friend Alfred Hitchcock."

The old man mopped his brow again. "Alfred is an old and dear friend, with much experience in the field of mystery. I knew if anybody could help me, he was the one. Now it will be up to you boys. The entire matter is in your hands."

"Thank you, Mr Allen," Jupiter said, "for your confidence. There have been other incidents of missing dogs in this town. Five of them, at last report, not including yours."

Mr Allen nodded. "I heard that on the news after my dog had disappeared. If I had heard of it before, I might not have let Red Rover run on his own as I did."

"Have you spoken to the other dog owners?" Jupiter asked.

The old man shook his head. "No. Not yet. I didn't want to mention what I'd seen."

"Do all the people round here own dogs?"

Mr Allen smiled. "Not all. Not the man across the street, Mr Carter. Nor my next-door neighbour on the right, Arthur Shelby. I don't know many of my neighbours. I live a quiet life with my books and paintings. And my dog."

Jupiter stood up. "We'll be going then, Mr Allen, and I promise you a full report of any progress we make."

Mr Allen shook hands and saw them out, thanking them again. The boys went out through the wooden gate, and Jupiter closed it behind them.

Pete smiled as Jupiter set the hook in place. "Keeping out the dragon, Jupe?"

"I doubt very much that a mere locked gate, or even a locked door, would stop a dragon, Pete," said Jupiter.

The Second Investigator gulped nervously. "I don't like the way you said that," he declared. He looked up the street, and then glanced at his watch. "Where's Hans?"

"It's much too early," Jupiter said. "We still have plenty of time."

He started to walk across the street.

Bob and Pete looked at him.

"Time for what?" Bob asked.

"To call on Mr Carter," Jupiter said. "After him,

Mr Arthur Shelby. Aren't you curious about men who live in this lonely section and don't need dogs to protect them?"

"No, I'm not," Pete said. "As a matter of fact, I'm wondering why I haven't bought a dog yet to protect *me!* A large one that's not afraid of dragons!"

Jupiter smiled and the boys followed him to the other side of the narrow street. Mr Carter's grounds were well kept up and his house was freshly painted.

"Notice," Jupiter told his friends as they went up the path, "that the hedges are evenly clipped and the lawn neatly mowed. His trees are pruned and his flower beds are well tended. Mr Carter must be a neat man."

Jupiter pressed the bell. Almost immediately the front door was flung open and a heavyset man stood there glowering down at them.

"Yes? What do you kids want?" he demanded loudly.

"I beg your pardon, sir," Jupiter said politely. "We've just visited your neighbour, Mr Allen, across the street. His dog, Red Rover, is missing, as you may know. We were wondering if you knew anything about its disappearance."

The man's eyes narrowed and his thick eyebrows rose, then lowered. His mouth twisted into a snarling line.

"So Allen's lost his dog, has he? Like the others up the street, eh? Well, good riddance to them. Good riddance and let's hope they stay lost. I hate dogs!"

His eyes blazed furiously at them, with an almost insane glint. His hands clenched and for a moment the boys thought he was going to attack them.

Jupiter managed to keep his voice calm, and his placid-looking exterior unruffled. "I'm sure you must have a good reason for disliking the animals, sir," he said. "Perhaps if you could tell us what they've done—"

"What they've done?" the man echoed sarcastically. "Done what they've always done. Barked and howled at the moon all night. Trampled my flower beds. Ripped up my lawn. Upset my dustbins, littering the path. That enough for you?"

"I'm sorry," Jupe said sympathetically. "We're new to the neighbourhood. It's Mr Allen's dog we're trying to find. If it's damaged your property, I'm sure Mr Allen would pay for it. He misses his dog terribly and I'm sure he'd do anything—"

"Do anything, would be?" the man asked. "Well, so would I. Wait here!"

He ducked inside behind the door. The boys hardly had time to exchange baffled glances than the door was flung open again and Mr Carter was back.

He was holding a large shotgun.

"Here's what I'd do," he said, raging. "Fill him with lead! This one carries double ought. That's the largest ammunition made for this weapon. And if I set eyes on that dog of Allen's or any other pesky beast hereabouts on my property, here's what they'll get."

He raised the gun threateningly.

3

The Test of Terror

THE ANGRY MAN tightened his finger on the trigger. "I'm a good shot and I never miss. Any more questions?"

Jupiter shook his head, trying not to look unnerved by the gun a foot from his face. "No, sir," he said. "I'm very sorry if we have disturbed you. Good day, sir."

Mr Carter's lips tightened. "If I never see any of those pesky dogs around again, that's when it'll be a good day. Now git!"

He thrust the muzzle outwards as he spat out the words, and the boys backed off slowly.

"Turn round," the man said. "I don't want you spoiling my lawn!"

Jupiter looked at his two companions and shrugged. With hearts quaking, they turned their backs on the ill-tempered man with the gun and went down the path.

"Don't run, walk slowly," Jupiter whispered.

Bob and Pete nodded, wondering when the shotgun blast would come, trying not to panic.

Then they all jumped at the loud sound behind them!

"It's all right, fellows," Jupiter said. "That was just Mr Carter slamming his front door."

The boys turned, saw Jupiter was correct, and ran. They were halfway down the street before they stopped. They looked back. Nobody was after them. Mr Carter's door remained closed.

"Whew!" Bob muttered. "That was close!"

"A shotgun with double-ought ammunition," Pete said, testing his forehead for sweat. "One more second and that stuff would have ripped right through us."

"Not too likely," Jupe said. "The locking bolt was in the off and therefore safe position."

Bob and Pete glared at him. "You knew that all the time," Pete said accusingly. "No wonder you acted so calm."

"I don't believe Mr Carter ever intended to shoot us," Jupiter said. "He was merely acting out his anger. I happened to trigger him off by bringing up the one subject that annoys him. Dogs!"

"I think he's got another subject now," Pete said. "People!"

Jupiter pursed his lips thoughtfully. "We'll have to be more careful the next time we approach Mr Carter."

Pete shook his head. "No, sir. The next time you can be careful approaching Mr Carter all you want. You won't have to worry about me, because I won't be there. I forgot to tell you, I have a very delicate skin. It's allergic to lead."

"Me, too," Bob said. "If I'm going to be shot at, I prefer a water pistol at ten paces."

"There's a possibility," Jupiter said, "that Mr Carter is a far better actor than I give him credit for, and had something to do with the disappearance of the dogs."

"Sounds reasonable," Bob said.

"It will be a simple matter now to compare Mr Carter's irascible response with our next subject's."

"What's he talking about now?" Pete asked Bob.

Jupiter pointed across the street.

"There were two neighbours Mr Allen mentioned who did not own dogs. We met the first one, Carter. Now we have a few questions to ask the other one, Arthur Shelby."

A closed metal gate running chest high barred their way. The boys looked over it to the large house set back on the property of Mr Arthur Shelby.

"Looks okay," Bob said. "I don't see a cannon emplacement anywhere."

Pete inched a little closer to look at the windows on the lower and upper storeys. "I don't see anybody watching us," he said. "Maybe Mr Shelby isn't home."

Jupiter stepped forward. "It's easy to find out," he said. "All we have to do is go through this gate, and—"

He stopped, open-mouthed. His companions gaped too. The gate had opened without Jupiter touching it.

"How did you do that?" Pete demanded. "You developing magical powers?"

"Maybe the wind blew it open," Bob suggested.

Jupiter shook his head. He held out his arms, stopping his companions from advancing, and stepped back. The metal gate swung shut.

Jupiter took a step closer. The gate opened.

"A very simple explanation," he said. "The gate works on an electronic seeing-eye principle. You've all seen that at airports, supermarkets and other modern buildings."

Pete looked at the gate sceptically. "Sure I have," he said. "Only I've never seen one in a private house before."

"Any sign of progress and modernity is a good sign," Jupiter said cheerfully. "The fact that Mr Shelby uses such a device on his gate shows he is not superstitious or hidebound by convention. Just the kind of person we want to talk to, especially about such an unlikely topic as a dragon in the neighbourhood."

He stepped through the gate and the other boys followed. Off to the side of the path, the boys saw a large, ornate sundial set in the centre of the lawn. Ahead of them was a large flower laden trellis. They walked under it.

Suddenly the trellis dropped.

The boys stopped, bumping into each other. The front part of the trellis had dropped in front of them. Behind them, the back part of the trellis hissed downwards with a slight clanging sound, barring their retreat.

They were trapped in a huge metal cage decorated with flowers!

"I hope this is only a joke," Jupiter said, licking his lips nervously. "It's like a portcullis."

"What's a portcullis?" Pete asked in a panicky voice.

"It was usually a large, heavy iron grating suspended by chains and lowered between grooves to bar the gateway of a castle or fortified town," Jupiter explained.

"I've seen pictures of them in old books at the library," Bob said excitedly. "It's usually the last defence after you cross the moat of the castle."

"I don't remember crossing any moat," Pete complained fretfully.

There was a slight hissing sound, and as suddenly as it had fallen, the trellis lifted above their heads.

The boys looked at each other.

"I think Mr Arthur Shelby has a keen sense of humour," Jupiter said, relieved. "Let's go."

He took a step forward and Pete grabbed his arm. "You're going the wrong way, Jupe," he said. "Maybe they don't want us in this castle."

Jupiter shook his head, smiling. "First an automatic-opening gate. Then an electronic controlled trellis. Mr Shelby seems to be unusually preoccupied with scientific gadgets. It would be a shame not to meet him."

The menacing bird dived at the boys!

Jupe moved forward again and his companions followed reluctantly. He grinned as he stepped up and pressed the doorbell.

"Yow-wh!" he yelled, and leaped back, shaking his arm. "That doorbell has an electric charge on it! I got a shock!"

"Okay, I've had enough of this Mr Shelby's jokes," Pete said. "I vote we call off the interview with this joker right away."

"I'm with Pete," Bob said. "I've got a funny feeling Mr Shelby is trying to tell us he doesn't want us here."

"I don't think so," Jupiter said. "He's testing us. He's put us through a sequence calculated to scare us off."

As if in answer to Jupiter's reasoning, the front door clicked and swung silently open.

"Neat," Bob said admiringly. "He's got this place bugged all around."

The boys cautiously stepped over the threshold. The interior was dark and quiet.

Jupiter cleared his throat, trying to speak with confidence. "Good day, Mr Shelby. We are The Three Investigators, calling at the suggestion of your next-door neighbour, Mr Allen. May we come in, sir?"

There was no answer. Then faintly they heard a slight flapping sound. It came closer, and they heard it more distinctly. It appeared to be coming from high in the gloomy interior of the house. Suddenly they froze. A huge, dark form was hurtling towards them with a shrill whistling sound.

A big, black, hawklike bird, screeching fiercely, its sharp beak open, cruel talons outstretched, and eyes blazing madly, swooped down on them!

4

A Surprising Hand

"DUCK!" Pete yelled.

The boys flung themselves to the floor.

The screeching bird plummeted towards them, its huge talons curled menacingly.

Then it slowed to hover a foot above them.

Surprisingly, it remained there.

The shrill screeching sound stopped.

Jupiter had flung his hands over his face to protect his eyes. He peeked cautiously between his fingers. Then he sat up, his expression changed from fear to chagrin.

"It's okay, fellows," he said. "It's not a real bird."

"What?" Pete cried.

He lifted his head unbelievingly. Bob did the same.

The dark bird hung there limply, dangling at the end of a thin copper wire. Its yellow eyes glared at them with a dull expression.

"It's a toy," Jupiter said. He reached out and touched the bird. "Seems to be made out of plastic and chicken wire!"

"Oh, boy!" Pete said disgustedly.

From the dark interior of the room came the sound of rasping, breathless laughter. Lights flashed on suddenly overhead.

A tall, thin man wearing dark overalls stood there looking down at them. His hair was short and coppery red.

"Welcome to Mystery Castle," he said in a deep and sepulchral voice.

Then he doubled over, laughing. His laughter became riddled by a spasm of coughing.

"He's sure got a keen sense of humour," Pete muttered.

The tall, red-headed man straightened up slowly. His blue eyes were bright and watery. "Arthur Shelby here. I'd better take my bird back before it bites you."

The boys scrambled to their feet. The man came closer, stooped and unhooked the wires holding the motionless bird. Jupiter looked up at the ceiling and smiled.

"He had it running on those narrow-gauge tracks up there," he said. "Just like electric toy trains."

Bob and Pete looked up at the tracks stretching across the ceiling. "I like electric trains better," Pete said. "They don't scare me."

Mr Shelby was grinning. "Fooled you, did I? Sorry. It's my hobby—making crazy gadgets," He waved his hand to the room behind him. The boys saw a large workshop cluttered with tools and scraps of wood and wire.

Mr Shelby set his bird down on a work table. His voice was normal now, not deep and mournful, merely husky. "What brings you boys here?" he asked.

Jupiter handed Mr Shelby one of their business cards. "That may explain it, sir," he said. "We like to solve mysteries."

The red-haired man studied the card, making no comment about the question marks. Then he returned it, smiling.

"I suppose the mysteries round here are the missing dogs, eh?"

"When we learn all the facts of the matter," Jupiter said slowly, "it may turn out to be a single mystery. We're trying to help Mr Allen find his Irish setter. But I have a feeling his missing dog is linked somehow with the disappearance of the others in Seaside."

"Could be," Mr Shelby said. "I don't have much to do with my neighbours here but I heard the report on the news. Allen's been away and I wasn't even aware he had come back until I heard Red Rover was missing, too. I hope you find him."

"That's our job," Jupiter said. "But we can use some information. I thought talking to some of Mr Allen's neighbours would help. We've just been across the street to speak to Mr Carter. Do you know him?"

Shelby laughed. "Who doesn't round here? I've got the red hair but Carter has the temper. I suppose he let you see his shotgun?"

Jupiter shrugged. "He tried to frighten us off. Fortunately, he had the safety catch on when he threatened us. He said dogs round here have been trespassing on his property. He made it clear he hates dogs."

Shelby grinned. "Carter hates everything and everybody."

"You scare people off in a different way," Pete said suddenly. "What's the idea of all those tricks you've got set up round your house?"

The red-haired man glanced at Pete, amused. "I wondered when you'd get round to me. I don't hate people so much as I hate to be *bothered* by them. I've worked out a few ways to keep the pedlars and daily nuisances away. Scared you, did I?"

"You can say that again," Pete muttered.

Shelby laughed again. "My background is engineering. I'm an amateur inventor It's fun for me to rig up these gadgets. But nobody gets hurt."

He glanced at his watch. "Now, how can I help you boys?"

"About the missing dogs," Jupiter said, "do you have any ideas that might help us?"

Their host shook his head. "Sorry. All I know is they've been reported missing. You'd do better speaking to the owners."

"The only one we've spoken to is Mr Allen next door," Jupiter said. "He gave us a clue but it's kind of hard to believe."

"Oh?" The red-haired man's bushy eyebrows flew upward. "What was that?"

Jupiter pursed his lips, frowning. "The trouble is, I don't know if I'm allowed to tell you about it."

"Why not?" Shelby demanded.

"I think maybe Mr Allen might be embarrassed if word of it got about," Jupiter said. "I'm sorry, Mr Shelby."

The tall man shrugged. "I guess you've got to act like a lawyer in these matters. Protect your client's confidences. Something like that?"

Jupiter nodded. "And yet, it's odd. You live next to him. It doesn't seem likely that he saw something mysterious round here that you didn't see."

Mr Shelby grinned. "You seem to have a pretty good vocabulary. Seems to me you could talk a lot clearer, if you wanted to."

"You're not kidding," Pete said, impatiently. "What Jupe is trying *not* to say is that Mr Allen saw a dragon come out of the ocean the other night."

"You shouldn't have said that, Pete," Jupiter said. "We have to keep what our clients tell us in confidence."

"Sorry," Pete muttered. "I guess I get too nervous just thinking about it."

"A dragon?" Mr Shelby said. "Is that what Allen claims he saw?"

Jupiter hesitated. Then he shrugged. "Well, it's out now. I guess he was afraid people would think he was losing his mind if he talked about seeing a dragon. But that's what he claims he saw."

Mr Shelby was shaking his head. "Impossible."

"He said he heard it, too," Bob said. "That is, when it entered the cave under his house."

Jupiter blew out his cheeks. "Well, I guess we just don't keep any secrets at all, Mr Shelby. But if there really is a dragon, or something dangerous like that down there, you ought to know about it, too. I mean, in case you go down there at times."

"Thanks for the warning," Mr Shelby said. "But I rarely go down to the beach. I'm not much of a swimmer, you see. And as for the caves, I learned long ago not to go into them. They're dangerous."

"What makes them dangerous?" Bob asked.

Mr Shelby smiled. "They were dangerous before there was any talk of a dragon in them. Landslides are common here along the coast. You could be buried alive."

"I heard they were used by smugglers and rum-runners," Jupiter said.

Shelby nodded. "That was a long time ago. As for the landslides, just take a walk along the cliff. You'll see how the earth has slipped. Sometimes a house goes down with it."

He looked intently at the boys, his eyes shining. "I know how it is being young. I suppose if I were your age again, and heard a wild story about a dragon, I might be tempted to go down and take a look myself. If you do, remember, those caves are very dangerous."

"Thanks, Mr Shelby," Jupiter said. "Then in your opinion, there's nothing to Mr Allen's dragon?"

Shelby smiled. "What do you think?"

Jupiter threw up his hands. "Well—"

Mr Shelby laughed again.

"Well," Jupiter said, "thanks a lot for talking to us. Maybe we'll find out exactly what he did see."

"I hope so," Mr Shelby said. "I know Allen's made a lot of horror films in his time. Maybe he has a friend or enemy who's playing a practical joke on him."

"That's possible," Jupiter admitted.

"Sometimes people will go to extremes in a case like that. Sorry I can't help you boys. I'll see you out now."

He led them to the door and opened it. As they filed out, he stopped Jupiter, offering his hand. "Good luck, son."

Jupiter took the hand extended to him. "Thank you, sir."

The door closed softly behind him.

Then he stared down open-mouthed, a shiver running through him.

Mr Shelby's right hand had come off, and Jupiter was holding it in his own!

5

Trouble Below!

"ULP!" Jupiter stared, horrified, at Mr Shelby's hand. It was flesh-coloured and looked real. It even *felt* real!

It was too much for even level-headed Jupiter. He gasped and dropped it.

The other investigators heard his cry and turned.

"Yipes! What's that?" cried Pete.

"Whiskers!" Bob said, looking closer. "It's a hand!"

Jupiter found his voice. "It's Mr S-Shelby's. It c-came off when we were shaking hands!"

"What?" Pet asked.

"It came off," Jupiter repeated dully. "I don't know how."

Loud laughter came from inside the house. It was followed by strangling, coughing sounds.

Jupiter flushed. "My fault, guys. I forgot what a practical joker Mr Shelby is."

He picked up the hand gingerly and held it out to Bob and Pete. Pete shook his head, and Bob took it. "It even feels real," Bob said. "Maybe Mr Shelby wears an artificial arm, and his hand just happened to come off accidentally when you shook hands."

Jupiter shook his head. "You heard him laughing a moment ago. No, it's just another one of his practical jokes. That's all. He's got a funny way of scaring people."

"Yeah," Pete said sarcastically. "Very funny. Let's

get out of here before he thinks of something else."

Bob tossed the fake hand away. The boys turned and raced down the walk.

Avoiding Mr Shelby's portcullis, the boys zigzagged across the path. They slowed down as they approached the closed metal gate.

It swung open noiselessly, as before, and The Three Investigators hurried through.

"He's a good sport anyway," Bob said, as they ran down the street. "At least he didn't have his gate bite us on the way out."

"Keep going," Pete muttered. "I'll thank him when I'm far enough away."

Finally they slowed and came to a breathless halt.

"Now what do we do?" Bob asked. "Wait for Hans to pick us up?"

"I move that we keep running all the way back to Rocky Beach," Pete said. "What's twenty miles when you consider how much safer it is there?"

Jupiter plucked at his lower lip. He glanced at his wrist watch. "There's still a little time. How do you fellows feel about taking a quick look at that cave down below, before we go home?"

Pete looked towards the cliff ridge. "You mean the one the dragon's supposed to have gone into? I'll give you my vote in two words, Jupe. Forget it."

Jupiter nodded. "How do you feel, Bob?"

"Like Pete," Bob answered. "Besides, you heard Mr Shelby telling us how dangerous it is. I don't know about the dragon, but I don't think I'd be any happier under a landslide."

Jupiter was walking to the cliff edge. He put his hand on the old weatherbeaten stair handrail that ran steeply down to the beach.

"I suggest we take a look," he said. "Then, when

we get home, we'll have a better idea of what we're up against."

With that, he took a step down and quickly disappeared from view.

Pete looked at Bob. "How come he always outvotes us, one to two?"

Bob shrugged. "He's just more stubborn than we are. You and I are probably nicer people."

"Yeah," Pete muttered. "A lot of good it does us. Come on. We'd better go down after him before Mr Shelby sends a flying object after us. Or that Mr Carter across the street decides he needs some target practice."

With that, Pete reached for the handrail and started down. Bob followed. The steps were narrow and old, set close together, and the descent to the beach was steep. As they ran down, Pete and Bob grabbed the rails at first. Then, as they gained momentum and confidence, they merely reached out and slapped at them.

Jupiter couldn't help but hear the clatter behind him. He glanced back once, saw what was happening, and grinned. It was a race to the bottom now.

Not as agile as the others, Jupe could still make an effort when he wanted to. He increased his pace as he bounced from step to step.

He was perhaps fifteen feet from the bottom when it happened.

Suddenly, without warning, a step collapsed under his weight. His momentum carried him downwards. The next step cracked and broke away, too. He attempted to brake by grabbing the handrail.

It tore loose and came off in his hand. Then he was yelling and fallng in space.

Immediately behind, Bob and Pete heard his warning cry too late. The entire staircase below was collapsing like a deck of cards on end. The railing above the section that Jupiter had clung to was their only chance. They threw themselves at it frantically.

It tore loose, too.

Helplessly, they plunged headlong downwards. Loose boards hurled after them.

Jupiter's mind worked quickly as he fell. In the split second before he landed, he had two nagging thoughts.

Was this accident a real one?

Or was it to keep The Three Investigators from investigating the mystery of the dragon on the beach?

That was all he had time for.

He landed with stunning force. Bodies and boards crashed about his head.

Everything went black!

6

Trapped!

"JUPE, are you all right?"

Jupiter blinked and opened his eyes. He saw the blurred faces of Pete and Bob looking down at him.

He grunted and sat up. There was a lot of sand on his face, and he brushed it off carefully before replying.

"Of course I'm all right," he said finally. "Not that the effect of both of you landing on me at once did me any good. In addition to knocking the breath out of me, you practically buried my face in the sand."

Pete grinned. "He's okay. He can still talk."

"I hear him," Bob said. "As usual, he's making it seem our fault. As I recall, his weight broke the steps and railing first. What were we supposed to do—fly over him?"

Jupiter got to his feet slowly. He kicked at the litter of broken boards all round them. Then he picked up a splintered piece and studied it. He stooped and picked up another, comparing it with the first. He nodded as if satisfied.

"Your statement is correct, Bob," Jupiter said. "My weight did break the steps first. But I'm inclined to believe that I had help. These steps appear to have been tampered with. Enough to make them give way at the slightest pressure."

He extended the boards to his two partners.

"If you notice, the top part is splintered sharply. See how jagged it is? The bottom part is broken more evenly. Almost as if it had been partly sawn through before we came down the steps."

Bob and Pete looked at the boards closely.

"Maybe you're right," Bob admitted. "But who knew we were coming down them?"

"Sure." Pete said. "It was your own idea, Jupe. If we never went down the steps, the accident could have happened to anybody in the neighbourhood. We've only met Mr Carter, Mr Allen and Mr Shelby, so far. There must be a lot of others who use this staircase."

He pointed up the beach. "It's a long walk to the other one. And a longer walk to the next one. Anybody could have come down here."

Jupiter sighed and threw the boards down. "We don't have the equipment to examine these boards anyway, to find out if they were actually sawed or not. Maybe I'm wrong in my deduction."

Pete and Bob stared at each other. It was a rare day when Jupiter ever admitted to a wrong .guess about anything.

Jupiter set his lips firmly. "However, " he said, "we can't let ourselves be sidetracked by the accident on the steps. Our main purpose in coming down was to examine the beach here and the cave for evidence of the dragon. Let's get on with it."

Without a backward glance, Jupe started walking towards the sea. "We'll look for tracks leading from the water inland towards the cave first. What Mr Allen claimed he saw took that direction."

Bob and Pete joined him, and the three advanced slowly over the sand. The wide expanse of beach appeared deserted. Overhead a few seagulls, screaming raucously, swooped about in erratic flight.

Pete pointed to one of the gulls who had just landed. "Maybe we ought to ask one of them if he saw a dragon recently. That would save us a lot of trouble."

"Good idea," Bob said. "And if they won't talk, there's that tug with the salvage rig about a mile out."

He pointed offshore to a clumsy-looking craft trailing its rig. "They don't look like they're going anywhere in a hurry. Maybe they're on a dragon hunt, too."

Jupiter looked out and shook his head. "We don't have to worry about what's out that far. All we have to do is cover the shoreline round here."

He ran his eye from the cave in the distance towards the water. "We should see tracks somewhere in this area. I suggest we spread out a little."

They separated and walked slowly along the beach, scrutinizing the sand closely.

"All I see is a lot of seaweed piled up," Bob said.

"Me, too," Pete said. "Plus some seashells and a lot of driftwood."

Bob shook his head finally. "No sign of any kind of tracks, Jupe. Could the tide have washed them away?"

Jupe tugged at his lip. "Possibly here, close to the water. But there's plenty of dry sand for tracks all the way up to the cave. Let's go up and look."

"Do we have to?" asked Pete. "What if the dragon is in the cave? What are we supposed to do—fight it off with our bare hands?"

"I don't expect us to have to fight anything, Pete," Jupe said. "We'll approach the cave entrance carefully. And we won't go inside unless we're certain it's safe enough."

Pete scowled. Then he stooped and picked up a long piece of driftwood. "Well, I don't know how much good this will do me. But I'll feel a lot safer with some kind of club in my hands."

Bob picked up another piece of wood, part of an

oar with the blade broken off. "You have the right idea, Pete," he said. "I remember seeing pictures of St George and the dragon. He didn't use old driftwood, either. He was smart. He had a nice long sword."

He brandished his long oar, then glanced at Jupiter. "Don't you want some kind of weapon, too, Jupe? We can go back for those broken railings, if you like. They've still got some of the nails set in them. Nice long ones."

Jupiter smiled and shrugged. "I suppose it won't hurt to carry something."

With that, he reached down and picked up a long, wet plank from the debris along the shore. He put it on his shoulder and glanced at his companions.

Bob and Pete smiled weakly. Then, with resolutely set faces and quaking hearts, the boys walked slowly towards the dark opening in the face of the cliff.

They crossed the slight ridge near the waterline, scanning the sand each foot of the way. Suddenly Jupiter stopped. His eyes were bright.

"Here's something," he said softly.

Bob and Pete looked down. There were unmistakable depressions in the loose soft sand.

"This dragon must be a new type," Bob said finally. "It looks like it's running on wheels."

Jupiter nodded. He looked up and down the beach. "I don't see anything. But these look like the tracks of some kind of vehicle. Maybe a beach buggy. Sometimes lifeguards use a jeep or beach buggy to patrol a long area, such as this."

"Maybe," Bob said. "But if they were on patrol, these tracks would be heading north and south—the way the beach runs. Instead, they're heading towards the cave."

"You're right, Records," Jupiter said. He dropped to his knees and studied the depressions.

Bob was scowling, looking back at the water. "I don't get it. If the tracks show here, why couldn't we see them near the water?"

"A heavy running tide and high breakers would wash them away, I guess," Jupiter said.

Pete grinned. "I guess old Mr Allen's eyes aren't too reliable. Instead of a dragon, what he probably saw was a jeep or something."

"Possibly," Jupiter answered. "In any event, when we get to the cave we'll find out one way or the other."

Ten yards from the cave, the tracks disappeared completely.

The boys looked at each other.

"Another mystery," Pete said.

They reached the mouth of the cave. It looked empty.

"This opening is almost big enough for a bus," Bob said. "I'll take a look inside and see how far back it goes."

Jupiter peered inside the cave. "All right, Bob. But stay within shouting distance. Pete and I will be with you, as soon as we check the entrance for any clues."

Bob brandished his spearlike weapon and walked into the cave.

"What makes him so brave, all of a sudden?" Pete asked.

Jupiter smiled. "Once we saw the tracks were made by a man-made vehicle, rather than a fantastic creature such as a dragon, I think we all got a lot braver."

He cocked his head, as if listening.

"Perhaps we can tell from the echo of Bob's voice

how large the cave is." He raised his voice. "Just checking, Bob—how are things in there?"

Pete inclined his head, too, in a listening attitude. They heard the sound together. A heavy plopping sound.

Then they heard Bob's voice. It was thin and high-pitched. He spoke only one word but it filled them with terror.

"Help!"

7

A Mysterious Warning

As Jupiter and Pete stared wide-eyed into the dimly lit cave, they heard Bob cry out again.

"Help! Help me!"

"Bob's in trouble!" Pete exclaimed. "Come on!"

Pete, the most muscular and athletic of the trio, darted into the cave. Jupiter tried to keep up with Pete's flying feet.

"Not so fast, Pete," Jupiter said. "He's not too far away, and we have to be careful not to—"

He never completed his sentence. In the gloom of the cave, he suddenly ran into something hard that knocked the wind out of him. He fell to his knees.

Then he heard Pete's voice.

"Stay back, Jupe! I've found him!"

"Where, Pete? I can't see."

Jupiter blinked. Then his eyes adjusted to the darkness of the cave. He saw Pete was on his hands and knees in front of him.

"He's down a hole," Pete said. "I stopped just in time."

"I can't see," Jupiter said. He tried to peer around Pete's shoulder. "Bob," he called. "Where are you?"

Bob's voice was so close, he jumped.

"Down here!" Bob cried. "I fell into some kind of a pit. It seems to be dragging me down!"

"Yipes!" Pete exclaimed. "Quicksand!"

"Impossible," Jupiter said. "Quicksand is usually found in tropical countries."

He wriggled round Pete, carefully feeling the cavern floor with his hands. "I still can't see him. Bob, can you see us?"

"Yes," Bob said. "I'm almost directly under you."

Jupiter leaned over, extending his arm. "Just reach up and grab my hand, Bob. Pete and I will pull you out."

They heard dull plopping sounds below.

"I c-can't!" they heard Bob say after a moment. "Whenever I try, I seem to sink deeper!"

"Push your stick up," Pete suggested. "That broken oar you were holding. Jupe and I could pull you out in a second."

"I can't", Bob said despairingly. "I dropped it when I fell in here."

Pete looked at his piece of driftwood and groaned. "Mine's too light to hold you."

Jupiter was wriggling cautiously round the edge of the pit. "Hang on, Bob," he said. "I'm circling the pit to try to get some idea of its size."

He crawled slowly away.

"Hurry!" Bob cried. "This is no time for measuring things."

"I've got to," Jupiter replied. "It's the only way I can think of to get you out."

He made his way in the darkness on his hands and knees. Bits of earth dropped into the pit, despite his care.

"Watch it!" Bob cried out. "You're starting a landslide!"

"Sorry," Jupiter said. "It's the loose dirt round the edges."

In another moment, he had completely circled the pit and rejoined Pete. "I think we can manage it." He called down to Bob again. "Bob, can you tell us if you are touching bottom?" They heard thrashing sounds below. Then spluttering, spitting noises.

"Not yet," Bob replied testily. "Maybe by the time you geniuses up there think of a way to get me out, I will be."

"If you hold my legs, Jupe, I can reach down for him," Pete said. "We don't have time for anything fancy."

Jupiter shook his head. "I think we can use my plank. Not for pulling him out directly—we'd never get enough leverage on this sandy ground. But the plank is just long enough to reach across the pit and wedge into the sides."

"Then what good is that?" Pete asked. "Bob can't reach that high."

"Yes he can, if we can place it at the right angle," Jupiter said. "I think we can wedge it in from the opposite side."

Pete looked at the thin plank Jupiter held. He nodded, wetting his lips. "It's worth a try. If it will hold his weight."

Jupiter leaned over the ledge. "We'll be trying to reach over your head, Bob," he explained. "It will be up to you to see that the plank is wedged in firmly enough to sustain your weight.

"Because if it slips," he added, "we'll not only lose the plank, but you."

"Thanks a lot," Bob answered. "Only hurry it up. I think I've sunk another couple of inches."

Jupiter left Pete and hurried to the far side. He leaned over the edge and extended the plank.

"I'm pushing it out now," he told his friends. "I don't know if you can see it, Bob. But in a moment it should be passing over your head."

Lying on his stomach, he shoved the plank out foot

by foot. Finally he heard a shout from below.

"I can see it now," Bob called. Then, on a higher despairing note, "I can't reach it. It's too high."

"It's coming down now," Jupiter said. "I'm trying to get the precise angle where it will fit."

He extended the plank a few more inches.

"You're doing fine, Jupe," Bob called. "It's coming in all right. Just another couple of inches."

He waited for Jupiter's next move. Then he heard a scuffling sound. "Come on, Jupe. What's holding you up?"

Jupiter's voice was hoarse. "I'm out too far. I—I'm beginning to fall in myself!"

"Oh, no!" Pete groaned. He leaped to his feet and dashed for the other side.

Jupiter's feet were clawing wildly for purchase on the slippery ground. The rest of him was already tilted downwards over the dark pit. Bits of earth crumbled under his weight and rolled away.

Pete threw himself forward and landed on Jupiter's legs, pinning him there. Then, grabbing Jupiter's belt, he threw his weight backwards.

"Easy, Jupe," he said, panting. "I've got you."

In another moment, he had enough of Jupiter back for the stocky boy to recover his balance.

"Thanks, Pete," Jupiter said breathlessly. "Now if you would just remain over me another few seconds until I get this plank extended all the way—"

They both heard Bob's joyous shout.

"You got it, Jupe!"

"Okay, Bob. Pete and I will now wedge it into the pit at this side. Then it will be up to you to come up it, hand over hand. Can you reach it?"

There was a second's pause. Then, "I got it!"

"All right, Bob," Jupiter said. "Come on, then."

"Roger!" Bob said.

They heard a warning creak. The plank shook under their hands.

"Here he comes!" Pete yelled.

As the plank swayed and shivered under Bob's advancing weight, Jupiter leaned on his end with all his strength.

"It may still break," he whispered to Pete. "Get ready to grab him."

They heard Bob breathing heavily.

"Okay," he panted. "Here I am. Now what?"

Pete leaned over. "Grab my hand, Bob."

Bob's hand shot up quickly. For a brief moment, their grips held together. Then Bob's hand slipped away. He moved frantically to grab the wet plank again.

"He's harder to hold than a greased pig. Jupe," Pete complained. "You want to try it?"

Jupiter shook his head. "I doubt that I'd do it any better than you. We'll have to grab him together."

Bob glared at them from below, as he dangled from the swaying plank. "For Pete's sake, will you guys stop holding these conferences and get me out of here? I'm weighed down with so much mud, I can hardly hold myself up. And my hands are slipping, too—"

Jupe's eyes darted round the interior of the cave. "What we need is a rope," he said. "Something we can throw and loop over him—"

"There's no rope," Pete muttered. "And no time. We're only a couple of inches short. There must be something—"

Suddenly Jupiter's eyes brightened. "I have it!"

His hands went for his belt buckle. Swiftly, he opened it and drew the belt off his waist. Pete watched open-mouthed as Jupiter inserted the end of his belt through the buckle. It made a small loop.

Jupiter let the other end dangle and leaned over the pit again. "I've made a small loop out of my belt, Bob." he said. "When I lower it, let it go over your hand. Your weight will tighten it. Then Pete and I can pull you out."

He slowly let the belt out, lowering it into the pit. Then he braced himself for a tug from below.

"I got it!" Bob yelled. "Pull!"

Jupiter sighed with relief. Pete grinned and reached for his share of the belt. Together, they leaned back and pulled.

Something dark and wet, covered with ooze and slime, slowly came up out of the pit.

8

A Forced Retreat

THE WET FIGURE dropped beside them, panting heavily. "Thanks, fellows."

"It was Jupe's idea," Pete said. He glanced down ruefully at his own belt. "I'm wearing a belt, too. I just never thought of using it."

"Perhaps that's because you're not as weight conscious as I am," Jupiter said, smiling. "Besides, since my waist is wider than yours, my belt is longer."

Bob wiped mud from his face. "It worked fine, Jupe. I'll never kid you about being overweight again." He glanced down into the pit and drew back, shuddering. "Otherwise I might still be down there."

"All's well that ends well," Pete said. "Now what do we do?"

"We go home," Jupiter said firmly. "Bob's wet and needs a change of clothing. I'm sorry. It was my fault for insisting we investigate the cave without our torches handy."

"It would have been a good idea," Bob agreed. "But I guess it was dumb of me to dash ahead without looking where I was going."

Jupiter stood up, frowning.

"Odd that such a dangerous pit should be so close to the entrance to the cave. I imagine that would keep a lot of curious people out."

"Not if they do things my way," Bob said, grinning weakly. "That would keep a lot of those curious people *in!*"

"Golly," Pete said, a serious note in his voice. "Maybe that's what happened to Mr Allen's dog, and the other missing ones. They might have fallen into that pit, too, and been sucked down."

Jupiter nodded. "It's a possibility. But we were looking for evidence of their tracks before Bob cried for help, and didn't find any."

"Oh?" Pete exclaimed. "Is that what we were doing?" He took a quick look behind him. "Well, let's get out of here while we still can. This place is scary."

In complete agreement, they walked quickly out of the cave.

Jupiter looked back. There were giant boulders on the other side of the cave opening.

"I wonder how far back that cave goes," he said, thoughtfully. "We were told it had been used by smugglers and rum-runners in the past."

"That's right," Pete said. "What about it?"

"The part we were in didn't seem ideal for hiding things. It was too open and easy to get into."

"Maybe there are other passages," Bob said. "Sometimes water erosion wears away the softer rocks. It takes millions of years sometimes. Maybe this area was under water a long time ago. If so, there would be a lot of natural passages."

"Probably," Jupiter agreed, "but we don't have the time to investigate that now. We will have to postpone our search until another time."

"Suits me," Pete said with enthusiasm. "Just as long as we can call it quits for today. I've had it with scares."

"We've all agreed on that," Jupiter said. "The trouble is, we seem to have one more ahead of us."

"What do you mean?" Pete demanded.

Jupiter pointed towards the sea. His companions

looked in that direction. They blinked. It wasn't possible!

Something dark and glittering was rising out of the water.

"I can't make out what it is," Bob whispered.

"It's got a small dark head—like a dragon has, I think," Pete said, shakily.

A large wave came rolling in. It loomed high over the dark shape, then swept over it, covering it completely.

The boys held their ground nervously, peering intently at the swirling water.

The rolling wave crashed and broke on the beach. Another came in after it. Then, as the swirling water eddied back, they saw the dark shape again.

It stood up. It was sleek, black and shining, down to its webbed feet. Slowly it walked ashore.

"Skin diver," Pete said, relieved. "Wearing a face mask and flippers. What a thing to get scared over. Come on. Let's go."

As they turned away, Jupiter spoke softly into their ears. "Red alert! He's carrying a speargun!"

Pete laughed. "So what? He's probably hunting fish or something."

Jupiter shook his head. "He's heading this way."

Suddenly the masked man in the black wetsuit dropped to his knees. He extended his speargun, and then fell prone, aiming it.

"Uh-oh! Look out!" Bob cried. "He's aiming at us!"

"Huh?" Pete said. "Why would he do that?"

He squinted and his face paled. "Excuse me! Bob's right!" He whirled around. "It's got to be us—there's nobody else around!"

Jupiter Jones saw the man lying facing them less

than a hundred yards away. The speargun was cradled in his arms and definitely appeared to be pointed at them.

Jupiter had a logical mind. One that worked with almost lightning speed sometimes. He appraised the situation and frowned. It defied all logic.

When logic failed, Jupiter could still depend on a keen sense of preservation. "Red alert," he said. "Scatter and run!"

They whirled instantly and ran for the staircase. As they got closer to it, they saw immediately it was useless. In the excitement, they had forgotten the accident a short while before. They saw the litter of broken steps and railings again. Behind loomed the cliff wall, rising steeply at an angle impossible to climb.

Jupe looked towards the next staircase. It was too far away, requiring a long run over heavy sand that would slow them down. They'd be an easy target on the open beach.

Quickly he made his calculation. "We've got only one chance. Quick! Back into the cave!"

The boys veered off, changed direction and sprinted for the cave opening. They ran desperately, expecting at any moment to hear the sharp retort of the speargun.

Or perhaps to feel the long and deadly steel shaft it propelled.

The sand flew under their feet.

"Almost there!" Jupiter gasped. "Dive!"

The three leaped headlong for the mouth of the cave, almost as one. Then they scurried on hands and knees behind the big boulders for protection.

"Made it!" Pete grunted. "Now what?"

"We hide," Jupiter said, struggling to catch his

breath. "It will give us time—to work out a plan."

"Maybe now's the time to look for those other passages," Bob said.

Jupiter nodded, his cheeks pink with excitement. "Agreed, Bob. But we'll let him make the first move. If he comes this way, then I'll admit our situation demands emergency procedure—such as going deeper into this cave."

Pete was peering over Jupiter's shoulder. His voice was tight. "We'll have to, Jupe—here he comes!"

"Whiskers!" Bob exclaimed. "What'll we do? I don't feel like dropping into that pit again."

Jupiter had backed into the cavern wall.

"Look!" he suddenly called to them.

In the wall, they saw some vertical planking, running up to the ceiling of the cave.

"Jeepers," Pete said. "How did we miss that before?"

"The sand and dust provided a natural covering," Jupiter said. He tapped the panel with his hand. It brought a hollow sound.

"It must be a secret passage," he said. He pushed at the boards. "They appear loose enough to be moved. Take another quick look, Pete. See if that skin diver is still coming for the cave."

Pete peered out and quickly ducked back.

"We've got double trouble," he said, his voice shaking. "Now there are two of them!"

Jupiter frowned. "Two? In that case, we'd better work fast. Help me with these planks."

They tugged and pushed at the planks.

"It's no use," Bob said. "They're wedged in too tightly."

Jupiter shook his head. "There has to be a way." His eyes gleamed suddenly. "Of course! Stupid of me."

The boys held their breath as the divers searched . . .

He kicked at the loose sand under the plank. "All we have to do is dig down a little. Get some of that sand out. That will loosen them up."

Quickly, they dropped to their knees and scooped away at the sand. The wide plank above it suddenly moved.

"That's it," Jupiter said. "Now, if we can turn it enough for us to slip through—"

Once they had disturbed its base, the plank was easy to manage. Bob and Pete went through. Then it was Jupiter's turn.

He struggled to get through the narrow opening.

"Can't—do it," he gasped. "Still—too fat!"

Bob and Pete hastily scooped out more sand below, from the other side. The plank swung open, and Jupiter heaved himself through.

"Let's leave a little crack to see through," he whispered.

They swung the heavy board back into place, making sure it didn't fit tightly against its neighbour.

They were still on their knees in the dark pocket of the cavern, when they heard voices.

The first skin diver flicked on a torch.

"I could have sworn those kids ran in here, Harry. Too bad you let that wave knock you down and I had to take my eyes off them."

"We'll find them soon enough, if they're in here," the other answered. "If they're not, we can get to work."

The Three Investigators held their breath as the first man played his torch round the cave. Jupiter, on hands and knees, pressed his face to the opening between the long boards.

Bob and Pete stooped over him, each with an eye at the crack.

The men in the black wetsuits walked ahead. The light faded, as did the sound of their shuffling flippered feet.

The rasping voice of the second man echoed from the pit area. "You must have been imagining it, Jack. Nobody here."

"Guess they got away up the other steps, then."

There was a faint plopping sound and then silence. Jupiter could hear and see nothing more, and drew his face back from the board. Dust and sand were making his nose itch. He wondered if his partners had the same symptoms. A sneeze would be a disaster for them now.

"No sneezing," he whispered. "Cover your noses."

They obeyed his warning, and waited nervously. The cave remained dark and silent. Finally Jupiter stood up.

"They've gone," he whispered. "Let's get out while we can."

They scooped away the loose sand again, and carefully eased back the plank.

"You first this time, Jupe," Pete whispered. "If *you* get through, Bob and I can make it easily."

Jupiter took the suggestion with a smile.

They slipped back into the mouth of the cave and listened. The cave remained silent. They put the board quietly back into place, and brushed in sand until it stood firm again.

Jupiter stood up, his heart beating wildly. He looked at his watch.

"We've had over three hours," he whispered. "Hans will be waiting."

9

Message from a Ghost

"WELL, what do you make of it?" Jupiter asked.

It was an hour after their return with Hans in the truck. Bob was at home getting a much needed shower and change of clothing. Pete and Jupiter were alone in Headquarters.

Pete shrugged. "I can't figure it out. I don't know who those skin divers were, except that their names were Harry and Jack. I don't know why Harry, or Jack, pointed that speargun at us. I don't know why they followed us into the cave. I don't know where they disappeared to or how. I don't even know how we got out of there alive."

Jupiter pinched his lip, and nodded. "Add to that the curious incident of the collapsing staircase, and it's obvious we're confronted with many questions before we try to solve the mystery of Mr Allen's missing dog."

"I've got an idea that will help," Pete said.

"Oh?" Jupiter wheeled round in his chair, his eyes sparkling with interest. "What?"

Pete gestured to the telephone on their desk. "Just pick up that telephone and call Mr Allen. Tell him we've decided not to find his missing dog for him. Tell him we nearly disappeared ourselves. Tell him we're willing to forget the whole thing."

Jupiter ignored the suggestion.

"Our first problem," he stated, "is to determine who

those skin divers were, and what they were doing in the cave."

Pete shook his head. "Why bother with those two tough characters? We were in there, too, and I don't even know what *we* were doing in there."

"Looking for clues of Mr Allen's dragon," Jupiter replied. "And tracks or traces of his Irish setter, Red Rover."

"Well, we didn't find much," Pete declared. "Except that pit. Bob found that for us."

"We found that passage behind the boards," Jupiter said. "It may be a secret tunnel in the cave. Or it could be one of the secret hiding places used by the rum-runners or smugglers in the old days."

"I don't see what that's got to do with us," Pete answered stubbornly. "It wasn't hiding Mr Allen's dog."

Jupiter frowned. "As investigators, we have to return and examine that cave more thoroughly. Don't you realize that?"

Pete nodded reluctantly. "Sure. All I'm wondering about is how those skin divers didn't fall into the pit Bob found? Doesn't that prove they know their way around in there?"

"Maybe, but they did have a torch," Jupiter said. "As to how or why they disappeared, perhaps when we return with torches, we'll discover—"

The telephone rang, for the second time that day.

They stared at it.

It rang again. "Well, answer it," Pete said.

"I will." Jupiter picked it up. "Hello?" he said into the phone. "Hello?"

He held the telephone close to the microphone so that Pete could hear what was said, too. They heard a rasping sound.

"Hello!" Jupe said again. There was no answer.

"Maybe it's a wrong number," Pete said.

"I—don't think so," Jupiter said. "Listen!"

They they heard the strange rasping sound again. The sound was like that of somebody trying to breathe, gasping for air with great difficulty.

The curious breathing sounds changed to a voice that seemed to be strangling, as if the speaker had only a few moments of life left.

"Keep—" the strangling voice said. Then, as if it were the most tremendous effort imaginable, the voice continued.

"Away," it said. "Keep . . . away."

Then it became a heavy breathing sound again.

"Keep away from what?" Jupiter asked the telephone.

"My . . . cave," the voice said. There was another long gasping sound and then silence.

"Why?" Jupiter asked. "Say, who is this?"

The voice sounded hollow now. "Dead . . . men," it said slowly, "tell . . . no . . . tales!"

There was a long trembling gasp, and then silence.

Jupiter hung up. For a moment, he and Pete sat staring at the phone. Then Pete hopped up.

"I just remembered we're having dinner early tonight," he said. "I'd better get on home."

Jupiter jumped up. "I'll leave, too. Aunt Mathilda might want me to clean up the yard a little."

Quickly both boys bolted from the trailer.

They hadn't had any trouble understanding what the ghostly voice had told them. It was a very simple message.

Keep away from my cave!

Dead men tell no tales!

Old Mr Allen had told them about a dragon entering a cave.

He hadn't mentioned a dead man—or a ghost!

10

The Death of Seaside

MEANWHILE, Bob had showered and changed his clothes. By the time he reached the Rocky Beach Public Library, where he had a part-time job, he felt more cheerful.

As he walked in, Miss Bennett, the librarian, looked up and smiled.

"Oh, Bob," she said, "I'm really glad to see you today. It's been one of those busy days. So many visitors, and now, of course, so many books to put back on the shelves. Could you get right to it?"

"Sure," Bob replied.

He picked up the sizable stack of returnable books and put them away one by one. Then he turned to the reading-room tables. A lot of books had been left out, and he gathered them up. The title of the one on top was *Legends of California.* He flipped the pages idly and saw one chapter entitled "Seaside: Dream of a City That Died".

"Hmmm," Bob said to himself. "That might be interesting."

He put it aside thoughtfully. This was a lucky find. Anxious to return to the book when he had finished his duties at the library, Bob attacked the stacks of books lying about with record speed.

When he had finished putting them all back on the shelves, Miss Bennett asked him to mend some books with torn bindings. He took them into the back storage room and secured the covers with plastic tape. In a little while, he had done everything that had to be done.

He returned to Miss Bennett's desk.

"Everything's in order, Miss Bennett. I have some research to do now, if there isn't anything else you need me to do—"

Miss Bennett shook her head, and Bob hurried to the reading table with the book of Californian legends. He didn't know very much about Seaside at all, he realized. Neither Jupiter nor Pete knew much about it either. Certainly none of them had ever heard a word about the town *dying!*

Quickly he opened the book to the chapter about Seaside. It started with these words:

> There are cities which are plagued by ill fortune, just as people. Seaside's dreams of becoming a key resort community went up in smoke fifty years ago.
>
> The bright and bustling city its planners had visualized and gambled their fortunes on, was never to be. The elaborate canals and waterways, constructed to remind visitors of Venice, have crumbled and been replaced with factories. The once elegant hotels have been boarded up or bulldozed to make way for motorway construction going north and south.
>
> Perhaps Seaside's most bitter disappointment was the failure of its underground railway, the first on the West Coast. Investors, as well as the public, were cool about plans for a rapid transport system linking the coastal part of Seaside with the business section and other nearby communities. As a result, the underground network was never

completed, and its few miles of tunnel remain boarded up and forgotten, a ghostly secret and costly reminder of the city that died before it had a chance to grow up.

"Wow!" Bob said to himself. The town of Seaside meant more to him now. It was more than fifty years since it had died—the book he was reading was several years old. If he hadn't found it by accident, he probably never would have known the story of the place they had visited.

He wrote down some of the main facts about Seaside and put the book away. Then he sat thinking. He had a great deal to tell Jupiter, but he decided to wait until after dinner. It was almost that time now and he was hungry.

He said goodbye to Miss Bennett and cycled home. His mother was preparing dinner, and his father was reading his newspaper and smoking his pipe. He greeted Bob with a smile.

"Hi, son," he said. "I understand you came home with enough mud on you to test our washing machine to the limit of the manufacturer's most exaggerated claims."

"Right, Dad," Bob said. "I fell into a hole. At first I thought it was quicksand, but it turned out to be mostly mud and water."

"Quicksand? Nothing like that round here, to my knowledge."

"Not Rocky Beach," Bob said. "It was at Seaside. We're on a case that took us down there. We were investigating one of the caves."

His father nodded, and put his paper down. "In the old days it would have been worth your life to stick your nose into one of them. A lot of the caves around Haggity's Point there were used by rum-runners, and before that by pirates."

"So I heard," Bob said. "And I just came across a book in the library that told all about how Seaside was a city that died before it grew up. Did you know that?"

His father was a newspaperman who always seemed to have a secret store of knowledge. He nodded again.

"A lot of people lost their shirts and went broke when they guessed wrong about that town. After the big fire at the amusement park, its luck turned bad."

"It didn't look that bad to me," Bob said. "It's as big as Rocky Beach here."

Mr Andrews smiled. "Since then, they've had fifty-odd years to rebuild and it's a bustling, thriving city now. But not what it was intended to be, a big resort. Now it's just another place to live and make money."

"Tough," Bob said. "I read they even started their own underground railway but never got round to finishing it."

Mr Andrews leaned forward. "That particular decision cost one of the early Seaside planners his life. He committed suicide after losing his personal fortune pledged to the building of the underground system." He frowned, and puffed on his pipe. "His name escapes me now, but he was the big man with the big dream. If enough people had shared his conviction and enthusiasm, Seaside might have become what he wanted—the biggest Fun City of them all."

Mrs Andrews' voice interrupted, clear and firm.

"Dinner's ready."

Bob wanted to hear more but his father got up and went to the table. Bob followed and sat down. There was a lot Jupiter should know.

"I say we forget all about finding Mr Allen's lost dog," Pete was saying firmly. "It may be only a missing pet to him, but to me it's also a dragon, and two nasty-looking skin divers with loaded spearguns who don't like kids. Not to mention that mud hole that sucks in people, and the staircase that falls apart when you run down it. Plus whatever it was that called on the telephone warning us to keep away from its cave. That sounds like good advice to me, especially coming from a dead man!"

Bob's eyes widened. "What's *that* all about?"

It was an hour after dinner, and the boys had met again in Headquarters to discuss their plans.

"After you went home to change, Bob," Jupiter explained, "we received a mysterious telephone call." He told Bob about it, repeating the message word for word.

"Sounds like a gag to me," Bob said, at last. He licked his lips. "If it's not, somebody is telling us we're not wanted near that cave."

Jupe's face had a familiar stubborn look. "We haven't seen anything of the mysterious dragon yet," he said. "I suggest we go back tonight for another look."

"Let's vote on it," Pete suggested hastily. "My vote is we abandon the case now. All in favour say aye!"

"Aye! Aye! Aye!" The word was repeated shrilly by Blackbeard, the trained mynah bird whose cage hung near the desk in Headquarters.

"Quiet, you!" Pete snapped. "You're not a paid-up member of this club. We only allow you to live here!"

"Dead men tell no tales!" Blackbeard called out and laughed shrilly.

Bob turned to Jupiter. "Maybe that's who you heard —Blackbeard."

Jupiter shook his head. "No, Bob. It came from somebody who seemed to have trouble breathing and speaking. If it was done deliberately to create the effect of a dying man—or even a ghost—it succeeded. It was actually scary, wasn't it, Pete?"

Pete shrugged. "No more than anything else that's happened so far." He pushed back his hair. "If I'm not grey yet, maybe I will be by tomorrow."

Jupiter grinned. "You're no more scared than any of us, Pete. You're just putting on an act."

"Want to bet?" Pete said.

Jupiter's answer was to pick up the phone.

"I'm betting that when Worthington shows up for us in the Rolls-Royce, you'll want to come along," he said.

Less than an hour later, Pete looked out of the window of the smooth-riding, gold-plated, luxuriously appointed old car. It purred almost silently along the Pacific Coast Highway heading for the outskirts of Seaside. Worthington, the tall and polite English chauffeur, was at the wheel, driving with his usual skill.

"Sometimes I wish you'd never won the use of this car in that contest, Jupe," Pete complained. "When I think of all the trouble it's got us into."

"*Out* of, too, Pete," Bob reminded him. "And when our first thirty days' use of it was up, you weren't too happy about it, either, as I recall."

An English boy they had helped at that critical time had made the necessary financial arrangements for the continued use of the car. The Three Investigators had almost unlimited access to the Rolls-Royce, as well as the services of its driver, Worthington.

Pete leaned back against the leather upholstery and

smiled. "I've got to admit this beats riding in the truck, not to mention walking."

Jupiter had given the directions needed to get them off the highway and on to the narrow ridge road overlooking the beach at Seaside. Now he leaned forward and tapped the chauffeur's shoulder.

"This will do fine, Worthington," he said. "Wait for us here."

"Very good, Master Jones," the chauffeur replied.

The big Rolls-Royce with the huge old headlights shining into the night eased up to the side of the road.

The boys tumbled out. Jupiter reached back into the car for their equipment.

"Torches, a camera and tape recorder," he said. "Now we'll be prepared for any emergency, and be able to document it, as well."

He handed Bob the recorder. "For recording any sounds of dragon, Bob, or ghosts who have trouble breathing and talking."

Pete took one of the three powerful torches. Jupe put a coil of rope on his other arm.

"What's the rope for?" Pete asked.

"It always pays to be prepared," Jupiter told him. "It's a hundred feet of light nylon. It should hold us if the other staircases have been tampered with and we have to get down from the cliff by our own means."

They walked a little way along the quiet, dark street. Jupiter led the way to the staircase he had chosen for their descent. It was several hundred yards from the one that had collapsed under their weight that morning.

His companions joined him on the ridge and looked down. The beach appeared deserted. The rising moon cast a dim glow through light clouds. The soft hiss of the waves lapping the sand below was periodically drowned out by the roar of the breakers that loomed up dark and menacing beyond.

Pete licked his lips nervously, grasped the handrail of the old staircase, and stood still for a moment listening. Bob and Jupe listened, too.

All they could hear was the dull roar of the surf and the beating of their hearts.

"Well, good luck one and all," Pete said tightly.

As the boys took the first step down, they felt certain they heard the ocean roar a little louder, as if in anticipation!

11

Terror in the Night

THE STAIRS were dark and the salty night wind stung their faces. The towering cliff wall jutted towards the ocean, casting long, gloomy shadows on the moonlit sand.

The staircase held their weight, and they ran down the last few steps with more confidence, jumping off to the sand with relieved sighs.

Jupiter looked up. Only an occasional light was burning in the houses along the ridge.

They trudged along the damp dark sand and passed the old staircase that had collapsed under them earlier.

As they approached the cave entrance, they came to a halt, listening intently and looking about carefully. No one, as far as they could detect, was moving inside or anywhere about.

Jupe looked up. The cliff wall jutted out blocking his view of the ridge. He scowled, feeling this was important somehow, but not sure why.

At last he nodded. "All clear." They slipped quickly inside and again Jupiter paused to listen. Pete was puzzled. Jupe was acting as if they were on a commando raid.

"Why the big act?" Pete whispered. "I thought this wasn't supposed to be so dangerous."

"It never pays to be careless," Jupe whispered back.

Pete flicked his torch on and let the light play on the walls of the cave. Then he lowered it to the ground ahead. He gasped in surprise.

"Do you see what I see?" he demanded. "The cave ends right there—just behind the pit. How did those two skin divers get out?"

Jupiter walked forward slowly and flashed his light around.

"It's a smaller cave than I expected," he said thoughtfully. "And that's a good question, Pete. How did those skin divers leave? And where did they disappear to?"

They walked about and tested the cave walls.

"Solid," Pete said. "That's great!"

"What do you mean, Pete?" Bob asked.

"Don't you get it?" Pete answered. "Look how small this cave is! And that pit is pretty small, too. What I mean is, no dragon could ever fit in here!"

Jupe looked puzzled. "And yet Mr Allen said he saw a dragon come out of the sea and enter this cave under the cliff." He looked intently down at the pit. "Those skin divers didn't just vanish into thin air. We'll have to assume there's another cave entrance here somewhere. Or another opening somewhere in this cave. There may be other, larger passages running close by."

"Wow!" Bob suddenly exclaimed. "I just remembered something!"

Quickly he told his companions what he had read in the library and heard from his father.

Jupiter's eyes were thoughtful. "A tunnel, you say?"

Bob nodded excitedly. "It was supposed to be the first underground railway system on the West Coast. It was never all finished, but part of it was, and still exists. Sort of like a ghost railway."

"That's interesting, Bob," Jupe said. "But that tunnel could be miles away. And we don't know that whoever started the tunnel came this far with it, or started at this end."

Bob looked deflated. "I guess you're right, Jupe."

"We'll look for it while we're here," Jupiter said. "But the best way to find the tunnel would be from a map. We could probably get one at the Seaside City Planning Board offices."

"After over fifty years?" Pete laughed. "Whoever drew up that map probably died a long time ago. And if the map is still around, my bet is it's buried somewhere under a lot of old papers and dust."

Jupiter nodded. "Could be, Pete. But as long as we're here tonight, we might look for the tunnel while we continue our investigation.

"I was thinking of that little passage we found this morning behind the boards. That should be safe enough to start with, I imagine."

Pete and Bob nodded in agreement and moved over to the boarded section. Jupe brushed some of the sand and dirt away from it, exposing a large board. As he did so, Bob saw Jupe's eyes suddenly gleam with excitement.

"What is it, Jupe?" Bob whispered.

Jupe was looking puzzled.

"I'm not quite sure yet," he said. "It looks like plywood."

"Plywood?" Bob repeated.

"I believe so," Jupe said, feeling the board. "But I'm not certain yet as to how it relates to this mystery. Just now we'd better go ahead with getting some of the sand away so we can move these boards."

Soon the plank they had moved before was loose enough. They got it out of the way, slipped through the narrow opening, then carefully replaced it. Then they flicked on their torches to see where they were.

They were in a small, narrow cave. The ceiling was low, leaving them just enough room to stand without stooping. It was damp and sloped abruptly to a low shelf of rock in the rear.

"Another dead end," Pete muttered. "It doesn't lead anywhere."

Jupiter shrugged. "However, it does make an ideal hiding place for smugglers or pirates. I imagine it's been used a lot in the past. The old planks indicate they they tried to keep it a secret place."

Bob flashed his light on the cave floor. "Pirates, eh? Maybe they left us a few gold doubloons."

He and Pete dropped to their hands and knees and felt carefully in the thin film of sand for treasure.

Pete was the first to give up. "Nothing," he said, disappointed. "If they ever did use it to hide their loot, they sure were careful about picking it all up when they left."

Bob kept searching on hands and knees until he reached the far end of the cave. "Maybe they swept some of it into the corner," he whispered.

Jupiter was flashing his light at the boarded-up section. He scraped some of the dust and sand off the boards and was examining them when he heard Bob cry out.

"What's up, Bob?" Jupe asked.

He heard a rumbling sound. Jupiter turned and stared.

Bob had disappeared.

"Bob!" Jupiter stepped towards the other side of the cave and then stopped in his tracks, dumbfounded.

"What happened?" Pete asked. He was on his feet, staring.

Jupiter could only point to the cave wall they were facing. "He was here a second ago. Didn't you see him? Then the wall seemed to swallow him up."

"What?" Pete leaped headlong for the wall. It

brought him up short. "I don't get it," he muttered, shining his torch on the floor. "There's no pit this time."

As he stooped to examine the floor of the cave, there was a rumbling noise. Pete's eyes widened and he gripped his heavy torch tighter. He looked up at Jupiter and was surprised to see the stocky boy smile.

"It's okay," Jupe said. "He's coming back now."

Pete whirled in time to see the movement in the wall. A small section was turning. The next moment there was a gaping hole where there had been a wall, and Bob was on his knees crawling through.

"How about that!" Bob exclaimed. "Whiskers! A secret moving rock panel. I just happened to lean on it and—wham! It opened!"

"What's on the other side?" Jupe asked excitedly.

Bob's jaw dropped. "I didn't get a chance to notice, Jupe. It happened too fast. Let's see if I can open it again."

He backed against the low cave wall, squatting. Nothing happened at first, and he shifted his shoulders. Suddenly, they heard a sharp clicking sound. Then the rock rumbled and Bob tilted back.

"Here I go again," he cried. "Better use it while it's open!"

He tumbled through the opening, and then Pete and Jupe slid through.

"Wow!" Pete exclaimed. "This is more like it!"

This cave was very wide and high. It extended back as far as their torches could reach, running inland parallel to the first cave they had entered.

The Three Investigators jumped to their feet to examine it.

As they did, they heard a slight rumbling noise behind them. They whirled, too late.

The secret rock opening had closed behind them!

"Uh-oh!" Pete muttered. "That does it!"

"That's what happened to Bob before. I'm sure we'll be able to work out how it works later," Jupe said. "Probably a simple leverage system. Let's forget it now while we investigate this cave."

Bob looked up at the high vaulted ceiling.

"Wow!" he gasped. "Look at the size of it, Jupe! This might be the tunnel I read about!"

Jupiter nodded. "Possibly, Bob. But if you notice, the walls and ceiling are rough, unfinished rock, as any cave is. The tunnel you told us about was completed. It would be in a more finished condition, with concrete walls possibly and a paved flooring. Perhaps tracks, too. Or the bedding for them."

He shook his head, and flashed his light about. "No, this looks like any large natural cave. There's no entrance to the beach and water behind us, either. The walls appear solid all the way round. But let's follow its course under the cliff. It may still lead us to the old underground railway tunnel you mentioned."

"What I like about it," Pete said, "is that there's no way out to the beach. That means, there's no way in for things like dragons!"

"Which means we're in luck," Jupiter said smiling. "There's one thing certain about this cave anyway. It happens to be large enough to contain a dragon or any other creature that size."

"Thanks for reminding me," Pete muttered. "I nearly felt good there for about half a second."

The cave floor was fairly smooth and level and they advanced along it steadily. Then they stopped short.

The passage ended suddenly in a high, vertical grey wall.

"End of the road," Pete said. "Looks like all we've

discovered is the world's biggest unused parking lot!"

Jupiter was pinching his lower lip and looking puzzled.

"What's wrong, Jupe?" Bob asked.

"That wall ahead of us," Jupe said. "There's something about it that doesn't look quite right."

Bob and Pete flashed their lights on it, and shook their heads.

"It looks like a wall to me," Bob said. "Naturally I'm as disappointed as you are. I wanted—"

Jupiter had his eyes half closed and wasn't listening. He peered closely at the wall and tapped it. Then he hit other parts of it, his ear close to the grey surface.

"It sounds funny, Jupe," Bob said.

Jupiter nodded, frowning, then walked to the side of the cave and tapped the wall there.

"There's a difference," he said finally. "I can't explain it exactly but—"

"Oh, come on, Jupe," Pete interrupted impatiently. "If you can't prove it's not a wall, then it is. Let's get out of here. I'm getting cold."

Jupiter's face lit up. "That's it!" he exclaimed. "Cold! The wall isn't cold. But the sides of the cave are. Feel the difference for yourselves."

Bob and Pete hastily compared the feeling of the wall and the sides of the cave.

"You're right," Pete admitted. "It's not as cold as the sides of the cave. But what does that prove? Don't forget it's under some of those houses along the ridge. Maybe heat comes down from them and warms the wall a little."

"Heat rises, Pete," Jupe said.

"There may be another pocket or passage inside," Bob suggested. "That could warm it, too, Jupe."

The monster loomed darkly above the terrified trio!

dragon loomed high above them. Then the long curving neck swung round and the dark head with its great staring yellow eyes lowered.

The long wet jaws opened and they saw its teeth, incredibly large and shining. It breathed again in its harsh rasping manner, and then it coughed and stopped.

Jupiter had read of the warning cough of the great jungle tiger as it prowled for prey. But he had never thought much about it. He remembered it now and shuddered.

His eyes were riveted on the dark head of the monster. It swayed back and forth hypnotically. Then, suddenly, it dipped closer towards them. Jupiter shrank back against his companions, his hands still frantically searching for the trigger point of the stubborn, unyielding rock behind him.

The dragon's wet jaws loomed closer. Now they opened again and the frightened boys felt its hot steaming breath.

Suddenly the rock behind them clicked and trembled. Jupiter turned as it opened and saw Bob fall through. Pete sat frozen, staring helplessly up at the dragon. Jupiter jerked his arm and shoved him through after Bob. Then, holding his breath, he hurled himself through the narrow opening.

The rock rumbled shut, and the boys sighed their relief. But it was short-lived.

They heard the muffled, angry roar of the dragon. Then they felt the rock tremble as something heavy clawed and pounded at it from the other side.

12

The Grip of Fear

"IT'S COMING AFTER US!" Pete cried.

The roaring noise from the other passage grew louder. The rock that linked the two caves trembled under the pounding. Sand and small rocks started to fall from the roof of the small cave they were huddled in. The air became clouded with dry, gritty dust.

"Landslide!" Pete said, coughing.

"We're trapped!" Bob cried. "We'll suffocate!"

Jupiter remembered what they had been told about the cave—the danger of landslides, of being buried alive.

It appeared Arthur Shelby had not been joking.

More rocks fell. The pounding and roaring seemed to grow in intensity. Jupe shook his head, trying to get rid of his helpless creeping terror.

Dazed and frightened, he found his eyes fixed on the planks at the other end of their cave. Of course! It was incredible how fear fogged one's mind.

"The planks!" he yelled. "We go out the same way we got in!"

The three frightened investigators leaped for the boards. Jupe and Bob scooped desperately at the loose sand at the bottom, while Pete stood pounding at the thick board, trying to move it. In another moment that seemed like a lifetime, it was free. They squirmed through.

They swung the big board back and hastily kicked

sand underneath it, wedging it in place. Then they looked at each other, panting.

Jupe's head bobbed.

"Now we run for it!" he said.

Jupiter didn't intend to lead the way. His feet did it for him. They took him straight out of the mouth of the cave. Then he was on the sand, running.

Right beside him was Pete. Pete was the best athlete of the trio, and the fastest runner. Bob was next. Ordinarily neither of them would have had any trouble passing Jupiter.

Their torches made erratic bobbing paths of light as they ran. They passed the broken staircase. Finally, they were at the steps of the second staircase that ran to the top of the ridge. Worthington was up there, they knew, and the powerful Rolls-Royce that could whisk them to safety. Behind them was the roaring creature that had come out of the sea, and was angrily looking for them.

They were halfway up and still there was nothing behind to snatch at them with cruel jaws and hot steaming breath. Then they were on the top, panting and gasping for breath.

Ahead of them, far in the distance, were the twinkling lights of Los Angeles. And parked down the street, was the waiting car with Worthington at the wheel.

They raced to the big, sleek Rolls-Royce, its metal parts and golden door handles gleaming in the moonlight. The door was flung open, and they piled into the rear seat.

"Worthington!" Jupiter panted. "Take us home."

"Very good, Master Jones," the tall, dignified chauffeur replied, and the big car came purring to life. It picked up speed and began its long sweeping turn down to the Pacific Coast Highway, going faster and faster.

"I didn't know you could run so fast, Jupe," gasped Pete.

"Neither did I," Jupe replied through puffed cheeks. "Maybe—it's because—I never saw—a dragon before."

"Whiskers!" Bob exclaimed, as he leaned back against the leather-cushioned seat. "Am I glad we've got the use of this car!"

"That goes double for me," Pete said. "But how do you figure that dragon showing up, after we had decided there couldn't be any such thing?"

"I don't know," Jupiter said, puffing as he tried to regain his breath.

"Well, if you ever find out, don't tell me," Pete said. "I'll have enough trouble forgetting that I saw it tonight!"

"How could it happen?" Bob asked. "According to all the books I've read, dragons are supposed to be extinct. There just aren't such things around today."

Jupiter shook his head.

"I don't know," He frowned and pinched at his lower lip. "The obvious answer would be that we didn't see one. If there aren't any, then we couldn't possibly have seen one."

"Are you kidding?" Pete demanded. "If we didn't see one, then what was that thing that came into the cave breathing hot steam at us?"

"It sure looked like a dragon," Bob said.

Worthington turned his head. "I beg your pardon, young gentlemen, but I couldn't help overhearing. Do I understand you correctly, that you saw a dragon this evening? A real live one?"

"We sure did, Worthington," Pete said. "It came out of the sea and headed straight for a cave we were investigating. Did you ever see one?"

The chauffeur shook his head. "No, I can't say that I've been that fortunate. But in Scotland, they had something equally terrifying that a few people were privileged to see. A long undulating sea serpent. It was called the Loch Ness monster and it still appears, I'm told, from time to time."

"Did you ever see it, Worthington?" Jupe asked.

"No, Master Jones," the chauffeur replied. "But when I was a lad, I travelled near the loch—as their lakes are called—and word would spread rapidly when it was sighted. I consider it one of the major disappointments of my life that I have never seen the Loch Ness monster. It was reputed to be at least a hundred feet long."

"Mmmm." Jupiter thought about it. "And you've never seen a dragon, either, you said."

"Not a real one," Worthington said, smiling. "Only the kind they use before the football game."

"Football game?" Bob asked.

The dignified chauffeur nodded. "That annual New Year's pageant you people have near here in Pasadena. The big floats of flowers. The Rose Bowl parade, I believe it's called."

"Well, the one we saw a little while ago wasn't made out of flowers," Pete said quickly. "I can tell you that. Right, Jupe?"

"Mmm," Jupe replied. "Definitely not made out of flowers. It was a real dragon, all right," He hesitated. "At least we're all agreed it *looked* like one."

"I'm glad you agree for once," Pete said.

Jupiter scowled. He was pinching his lower lip between his thumb and forefinger, always a sign he was in deep thought. He looked out of the window of the speeding car and continued to pinch his lip without replying.

When the Rolls-Royce reached the Jones Salvage Yard, Jupiter thanked Worthington and said he would call again the next time they needed transportation.

"Very good, Master Jones," Worthington said. "I must say I enjoyed the assignment this evening. It's a welcome change from driving wealthy old ladies and well-to-do businessmen. Before parting, however, I hope you don't mind answering one question that comes to mind. About your dragon, if I may."

"Sure, Worthington. What about it?"

"Well, sir," the chauffeur said, "one might say you were privileged this evening to see a real live dragon, in the flesh, so to speak. At close quarters, might I ask?"

"Too close," Pete answered abruptly. "It was practically right on top of us."

"Good," the chauffeur said, his usual reserved manner dissolved. "Then perhaps you gentlemen took notice. Is it true, as the legend would have it, that the monster breathes out smoke and fire?"

Jupiter thought and shook his head slowly. "No, Worthington. This one didn't. At least, all we saw was the smoke."

"Ah!" Worthington said. "A pity. I should have been most pleased if you had witnessed the total effect."

"Maybe *you* would, Worthington," Pete said. "But what we saw was enough, believe me. I've had enough effect to last me a lifetime. Just talking about it gives me goose-pimples."

The chauffeur nodded and drove off. Jupiter led his partners into the junkyard. His Uncle Titus and Aunt Mathilda were already asleep inside the little house that adjoined the yard. There was just a dim nightlight on for Jupiter.

Jupiter turned to Pete and Bob. "I don't know if

you'll like this, but we will have to return to the cave, dragon or not."

"What?" Pete howled. "Don't you realize we're lucky just to be back here alive?"

Jupe nodded. He held his arms up and showed his empty hands. "My torch is still in my belt, just like yours and Bob's. But in our panic when we ran out of the cave, we forgot all our equipment. My camera, the recorder, the rope. That's one reason for our going back there."

"Okay," Pete said grudgingly. "That makes a little sense, but not too much. What's your other reason?"

"The dragon itself," Jupiter said slowly. "I don't believe it was real!"

His partners stared at him.

"Not real?" Pete demanded. "Are you trying to tell us that thing that frightened us out of our wits wasn't *real?*"

Jupiter nodded.

Bob shook his head. "If that wasn't a real live dragon, I'll eat my shirt."

"I admit it looked like one," Jupe said.

Pete looked annoyed. "Then what are you talking about?"

"I admit the dragon looked like one," Jupe repeated. "But it didn't *act* like one!

"It's too late now to discuss it," Jupe said. "I'll give you my reasons for not believing that was a real live dragon tomorrow morning. And, if I'm proved wrong next time we visit the cave, I'll do as *you* threatened, Bob—I'll eat *my* shirt."

"You won't have to bother," Pete said. "The dragon will eat it for you. And whatever else is handy."

13

Jest of the Joker

Bob had trouble sleeping. Tired as he was from the harrowing events at the cave in Seaside, he had no sooner closed his eyes than he was being pursued from cave to cave by a monstrous dragon breathing hot steam at him. At last he managed to fall soundly asleep, only to be wakened by his mother calling him for breakfast.

His father was finishing his breakfast when Bob came to the table. He nodded to Bob, then glanced at his watch.

"Good morning, son. Did you have a good time with your friends last night?"

"Yes, Dad," Bob answered. "Kind of."

His father stood up, dropping his napkin on the table. "That's fine. By the way, I don't know if it's important, but you seemed interested in the Seaside tunnel yesterday, and after you left, I happened to recall the name of the man who had lost his fortune building it."

"Oh?" Bob asked. "Who was it, Dad?"

"Labron Carter."

"Carter?" Bob instantly thought of the Mr Carter they had met. The one with the bad temper and big shotgun.

"Yes. He lost his vigorous health, too, once the Seaside Town Council turned away from his plans to make Seaside the resort city he had envisaged. The combination of losing his health, fortune and reputation was too much for him—he killed himself."

"That's too bad. Did he have a family?"

Mr Andrews nodded. "His wife died shortly afterwards. His son is the sole survivor." Mr Andrews looked thoughtful for a moment. "That is, if he is still alive," he added. "Remember this all happened over fifty years ago."

Bob waved goodbye as his father left for the newspaper office where he worked. He added this latest information to his notes. He wondered what Jupe would say when he presented his own evidence. Proof that somebody was still alive who knew about the original tunnel. Somebody with a grudge to bear against the city that had broken his father's heart. Somebody who had a very nasty disposition.

Bob couldn't imagine how the present Mr Carter might try to get even. He put his notes in his pocket, finished his breakfast and hurriedly left.

Perhaps Jupe would be able to tie things up later at the Jones Salvage Yard.

"Golly," Pete Crenshaw said, an apprehensive note in his voice. "What Bob's told us about the Carter family sure makes sense, Jupe. More than your remark about the dragon being fake," he added.

The Three Investigators were gathered together again at Headquarters. Bob had started the meeting by reading his notes, as usual, and had first mentioned Labron Carter. But he had even more surprises for his friends.

"I remembered what you said last night about the dragon," Bob said. "And I went straight from my house to the library this morning and did a lot of research before our meeting."

Jupiter glanced at the papers in Bob's hand.

"I believe it would be most constructive to our meeting this morning, Bob, if you came directly to the point," Jupe said. "To wit, are there dragons living today, or not?"

Bob shook his head. "Not. No dragons. Not a single book gave any evidence of dragons living today."

"That's crazy!" Pete exploded. "Those guys just don't know where to look. If they spent a little time around a certain cave in Seaside at night, they'd find one, all right. A nice big one!"

Jupe held up his hands. "I suggest we listen while Bob reads his report. Then we'll discuss it. Continue, Bob."

Bob looked down at his notes. "The closest thing I found to a dragon is a huge lizard called the Dragon of Komodo. It's large for a lizard—grows up to ten feet long—but nowhere near as big as the dragon we saw."

"Maybe one of them got some extra vitamins," said Pete. "Maybe that's our dragon."

"No," said Bob. "The Dragon of Komodo doesn't breathe smoke, and it only lives on one small island in the East Indies. And it doesn't look much like that creature in the cave. I think we can safely say there are no dragons living today.

"But I did find a lot of living creatures that attack, kill and even *eat* man!" He glanced at his companions. "Do you want me to continue?"

Jupe nodded. "Certainly. We must know our natural enemies—as well as the ones intending to fool us by pretending to be natural. Read your list, Bob."

"Here goes," Bob said. "One million people killed each year by disease-carrying insects; forty thousand die of snakebite; two thousand from tigers; one thousand are eaten by crocodiles, and another thousand are food for sharks." He looked up.

"Notice if you will, Pete," Jupe said, "no mention so far of any statistics covering the incidence of dragons and humans. Continue, Records."

"Those are the big numbers," Bob said. "There are also a lot caused by elephant, hippo, rhino, wolf, lion, hyena and leopard. Some of these are accidents. There are man-killers and man-eaters. A lot are intentional 'rogue' killers.

"But according to this book—*Man Is the Prey* by James Clarke—the dangers from some beasts are greatly exaggerated. Like polar bears, pumas, eagles and alligators. He said tarantulas are absolutely harmless, that grizzly bears do very little real damage, and that the apes have enough intelligence to stay away from man. Also that the most likely places you can go if you want to be eaten are central Africa and the Indian subcontinent. The safest place, he says, is Ireland, with nothing there more dangerous than the bumblebee!"

Bob folded his notes. There was silence in the little room.

"Any comment?" Jupe asked Pete.

Pete shook his head. "Seaside sounds pretty safe after that," he said smiling. "All you have to do now is convince me that dragon last night wasn't real."

"Well, to begin with," Jupe said. "We didn't see—"

He was interrupted by the telephone ringing.

Jupe reached for it, and then hesitated.

"Go ahead. Pick it up," Pete said. "It might be another call from that dead guy—or ghost. He probably tried to tell that dragon to keep out of his cave, too."

Jupiter smiled and picked the telephone up. "Hello?" he said.

As usual, he held the telephone close to the microphone so Bob and Pete could hear the conversation.

"Hello," said a familiar voice. "Alfred Hitchcock here. Is that young Jupiter?"

"Yes. Hello, Mr Hitchcock. I suppose you're calling to find out how we're doing with our investigation for your friend?"

"Yes," the hearty voice replied. "I had assured Allen you boys would clear up the mystery of his missing dog with dispatch and ingenuity. I'm calling now to verify my own assurances. Have you found the dog yet?"

"Not yet, Mr Hitchcock," Jupe said. "We've got another mystery to solve first. A mystery of a coughing dragon."

"A coughing dragon?" Mr Hitchcock repeated. "You mean there actually *is* one? It coughs, you say? How odd! There is seemingly no end to life's mysteries. However, I would suggest if the appearance of a dragon confounds you, that you discuss it with the man who is considered the world's living expert on them."

"Who it that, sir?" Jupiter asked.

"Why, my old friend Henry Allen," Mr Hitchcock answered. "I'm surprised he didn't tell you. He used more dragons in his work than anyone before or since."

"Yes, he did mention he'd used dragons," said Jupiter, "but apparently they didn't prepare him for seeing one on his beach. Well, thank you for checking with us, Mr Hitchcock. I think we'd better report our progress to Mr Allen. I'll give him a call."

"No need to," Mr Hitchcock said surprisingly. "I have him on another line at my office. He just telephoned to tell me he was quite impressed with you boys. One moment, and I'll ask my secretary to switch him over."

There was a moment's pause, and then the boys heard the voice of the old film director.

"Hello, is that you, young Jones?" he asked.

"Yes, Mr Allen. I'm sorry to say that so far we haven't found a clue to your missing dog. But we aren't giving up."

"Good lad," Mr Allen said. "Actually I didn't expect results so soon. It's possible that my dog was simply picked up by a stranger and taken away. As I told you, he is an extremely friendly animal."

"We've taken that possibility into consideration, sir," Jupe said. "Have any of your neighbours recovered their missing dogs yet?"

"No," Mr Allen replied. "And I see what you're driving at, young man. The coincidence is still there, isn't it? That all our dogs disappeared at approximately the same time."

"Yes," Jupe said.

"Have you spoken with any of my neighbours?"

"Only the ones you mentioned who don't own dogs," Jupiter replied. "Mr Carter and Mr Shelby."

"Did they have anything to say?"

"They're rather strange neighbours, Mr Allen," Jupe said. "Mr Carter was very angry at being disturbed and threatened us with his shotgun. He doesn't like dogs. It appears they have been tracking over his garden, and he implied he was out to get them."

Mr Allen laughed. "Just bluster, my boy. Carter makes a lot of noise. I don't believe he'd go so far as to shoot a helpless animal. How did it go with my friend Arthur Shelby?"

"Well," Jupe replied, "he was a little better, but not much. He had his own ways of scaring us."

The old film director laughed again. "Oh, you're referring to those devices around his house for scaring off trespassers and pedlars. I suppose I should tell you that Arthur Shelby is quite a prankster."

"Tell him we've already found that out," Bob whispered.

"Perhaps he's trying to remind me that I'm not the only one around who can scare people," Mr Allen continued. "He knows of my old horror films, and maybe he's trying to give me a dose of my own medicine." He chuckled again. "As a matter of fact, Shelby's peculiar sense of humour once cost him an important job with the city. The city fathers didn't appreciate it."

Jupiter glanced at his companions. They all hunched closer in their chairs to hear better.

"What happened?" Jupe asked, trying to keep his voice casual.

"It was several years ago," Mr Allen said. "Shelby is an engineer. He worked with the City Planning Bureau. Knew how the city worked, you might say. One day he decided to take advantage of that fact."

"How?" Jupe asked. "What did he do?"

Mr Allen chuckled again. "It happened on his birthday. It was Shelby's own idea of a jest. Nothing really serious happened. What he did was manage to have all the city traffic lights disconnected at the same time. He said it was his idea of having a birthday cake without candles. Needless to say, city traffic was a hopeless snarl. Businessmen were late for appointments, and late going to work and returning home.

"It was only a temporary blackout—lasted only a few hours. But it raised a lot of indignation that something like that could happen in our busy, modern city. A lot of very important people were quite angry and resolved to get the person responsible. Oddly enough, Shelby admitted it. Said right out he did it to celebrate his birthday—just for the laughs."

"What did they do to him?" Jupe asked.

"Fired him, of course. And they saw to it that he was never again able to secure another job working for the city. He's like me in a way, a man who's been denied his livelihood."

"You mean, he can't make a living any more?" Jupiter asked.

"It hasn't been easy for him," the old man admitted. "Sometimes he does an occasional odd job for some business concern that needs advertising. Electrical signs that move or animate in a clever way. Things of that nature. Not much. He's had to pay for his private joke, you see."

"How about Rose Bowl parades?" Jupiter asked. "Did Mr Shelby ever make any of the floats for them?"

There was a brief silence. Then Mr Allen's voice returned, hesitating slightly. "Not to my knowledge. The floats are displays done in flowers. Shelby's work is more mechanical. Also the Rose Bowl people take their parades seriously. A lot of people pay for seats to watch the floats parade in Pasadena, and they appear on TV. No, young man, I doubt very much that a joker with the past reputation of Arthur Shelby would have been hired for that sort of thing."

"Too bad," Jupe said. "Well, anyway, he makes a lot of things for his own amusement now, and he says they don't hurt anybody."

"Some people don't like his kind of practical jokes, my boy. It's as simple as that. Well, goodbye for now—"

"Just one question, sir," Jupe said. "That dragon you saw the other night—are you sure it was coughing?"

"Quite sure," the old director said. "A coughing sound."

"And you saw it from the top ridge near your house when it went into the cave in the cliff below?"

"Yes, son. I'm sure of that, too. It was late at night, but I haven't lost my faculties yet, despite my lack of sponsors and films to do lately. I still have better than fair vision."

"Thank you, Mr Allen. We'll be in touch with you."

Jupiter hung up. Then he turned to face his partners. "Any comments?" he asked.

Bob and Pete shrugged.

"So he told us Shelby was a joker," Pete said. "I could have told him that myself. That bird scared me as much as that dragon in the cave."

"Which brings me to my next observation," Jupe said. "And that is, I have found Mr Allen, whom we are supposed to be working for, not altogether reliable in his statements in so far as the truth in concerned."

"Huh?" Pete scowled questioningly at Jupe.

"He's trying to tell us old man Allen is lying," Bob explained.

"Well, why didn't he say so?" Pete asked, aggrieved. He looked at Jupe. "See if you can tell me in words I can understand what the old boy was lying about."

Jupe nodded. "He stated that he was standing on the top ridge when he saw the dragon entering the cave below."

Pete looked puzzled. "So, what's wrong with that?"

Jupiter shook his head. "The cliff there juts out. It's quite impossible for anybody on the ridge to see the cave, or anything entering it. I noticed it last night."

Pete scratched his head, puzzled. "I don't know. Maybe you're right and he's wrong. Can you prove it?"

Jupiter looked solemn. "I intend to. This evening, when we return to the cave. Perhaps then I shall be able to expose not only Mr Allen's fabrication, but also the hoax of the dragon, as well.

"Don't forget," he continued, "we have several suspects in this case. Men who might know about the tunnel, and who also have a grudge against people. Mr Allen and Mr Shelby both lost their jobs and were prevented from working. Mr Carter, if he's the son of the original tunnel builder, would know about the tunnel, too, and have a grudge to settle with a lot of people. How this ties in with a dragon and with the cave we found, I don't know. But maybe we can discover something in the cave tonight."

"You mean," Pete asked, "we're going back to the cave tonight? Back there? With you-know-what waiting for us?"

Jupiter didn't reply and continued writing on the pad in front of him. Then he reached for the phone. "First, I have to find out something," he said. "I should have thought of it before."

14

Start of a Dragon Hunt

"PLEASE put me through to Mr Alfred Hitchcock," Jupiter said. "You may tell him Jupiter Jones is calling."

Pete and Bob looked blankly at each other, then at Jupe. He ignored their questioning glances, as he cradled the telephone with one hand and continued writing notes with the other.

After a moment, he heard the hearty voice of the famous film director. "Alfred Hitchcock here. Am I to take it that you have just solved the enigma of the disappearing dogs at Seaside?"

Jupiter smiled. "Not quite, Mr Hitchcock. I'm calling in reference to what you said a while ago. You mentioned that your old friend Mr Allen was an expert on dragons, and used them in his horror films."

"Indeed he did," replied the director. "Bats, werewolves, vampires, ghouls, zombies, dragons—anything calculated to scare a human being out of his wits! It's too bad they were all made long before your time. I can assure you that fans still tremble today and get goose-pimples, merely thinking about them."

"So I've heard," Jupiter replied. "I imagine that for Mr Allen to have achieved such effects, these monsters and creatures he used must have looked quite real."

"Of course they did," Mr Hitchcock said crisply. "You don't frighten people with weak imitations of things that are supposed to be frightening, lad. It has to look and act exactly like the real thing."

Jupiter nodded. "Who makes them?"

Mr Hitchcock laughed. "We have very clever studio prop men, naturally. Sometimes a horrendous creature is animated by some ingenious mechanical device inside, motor driven or through gears and a crank. At other times, depending upon the action required of it, we use a different technique. We move the creature a bit at a time and photograph it, and then again and again until we have made it do whatever is required. That is called the 'stop-motion' technique, for your information. When all the frames are run off together, the action seems continuous, you see."

"I understand," Jupe said. "And what happens to the monsters that were created, after the picture is completed?"

"Sometimes they are put away," Mr Hitchcock said, "and saved for another occasion. Sometimes they are sold to an auction house. Other times, they are simply destroyed. Does that answer your question?"

"Yes," Jupe said. "But I have another. Do you have any of Mr Allen's films available that we could see? One particularly to do with dragons."

"Odd you should ask that," the director said, after a moment's pause. "I've been looking through our film library for an old classic of his entitled *Creature of the Cave*, one that is almost entirely to do with a dragon. I've been meaning to make a close study of it for my next picture. Not that I intend using Allen's ideas," he added hastily, "but merely to assure myself that my picture will have to be very good indeed to beat his."

"It would be most helpful to us, Mr Hitchcock," Jupe said quickly, "if we could see this film. I would like very much to see for myself how a real dragon is supposed to look and act. Could you arrange it?"

Mr Hitchcock didn't hesitate a moment. "Be at my studio in an hour. I shall be at Projection Room Four."

The phone went dead. Jupiter put it down on its cradle slowly. He turned to Pete and Bob.

"Remember," he told them. "We will be looking at what is supposed to be an authentic dragon. Pay close attention to the film when we get there. Perhaps you may notice something that might save our lives later."

"What could that be?" Bob asked.

Jupiter got up and stretched. "I've been going on my theory that the dragon at Seaside is a fake. Perhaps I'm wrong. In that case, our dragon is real!"

Promptly on time, transported by Worthington in the grand old Rolls-Royce, The Three Investigators arrived at the bungalow on the Hollywood studio marked as Projection Room Four. Mr Hitchcock, seated at the rear with his secretary, nodded hello.

"Lads, take those seats down front," rumbled Alfred Hitchcock. "I'm just about to signal the projectionist, and we'll get started."

He pressed a button on the seat near him, and the room went dark. Light flickered from a small opening in the booth behind the director, followed by a whirring sound.

"Remember," warned Mr Hitchcock, "this picture was made a very long time ago. The print we are showing is perhaps the only one available. It is underexposed and will be dark and murky in spots. That cannot be helped.

"That is enough introduction. On with the film!"

Soon, the boys forgot where they were. Mr Hitchcock

had not exaggerated. The film was as suspenseful as he had indicated it would be. The story held their attention, and little by little they were led along the path of horror by the skill of the old film director who had made it.

The next scene on the screen dissolved to a cave. The next moment they were in it. And then, as their hearts pounded wildly again, they saw it once more—the dragon!

It filled the screen as it entered the cave, a grotesque creature, huge and frightening. Its short wings lifted, showing long muscles rippling and writhing like live snakes under its wet scaly skin. Then the small, dark head turned on its long, swaying neck to face them.

The long, powerful jaws opened as it roared.

"Wow!" Pete whispered. He shrank back in his seat involuntarily. "That's real, all right!"

Bob stared at the monster moving closer on the screen, and his hands gripped the arms of his seat tightly.

Jupiter sat quietly, concentrating on every move the screen dragon made.

Spellbound they watched the film until the finish. When the dark projection room was flooded suddenly with light, they were still tense and shaking from the film's impact.

As they walked to the rear of the room, their legs were rubbery.

"Whiskers!" Bob exclaimed. "I'm beat. It was just like last night, all over again. I forgot it was a movie!"

Jupiter nodded. "There's the proof of how a master of horror can achieve his effects. Mr Allen had the skill to make us accept and believe anything he wanted. He scared us all out of our wits with a make-believe dragon on a celluloid film. That was his intention and we let him. That's something we must always remember."

"Well?" asked Alfred Hitchcock. "Can you see now why my friend Allen was once regarded as the master of horror films?"

Jupiter nodded. He had a lot of questions to ask the mystery director, but he saw Mr Hitchcock was busy and his secretary waiting to take notes. Instead, he thanked him for providing the film

"You've seen your film dragon now," Alfred Hitchcock said. "I shall await with great anticipation your solution of the mystery of the one in Seaside "

He ushered the boys out and they headed for the gleaming Rolls-Royce where Worthington waited.

They settled back against the leather seats as the tall chauffeur drove slowly towards the gate.

"You told us to watch the dragon closely," Bob said after a moment, "and I did. I couldn't see any difference between this dragon and ours. Could you, Pete?"

Pete shook his head. "The only thing different was this dragon had a better roar than ours."

"I don't think it had a better roar," Bob replied. "It's just that ours seemed to cough a lot."

Jupiter smiled. "Exactly," he said.

"What do you mean, Jupe?" Pete asked.

"Apparently our dragon in Seaside is more susceptible to bad weather. It seems to have developed a cold."

Bob looked intently at Jupe who was sitting back looking quite content. He didn't trust that look. It meant as he had learned from the past, that Jupe was on to something. Something that had eluded both Pete and himself.

"How could a dragon catch a cold?" he asked.

"They're supposed to live in damp caves and water."

Jupiter nodded. "My thoughts exactly. And in a few more hours when we return, we shall be able to expose the mystery of why our cave dragon coughs. If my theory is correct, it might explain why we were allowed to leave the cave, and are still alive."

Pete thought about this and frowned. "That sounds pretty good, Jupe. But what if your theory isn't correct?"

Jupiter blew out his cheeks. "It had better be," he said. "After all, I'm betting our lives on it."

15

Questions and Answers

PETE suddenly exploded. "Maybe it's time you stopped being so mysterious, Jupe, and told us what's going on. We became The Three Investigators to solve riddles and unexplained mysteries. Nobody said anything about becoming Kamikaze suicide pilots. I like my life. Bob probably likes his, too. How about it, Bob?"

Bob nodded, smiling. "I do, I do! And if I lose it, who will you get to do your research and keep your records? Pete's right, Jupe. What gives?"

Jupe shrugged. "I'm not entirely sure, yet. Naturally I wasn't intending to risk our lives needlessly. But there are times when it becomes necessary to take a chance."

Pete shook his head. "Oh no you don't. You'll have to convince me first. I saw a film the other night that my Dad brought home. One with a lot of his special effects. The scientist hero in it took a chance, too, and I'd hate to tell you what happened to him."

Jupe frowned. "I'd forgotten your father was a special-effects man for pictures, Pete. What was it about?"

Pete grinned. "About bugs."

"Bugs?"

"Ants and beetles that take over the world," Pete explained. "One of those science-fiction films. And believe me, it was as scary as that old picture we just saw with the dragon. These insects were fifty to a hundred feet tall—as high as buildings."

"How did they do that?" Jupe asked.

"They used real insects," Pete replied.

"Come on, Pete," Bob said sarcastically. "Real insects as high as buildings?"

Pete nodded. "My Pop explained it to me. It's a different process from the ones Mr Hitchcock explained to us.

"They photograph real insects through a prism—like a monocle—and then blow them up and superimpose them—photograph them again next to pictures of buildings. Naturally they look real and scary because they *are* real! That's how they do a lot of these pictures about monsters that come from outer space."

Jupiter was pinching his lower lip again, his eyes thoughtful. "Do you still have the picture at your house?"

"It'll be there for at least another week," Pete said. "My Pop even suggested that you and Bob might like to see it. You're invited over, any night. Also, it's free!"

Jupiter looked impatient. "I'm afraid we'll need it sooner than that, Pete." He glanced at his watch, then turned to Pete again. "Is your projector battery operated?"

Pete nodded. "Sure. It works both ways."

Jupe pursed his lips. "Is it your own property, not a loan from the studio?"

"It's ours, all right," Pete said. "Or my Pop's, anyway. Say, what's all this about?"

"It's about saving our lives—and possibly solving a mystery at the same time. Do you think your Dad would loan us your projector and the film you saw, just for tonight?"

Pete blinked. "You mean, to take out?"

"To take out," Jupe repeated. "It sounds like the kind of picture I'd like to show somebody."

Pete rubbed at his nose, and then shrugged. "I don't know. I suppose so, Jupe. I'd have to phone him, of course, to get permission."

"That's great," Jupiter said.

"Okay," Pete said. "But before I try to convince my Pop of anything, I want to know where we are going tonight—and why. I'm tired of being in the dark."

Bob nodded in agreement.

They both looked at Jupiter Jones. For a moment, he tried to disregard their stares. Finally, he shrugged and threw his hands open.

"Very well," he said. "I was hoping to keep my clues and deductions a secret. Mostly because I'm not certain yet if they're entirely correct. And even if they are, I'm still at a loss as to where they lead. This investigation started with trying to locate a missing dog. Since then, we have unearthed other mysteries. None of which appear to have anything at all to do with the mystery of the missing dog or dogs of Seaside. Mr Allen hired us to find his dog, Red Rover. But I have felt from the start that the mystery of the other missing dogs would be cleared up when we found his. That was before we met the dragon."

"What *about* the dragon?" Bob inquired. "You've made it pretty clear you think it's a fake one. How come?"

"Yes," Jupe said. "Even though I panicked and ran as you both did, I have several reasons for doubting the authenticity of the dragon in the cave."

"Give us one, for a starter," Pete said. "What makes you think it wasn't real?"

"Several things. The cave wasn't real. The old tunnel wasn't real. The entrance to it wasn't real. Naturally, given those things to consider, one is inclined to doubt that the dragon is any more real."

"I didn't notice any of those things," Bob said.

"Start with the first cave we entered," Jupe said. "We found some boards and moved one aside to enter the smuggler's cave."

"I remember you were looking at them in a funny way," Bob said. "What wasn't real about them?"

"It was supposed to be an old cave, a hideout for smugglers and pirates. The boards were old—at least some were."

"Some?" Pete asked.

Jupe nodded. "The plank that we moved aside, for one. But there was a long, wide piece of plywood. Plywood, I don't have to remind you, is a fairly recent process in manufacturing wood products. There wasn't any available for pirates or even smugglers."

"Plywood?" Pete repeated. Then he frowned, "Well, maybe. But it doesn't sound like too much proof of anything."

Jupiter went on. "Let's take the next cave. The large one we discovered when Bob found the rock that moved. We still don't know who made that possible. If you recall, we advanced into that cave inland, because there was no other way to go. No outside opening, no mouth to it like the first.

"Then we had to stop. We were confronted by what appeared to be a solid wall at the end. We had hoped this cave would lead to the old tunnel Bob had discovered in his research."

Both his partners nodded.

"I remember you started to scrape away at it with your knife," Pete said, smiling. "What did you find out, aside from the fact that solid rock can ruin a good knife blade?"

Jupiter reached into his pocket. He took out his pocket knife and opened it.

"Notice the grey particles on the blade," he said. "Then smell them."

Pete and Bob did as he suggested.

"Paint!" they both exclaimed in unison.

Jupe nodded, folded the knife, and put it away.

"Walls of old caves are not painted," he said. "And as I scraped the covering away, my blade left a streak in the surface. In my opinion, the wall was not rock at all, but plasterboard—sprayed with a grey paint, with sand and small stones thrown roughly on to the surface to make it look like a real cave wall. Plasterboard is, you know, an industrial material commonly used for walls in houses, or partitions in offices. A lot of it is prefabricated, with built-in textures looking like cork or brick.

"I believe whoever put that wall up was trying to hide a fascinating and perhaps valuable discovery," Jupe said.

"Like what?" Bob asked.

"Something more important on the other side," Jupe said. "Something, I suspect, like the original old tunnel of the uncompleted rapid transport system!"

"That's it!" Pete exclaimed. "Somebody discovered the old tunnel and then closed it up so that nobody else could find it! They thought a fake wall would turn away anybody who managed to get in that far."

"Unless," Bob added, "unless that's the way they closed it up in the first place."

"Prefabricated board isn't fifty years old," Jupe said.

"Maybe not," Bob replied. "But we don't know exactly when the tunnel was boarded up, either. Maybe they did it later. To keep kids and animals out."

Jupe's eyes were thoughtful.

"Possibly, Bob, although I doubt it. However, we now have to consider the third mysterious happening. We were at the wall. I was testing it, I turned to show you what was on my knife, and then—"

Pete nodded, and gulped. "Then the cave opened up and it got lighter all of a sudden, and the dragon came in. I see what you mean." He scratched his head. "At least, I think I do. Maybe you'd better tell me."

"All right," Jupe said. "The cave opened up. How did it open? What made that possible? There was no opening outside that we could see. Otherwise, we certainly would have entered that cave rather than the first one, where Bob fell into the mud-hole."

"Okay," Bob admitted. "We couldn't see any opening. But the dragon knew about it, somehow. Because he managed to open it. Maybe he's a lot smarter than we are."

Jupe raised his hand. "Remember, my theory is based on my feeling that everything was false and contrived. Therefore, the dragon was, too. And if it's smarter than we are, then it's only because the dragon is not really a dragon, but something controlled by some human agency."

Pete blinked. He turned to Bob. "What's he saying?"

Bob shook his head. "I think he's saying our dragon is a robot, not a dragon. Is that it, Jupe?"

"I'm not certain yet," Jupiter admitted. "It may be a robot, or some construction similar to the dragon used by Mr Allen in his old horror film. We'll find out in due course.

"What I *am* certain about, however, is the cave entrance. That, too, was not real. Unfortunately, we never tested it or examined it closely from the outside.

I'm sure that if we do, we'll find it's a fake entrance—built of some lightweight material, just as any fake film set or prop is, covered and painted to make it look real. Anybody could build a fake rock. Whoever did it covered the true entrance to the cave. When he wanted to enter, or wanted his dragon to enter, he merely moved the fake opening aside.

"I'm sure you'll both admit," Jupe added, "that if the city of Seaside wanted to cover up a big cave or a tunnel, they wouldn't use any lightweight, painted boards inside and fake rocks outside. They would have sealed it up solidly—with concrete!"

Pete looked out of the window of the smooth-purring Rolls. He frowned, then nodded. "Maybe you're right, so far. If we go back tonight, we'll test those rocks near the first cave entrance. But rocks don't scare me. What I want to know about is the dragon. Why wasn't it real?"

Jupiter Jones sat back, folding his arms.

"We all saw it about the same time. We were about the same distance away. Our hearing and sight are all on a par. Now what did we hear? What did we see?"

Pete and Bob were silent a moment, thinking.

"I heard a humming sound," Bob said. "Then I saw it."

"I saw a bright light—its eyes were shining," Pete said. "About that humming sound, yes—I think I heard it, too. Just before it roared, anyway."

Jupe nodded. "How did it move?"

"How?" Pete asked. "*Very fast!*"

Jupe turned to Bob. "What do you say?"

"I'm thinking!" Bob mopped his forehead. "I agree with Pete. It came in very fast. Just sort of glided in."

Jupe was watching him intently. "Like the dragon

in the film Alfred Hitchcock showed us? Did it move the same way?"

Bob shook his head. "No. Mr Allen's dragon seemed to walk. Ours just kind of glided."

"My impression, too," Jupe said. "It wasn't flying. It didn't move its feet. It glided. Therefore my deduction—it was built merely to look like a dragon. Made to create a startling and frightening effect.

"And the explanation for its gliding is quite simple. Our dragon moved, or was propelled, on wheels! Don't you remember we saw wheel tracks in the sand when we first came down?"

Pete and Bob looked at Jupiter open-mouthed.

"A dragon on wheels?" Pete repeated. "You mean, that's what scared us half to death?"

"I remember something else," Bob said. "We talked about it before. Mr Allen's film dragon roared. Ours seemed to cough a lot."

Exactly!" Jupiter smiled. "That's what I meant about the human agency behind it. Or rather, I should have said, the human agency inside it."

"What are you talking about now?" Pete asked groaning.

Jupiter smiled. "The man inside our dragon had a cold."

The dignified voice of Worthington interrupted. "We're at the Jones Salvage Yard, Master Jones. Shall I wait?"

Jupe nodded. "Yes, Worthington. Pete has to make a telephone call. Then hopefully we'll go to his house and pick up something. And tonight, we're going back to Seaside."

He glanced at his partners. "Am I right, so far?"

Pete grinned. "I just hope you're right later—when we see the coughing dragon again!"

16

Return to Danger

JUPITER's respect for Pete's father increased when Mr Crenshaw gave the boys permission to use his projector and the new studio film without questioning their reasons.

"He didn't even warn us about taking good care of it," Jupe said. "I guess he trusts our judgment."

"I don't know about that," Pete replied. I'm the one who lives here. If anything happens to that film or Pop's projector, *I'm* the one who gets it!"

The boys were at Pete's home now, in the den used by Mr Crenshaw for his home movies. Pete was rewinding the spool from the take-up reel. Jupiter had asked for a preview of the film so that he could better judge how effective it would be.

"All set!" Pete called. "Lights out, Bob!"

When the room was in darkness, he pressed the switch and the film began. The wall screen blazed with light, and soon the boys discovered that Pete hadn't exaggerated. The photographed insects were terrifying when blown up to outsize proportions.

The sound track suddenly groaned down to silence, and Pete snapped off the image.

"Lights, please, Bob!" he called. "I'm sorry, but I'm showing you the wrong reel. This part comes later. I guess my Pop was running it through again to check on his effects."

He was rummaging through the stack of cylindrical

cans marked with various numbers when Jupe stopped him.

"I don't think it matters, Pete. We don't have to see the entire film now. This part showing the insects in natural surroundings is exactly what I had in mind."

"But that's Reel Six," Pete answered. "It's a flashback. That's just the ants themselves, in the hills and along the shore, getting ready for their invasion of our cities." He picked up another can. "This first reel shows them attacking the cities. The part I mentioned where they're as tall as buildings."

Jupiter shook his head. "We can't show buildings or cities. We want to make it appear as if the giant ants have invaded the cave!"

Pete and Bob looked at Jupe, surprised.

"Is that where we're going to show the picture?"

Jupe nodded. "With the built-in speaker in your projector, we'll have all the sound effects. The wide-angle lens I noticed will be very effective, too. And most important of all, your projector is battery operated so we can run it in the cave."

"We're lucky about that," Pete said. "The battery pack was specially made so my Dad could use it on location work."

Bob broke in. "Well, let's see the rest of this reel you have on now, Pete. Jupe and I can always come back some other night to see the rest of it."

Pete shrugged. "It's okay with me if you fellows like to see a picture backwards."

Bob put out the lights, and Pete resumed showing his film of the giant insects. The boys watched in absorbed silence from then on, giving way to only an occasional murmur of surprise or horror. When it was over, they sat back tingling with excitement.

"Whiskers!" Bob exclaimed. "That's some picture. I can hardly wait to see the whole thing."

Pete pressed the button to rewind the spool, and glanced at Jupiter. "Will that be enough, do you think?"

Jupiter smiled. "It should be perfect for our needs."

"Great," Pete said. "Only I still don't understand what you intend doing with it. Who's going to see it in the cave? That dead man, or ghost, who phoned us?"

"Perhaps," Jupe admitted. "But my main purpose is to find out how a joker responds when a joke is played on him instead."

"A joker?" Bob said. "I didn't think that Mr Carter was joking when he threatened us with his shotgun."

"I wasn't referring to Mr Carter," Jupe said, calmly.

"You weren't?" Bob asked. "Maybe you forgot that he could be the living descendant of the Carter I read about. Labron Carter, who lost his fortune building the tunnel at Seaside and then killed himself because he was ruined. You said yourself, he would certainly know about the old tunnel and cave. And that he might want to get even with the people at Seaside for ruining his father. And, with his kind of temper, he's the kind of guy who could sure do it, too!"

Jupiter shook his head. "Mr Carter's not the man I suspect of creating the dragon in the cave."

"Why not?" Pete interrupted. "What makes you so sure?"

"One thing," Jupe said. "When we met Mr Carter, he did a lot of yelling. But he didn't have a cold. We met a man who was very clever about making things that scared people. If you recall, he did have a cold. And I associate him with the dragon because, as you will remember, *it coughed!*"

Bob blinked. "You think Arthur Shelby is the joker

who made the dragon? I mean—if it's really a constructed one, and not real!"

Jupe nodded. "It could be Mr Allen, too. He knows a lot about dragons. But my guess is Shelby."

"But why Shelby?" Bob asked. "He made scary things to keep people from bothering him at his home. What does he have to do with the cave? It's not his."

"That's what we intend to find out this evening," Jupe said. He glanced at his watch. "I suggest we get ready."

"You're forgetting somebody else," Pete said. "You two are only guessing about Carter, Allen or Shelby. But there were two other men there, and we all saw them!"

"That's right!" Bob said. "The skin divers! And they said something about having to continue their work, before they disappeared."

Pete snapped the big box that locked up the projector. Then he glanced at Jupiter.

"Well?" he demanded. "Am I wrong? What about those two tough guys? Couldn't they have something to do with it?"

Jupiter nodded. "They certainly could. And, if they turn up tonight my suggestion is—project your film for *their* entertainment."

"What about the dragon?" Pete asked. "It might be there, too, you know."

Jupe nodded again. "That should be even more interesting. We've all heard how a mouse can frighten an elephant. It remains to be seen if an ant can scare a dragon!"

It was dark on the ridge above the beach at Seaside. The narrow, secluded street was quiet as Worthington eased the Rolls-Royce close to the kerb and stopped.

Bob stepped out first. He glanced quizzically along the quiet street. "Why so far away this time, Jupe?" he asked. "You've left us a good walk to the staircase."

"Merely being cautious," Jupiter replied. "The Rolls-Royce might have attracted attention here already. If Hans were available this evening, his truck might have provided better cover."

Pete staggered out, swinging the projector in its case. He looked at the long walk ahead of him and groaned. "Don't mind me. By the time I get there with this load, my arms will reach the ground."

"That wouldn't be too bad," Bob said smiling nervously. "You'd pass for an apeman, then. Maybe you'd scare our dragon!"

Pete grunted in reply, and shouldered the case.

"Wait, Pete, we'll give you a hand with that," Jupe offered.

The tall boy shook his head. "No, thanks. I can make it. It's my responsibility. I guess I'll be stuck with it all night, considering I'm the only one who knows how to work it."

Jupe smiled. "Your contribution may prove to be the deciding factor this evening, Pete. Let's hope it works!"

They left Worthington to wait in the car and moved swiftly along the deserted street. Dark clouds obscured the moon. Below they could hear the booming of the heavy surf as it thundered on the beach.

Pete glanced up at the sky nervously. "I wish it wasn't so dark tonight."

"We're all nervous," Jupe admitted. "But darkness is our best protection until we reach the cave."

They were perhaps twenty paces from the staircase leading down to the beach when they heard footsteps.

"Quick! Hit the ground!" Pete urged.

The Three Investigators hurled themselves to the side and rolled behind the thin bushes bordering the sandy vacant ground.

The footsteps came closer along the path. They sounded heavy, confident, and aggressive. Then they slowed and became softer, stealthier. The boys huddled closer, and hugged the ground. Somebody was stalking them!

From the shadows, they were able to see the figure as it came closer. Soon it was almost abreast of them. They stared in fright.

They had seen that bulky figure before. And as they saw it again, their eyes automatically travelled down his body. They recognized the object held close to it.

The menacing shotgun. The one that carried the biggest load of shot possible. The double-ought gun of Mr Carter, the man who hated dogs, kids and seemingly everything.

The disagreeable, hot-tempered man slowed his walk still more when he came level to them. They could see his head swinging suspiciously to the side as he squinted into the darkness. His eyes were black and angry, his lips set in a firm, tight line.

"That's funny," they heard him mutter. "Could have sworn I saw something moving—"

He shook his big head as if puzzled, then continued his walk. The cowering boys waited until they could no longer hear his footsteps before lifting their heads.

When they did, he was gone.

"Whew!" Bob breathed. "Am I glad he didn't see us!"

"Me, too," Pete said. "I guess he even goes to bed with that shotgun in his hand. I wonder who he's looking for?"

"Come on," Jupe whispered. "He's far enough away.

Now's our chance to slip down the staircase. Keep low."

Quickly, they ran the remaining distance to the stairs.

"All clear!" Pete signalled.

They hurried down the many steps as silently as they could. When they got closer to the beach, they relaxed. The rolling breakers were making so much noise that they knew their footsteps could not be heard.

Pete reached the sand first. "Okay. Here we go again. I can't wait to find out how that dragon in the cave likes science-fiction movies!"

"We'll find out soon enough," Jupe said, "if he's home."

"It's okay with me if he's not," Bob said. "All I want to find out about is the tunnel. You two can have the dragon."

They came to the original cave they had entered. To the surprise of his partners, Jupe continued walking past.

"Psst! You passed the cave," Bob whispered.

Jupe nodded silently. He pointed ahead to the bluff jutting out to the beach.

"Round the cliff is the entrance to the big cave. We'd better see if it's open or not."

They rounded the bend in the cliff wall and stopped. Three giant-sized boulders crowded against the cliff wall, towering over their heads.

"Those are probably the fake rocks that mask the entrance," Jupe whispered. "Apparently it's closed now."

Pete approached the largest boulder. He put his ear close to it and then tapped it with his hand.

The sound he produced was dull and muffled.

Pete smiled. "You're right, Jupe. It's not solid rock—just like the props made at the studios. Made out of light balsa wood framing, or plaster over wire."

Jupe nodded and turned back. "We'll get you set up in the cave first, so Bob and I can look round."

"What?" Pete spluttered. "Leave me alone while you two—"

"You'll be a lot safer than Bob and me," Jupe said, leading the way back into the smaller cave. "We'll be doing some dangerous investigating. All you have to do is sit tight. And get ready to show your picture."

Pete continued to look puzzled. He looked round. "Who am I going to show it to? Are there any bats flying round here for tonight's audience?"

Jupe had already removed the board leading to the small inner cave pocket. He crawled through and Bob and Pete followed. Then, carefully, they replaced the board.

Jupe whistled softly. "The equipment we forgot last time is still here! Try to find the spot that moves the rock, Bob. We'll pick our stuff up later when we leave."

Bob stooped over the rock in the wall. "Got it," he said happily.

With a slight rumbling sound, the rock turned in the cave wall.

"Here is where you'll stay, Pete," Jupe said. "Inside this small cave. Use the opening in the wall for projecting your film. We're going to wedge the rock in place now so it won't close. When you get the signal, flash your picture on that big grey wall we found inside."

Pete settled down to get his machine ready. He picked up the can of film, then flicked his torch on. "Okay. What will the signal be?"

Jupe thought briefly. "*Help*, I imagine," he said.

17

Mystery of the Old Tunnel

LEAVING PETE BEHIND, Bob and Jupe advanced slowly through the huge vaulted cavern. The air was damp and cold, and they shivered.

They hadn't gone far when Bob whispered, "It's not all there!"

Jupe blinked. "What?"

Bob moved his torch beam ahead, and then swung its light from side to side.

"That big wall—it's—it's open in the centre!"

Jupe followed the arc of Bob's torch with interest. The opening in the grey wall extended from floor to ceiling.

"Bob, I think we've found your lost tunnel!" he cried softly.

Cautiously, the boys stepped through the opening.

The tunnel gradually became larger. It seemed to extend smoothly inwards as far as they could see. Then both boys stopped, their skin prickling, their hearts suddenly pounding.

A huge, shadowy figure was facing them, lying very still and quiet.

It appeared to be waiting for them!

The boys threw themselves flat on the ground, trying not to move, hardly daring to breathe.

They waited and waited. Nothing happened.

The dragon lay there, crouching, a long, dark, humped frightening figure. Its head drooped downwards on the end of its long neck.

"M-maybe it's sleeping," Bob whispered.

Jupe shook his head. He tried to keep his voice low and calm. "Remember," he breathed in Bob's ear. "It's not a real dragon."

Bob nodded curtly. "I know. That's what you've been telling us. Let's hope you're right."

The boys waited another long moment. Then Jupe flicked his light on again, and ran its beam along the ground.

He smiled now, relieved.

"Look at the dragon's feet, and tell me what you see."

Bob stared along the yellow path of light. He blinked.

"Tracks," he said. "Right under the dragon. They look like railway tracks."

Jupe heaved a sigh of relief.

"We were both right. The dragon's a fake, all right. And you've found the underground rapid transport railway that Labron Carter built more than fifty years ago. But you were wrong about one thing, Bob. You said it had never been used!"

"What do you mean?"

"The dragon's been using it," Jupe replied.

"But why? I don't get it," Bob answered, puzzled.

Who would build a dragon to lie in an underground railway tunnel that hadn't been used for fifty years? A railway that wasn't going anywhere. One that would probably never be used again. It didn't make sense.

Why? Bob wondered.

"We're going to find out now." Jupe was tugging at his sleeve. "Let's go before they return."

Bob followed Jupe slowly. "Before who returns?"

Jupe didn't answer. He kept going.

They came up to the monstrous shape huddled in the centre of the tunnel.

Jupiter frowned, puzzled.

"What's wrong?" Bob whispered.

"I can't figure it out," Jupe admitted. "It's facing the other way. Outwards, towards the beach. The fake inside wall is open, yet the outside cave entrance is still closed. What do you make of it?"

Bob shrugged. It wasn't too often that Jupe was stumped and asked what *he* thought about a puzzling situation.

"It looks like whoever's in this thing is heading out—to sea, maybe. But meanwhile they don't want anybody coming in," Bob said.

Jupiter nodded, his eyes bright. "I think you've made an excellent deduction, Bob. Let's look over this remarkable dragon now, before it gets away from us. It could be our last chance."

The drooping head of the dragon lay still as they circled it warily. The eyes appeared closed, lifeless.

Jupe flicked his light against it briefly.

"Hmmm," he said. "They're not eyes at all, but small headlights! Remember how the cave lit up the last time when it entered? And how it created the illusion of blazing eyes?" Jupe chuckled. "It's very simple. All they had to do was use lights, running lights, like a ship, or plane, or train."

They were at the side of the still dragon now. Jupe extended his arm. His fingers seized something that gleamed oddly in the dark, scaly skin.

"Door handle," he muttered. "That's odd. I don't see any door."

Bob peered over Jupe's shoulder. He pointed upwards. "There's another one above it. And another above that."

Jupe laughed shortly. "Fooled me again. It's not a door handle. These are metal ridges to put your feet on. I'm climbing up."

Bob followed Jupe up the footholds. When Jupe was at the top of the dragon, he lifted something up and held it there. He looked down, his lips parted in amazement.

"It's a hatch," he whispered to Bob. "Stand guard. I'm going down to take a look."

Bob gulped and nodded. Jupe heaved his stocky body. Then he was gone. The hatch slowly closed.

Bob started as he heard a thump inside.

It was as if the dragon had finally swallowed Jupe, Bob thought nervously.

He peered into the darkness ahead. In the light of his torch he could see the tunnel curving slightly in the distance. The tracks disappeared as the rounded wall cut off his view. The sides of the tunnel were smooth, showing ribs of steel extending to the ceiling, and patches of concrete.

He heard a rustling noise and jumped.

The hatch had opened.

"Take a look," Jupe urged softly.

Bob clambered up quickly. As Jupe dropped below him, his feet found a narrow ladder. When he touched bottom, Jupe flashed his light round the interior.

"Neat, isn't it? It looks like a dragon. It runs on tracks like a train. But look at this—a periscope! And this porthole. Unless I'm very much mistaken, Bob—this dragon is actually a midget submarine!"

Bob rapped the curved side wall. He rubbed his knuckles. "Whatever it's made of, it's pretty hard stuff."

Jupe nodded. "It would have to be iron or steel in order to remain submerged. But I don't think it is. Let's see what the engine room is like."

The boys walked forward down a narrow aisle.

"Gearshift, dashboard, brakes and pedals!" Bob exclaimed. "What kind of a sub is this?"

Jupe snapped his fingers. "I remember reading of one of the first submarines ever built. It ran along the ocean floor like a car. The inventor had windows built in the sides so people could look out, and charged his passengers admission. There were special air compartments in it to withstand the water pressure.

"The dragon builder might have taken his idea from that or the Rose Bowl floats—mounted on a car chassis, covered by the roses and design of the float. They travel in low gear, directed by a driver hidden below."

Bob snapped his fingers excitedly. "So that's how the dragon moved along the sand without seeming to. I mean, its legs didn't work like the dragon in the film Mr Hitchcock showed us."

"It's understandable," Jupe said. "Mr Allen needed a more realistic type of dragon for the film he directed. The builder of this one just needed something that looks like one. Just enough to get the scare effect he wanted. Only I wish I knew why—or who he's trying to scare."

Suddenly an eerie sound floated through the dragon.

"*Aaaaa . . . ooooo . . . oo!*"

Both boys jumped.

"What was that?" Bob whispered.

Jupiter hesitated. "It came from the rear section."

Bob looked at him. "Are you sure? I don't want to be in this thing if it suddenly decides it wants to take a dip in the sea."

The moaning sound came again, long, drawn-out, and chilling.

"*Aaaaaaahh . . . ooooooo . . . oooo!*"

Bob shivered. "I don't like the sound of that."

To his amazement, Jupe turned and trotted down the narrow aisle to the rear of the dragon. He stopped. The moaning sound came again. Jupe listened carefully, his head bent low to the floor.

"W-what is it?" Bob asked nervously, coming closer.

Jupiter didn't answer. He turned and directed his torch beam along the interior wall of the dragon. Then to Bob's surprise, he smiled.

"I believe we've finally solved our mystery," he said with a chuckle.

"We have?"

Bob cocked his head, listening intently. "I hear it," he said. "I still don't like the sound of it."

"That's because you've allowed your fear of the dragon to overcome your senses," Jupe said, smiling. He opened a narrow door and flashed his light inside the dark opening.

The moans became louder.

Bob blinked suddenly. "Hey—wait a minute! That sounds like—"

He craned his neck and looked inside. His jaw dropped.

"Dogs!" he exclaimed. "Whiskers! A whole cupboard full of dogs!"

"That's the mystery solved," Jupe said. "The mystery of the missing dogs."

"What's wrong with them?" Bob asked. "They look as if they're too sleepy to move, unless they're ill—"

Jupiter shook his head. "Not ill. Sleepy, perhaps. My deduction is they've been tranquillized!"

"Tranquillized?" Bob repeated. "Why?"

Jupe shrugged. "Perhaps they got in somebody's way. And he didn't want to hurt them. Scientists often stun an animal with a tranquillizing dart or needle to render it harmless so they can examine it."

One of the dogs moaned again. "*Aaaaahhh . . . oooooo . . . oo!*"

"That's an Irish setter," Bob said excitedly. "It must be Mr Allen's dog!"

"Red Rover!"

The red-coated dog stretched and yawned. Then it got to its feet and shook its head, its long ears flopping.

"Red Rover!" Jupe called. "Come on out, boy. Come on."

He extended his hand, palm up. The dog looked at it, sniffed and started to wag its long tail.

It took a few tentative steps, staggered and then, regaining its balance, walked out of the cupboard. Then it was rubbing its muzzle against Jupe's knee and whining softly.

"Nice fellow," Jupe said, stroking its head. "Good dog!"

Bob smiled. "Mr Allen was right—it's a friendly dog, all right!"

He extended his hand and knelt. The setter left Jupiter and came to Bob, wagging its tail slowly.

"Good boy," Bob said, rubbing its ears. He looked up at Jupe. "We found it. What do we do now?"

Jupe had taken a slip of paper out of his pocket. He folded it several times. Then he slipped it under the Irish setter's collar.

Jupe leaned forward, until his head was close to the big dog's ear. "Go home, boy!" Jupe ordered. "Home!"

The dog craned its head, and wagged its tail happily.

"Home!" Jupe repeated, extending his arm.

The dog uttered a happy bark. At the sound, other moans and whines came from the open cupboard. Slowly the other dogs emerged, walking stiffly, their tails wagging.

Bob grinned. "Whiskers! I counted—six! We've found them!"

Jupe nodded. As each dog wobbled out, he bent and folded a piece of paper under its collar.

"They're wide awake now. Hand them up to me."

"What's that about?" Bob asked.

"I prepared a brief message for each dog owner in the event we found the dogs," Jupe replied. "Like other successful firms, I think our organization should advertise and get credit for public service."

Red Rover whined.

Jupe turned and knelt. "All right, Red Rover. You're going home first."

He lifted the big dog and carried it up the ladder.

"Home, Red Rover. Home!" he whispered in its ear.

The setter whined happily and scrambled over the top. With long bounds, it raced for the wall opening.

Jupe grinned. "He's wide awake now. Hand the others up to me, Bob. Maybe the fresh air outside will revive them."

One by one, Bob passed them up and Jupe released them. They all came to life soon and ran off after the setter.

Bob brushed off his hands. "Pete can let them out of the cave. Okay, that accomplishes our mission. I'm ready to leave now myself."

His mouth opened in surprise as Jupe lowered the hatch and came down. "We can't leave," Jupe said.

"Why not?" Bob demanded.

"I just saw shadows moving on the tunnel wall. Somebody is coming this way."

"Oh, no!" Bob exclaimed. "We're trapped! Where can we hide?"

Jupe was walking down the narrow aisle. He opened the door of the small cupboard that had contained the dogs.

Pete rubbed his arms to get the chill off. He had already finished setting up the projector. A small rock had been wedged in place to hold the big turning rock firmly open. The reel of film was on the spool, and he crouched nervously waiting for the signal. Then he would flick the starter switch and run the picture.

He fussed once more with his machine to make sure it was aimed at the correct angle through the rock opening. Then he stretched out face down and waited.

He heard a sound behind him, and his flesh crawled.

He froze, listening intently. He heard it again.

Somebody, or something, was in the shallow outer cave they had entered first. He was able to hear it now, moving inside. Then, after a long wait, he heard the sound returning.

He heard a scuffing sound in the sand. Then he saw something that made him tremble still more. A big board hiding his smaller cave was moving.

Pete bit his lip. Reluctantly, he reached for his father's projector and pulled it back. He was on his knees now, wondering what to do. There was still time for him to wriggle through the rock opening. He could join Bob and Jupe in the big cave, and let the rock close behind him.

But they were depending upon him to hold his post, he remembered. Those were Jupe's instructions.

The big board moved again. It opened slowly.

Pete moved away until his back was against the cave wall. He waited, watching the boarded opening to the cave give way to the intruder.

Desperately, his hand searched the cave floor, seeking a weapon. Then he remembered his torch and his hand closed on it. The darkness of the cave might not be enough protection.

Then the big board was thrust aside. A burly form stood silhouetted in the faint light of the opening. It was so large that it had to turn sideways to enter the small cave.

Pete sucked in air.

He recognized the ill-tempered Mr Carter and his shotgun.

The roof of the cave was low, and Mr Carter had to stoop to advance farther. He bent and took a step forward. Then he stopped, listening.

Pete heard it, too, his heart pounding wildly.

"*Aaaaaahh . . . ooooo . . . oo!*"

He shrank against the wall. He drew up his legs and gripped his weapon tighter.

Then he heard something else, the sound of running feet. It came closer, accompanied by a panting breath.

Other feet were following. Again he heard the moaning, wailing sound. "*Aaaaahh . . . ooooo . . . oo!*"

It had to be Jupe and Bob running. And being chased.

He gulped. He couldn't close the moving rock now. It was their only way out of the big cave. Their only chance for safety.

But how safe was it? Pete wondered, with the terrible-tempered Mr Carter standing crouched a few feet from him in the darkness, his shotgun at the ready.

There was a sudden whirling, skidding movement. Yellow eyes blazed in the opening in the rock.

Something moaned and bolted through.

It was followed almost immediately by something dark and growling. Then another. And another.

Pete's mouth gaped open as he shrank against the cold cave wall.

He had been prepared for a dragon. This was a pack of wild, furry animals.

Mr Carter grunted as something hit him.

He went down. Pete swallowed nervously. After the pack attacked the fallen man, they would be upon him.

He lifted the torch in his hand.

18

Caught!

Bob and Jupiter huddled inside the narrow cupboard, straining their ears to hear.

"That's a lot of track to check and clear," a man's voice complained. "As if we didn't have enough to do with all that drilling. But we're all set now."

"It'll be worth the trouble, Harry," another deep voice said. "Let's move it."

"Sure," the first man replied. "He's a slippery character, Jack. Do you think we can trust him?"

The other man laughed. "There's only one of him, brother. And there's two of us. It's our boat. Maybe he ought to be worrying if he can trust us!"

The hatch opened and the men climbed down the ladder. Bob and Jupe, their ears pressed tightly against the thin door, heard one of them walking forward.

An engine whined and caught. They felt a sudden jerk and a slight bump. Then they were moving smoothly on the rails.

Bob touched Jupe's knee in the darkness. "They sound like those two skin divers. Are we going into the ocean?" he whispered.

"I don't think so," Jupe said softly. "There's still not enough ballast in the dragon to keep it submerged."

"Whew!" Bob sighed. "That's a relief."

The dragon moved with only a slight swaying motion to indicate its progress.

"We're going backwards," Jupe whispered, "into the old tunnel."

"I know," Bob whispered. "But why? What are they up to?"

Jupiter shrugged. "I wish I knew. Whatever it is, it sounds important."

The dragon stopped suddenly with a lurch, and Bob and Jupe fell back, bumping against the thin wall.

The man who had been driving came back. "Okay, Harry," his voice rasped. "It's time to load up. Watch yourself!"

"He'd better not try any tricks on us," the other grumbled. "Or I'll crown him with one of those bars."

"Yeah, sure," the first one said. "Well, that's the chance we're taking. For a million bucks, it's worth it!"

Jupe and Bob stared into the darkness of the tiny compartment. One million dollars? They wondered if they had heard correctly.

The men walked away and climbed the ladder. The hatch opened, and fell back into place with a clanging sound.

Jupe tapped Bob's shoulder. "Let's see what they're up to," he whispered.

Stealthily, they opened the cupboard door.

They had taken only a few steps when they halted abruptly. A man was speaking, his voice hoarse and rasping, his words interrupted by spasms of coughing.

"Hurry it up," he said. "I've taken care of the night watchman with some knockout drops. He'll be out for a few hours. We should have the three hundred bars out of there before he wakes up."

Bob nudged Jupe. "You were right. It's Arthur Shelby. I recognize his voice and his cough."

"That's the second mystery solved," Jupe whispered. "The mystery of the coughing dragon. Only one remains."

"You mean this one—what they're doing here?" Bob asked.

"The mystery of the three hundred bars," Jupe replied. "Three hundred bars of what?"

He tapped Bob's shoulder and moved along the dimly-lit aisle of the dragon again. Then, carefully mounting the narrow steps, he raised the hatch with his hands and peeped out.

His mouth gaped open. He was looking at a concrete wall alongside the dragon. A large hole had been drilled in it—a hole big enough for men to walk through. A man emerged from it carrying something in his arms and leaning back to balance the weight.

"Hey! This stuff weighs a ton," he complained.

"Sure," Shelby answered. "Why do you think you Morgans were hired—just because you have a handy boat? What this job needed was a lot of muscle power. The kind you used drilling our way into the vault. You and your brother were hired to take care of that and the loading from here to your boat."

"Sure," the man grunted. "I ain't complaining. How much does each one of these things weigh?"

"About seventy pounds," Shelby replied. "Just stack them alongside the dragon. When we've got the three hundred out of there, we'll load up the dragon and head for sea."

The husky Morgan brother put his load down and turned back to the hole in the wall. His brother came out, leaning back and breathing heavily.

"Okay, Jack," he grunted. "Three less to go now."

He set his bars down as Shelby directed and returned to the wall and disappeared inside.

Jupiter lowered the hatch.

"Mr Shelby said each bar weighed about seventy pounds," he whispered. "The Morgan brothers were talking about a million dollars. I think I know what those bars are. Gold!"

"Gold?" Bob exclaimed. "Where's it coming from?"

"The large standard gold brick or bullion bar the government makes," Jupe said, "is seventy pounds! The smaller standard gold bar weighs twenty pounds and is worth nine thousand, six hundred dollars alone! Shelby and the Morgan brothers appear to be robbing a Federal Reserve Bank!"

"Whiskers!" Bob exclaimed softly. "How much is one of those seventy pound bars worth?"

Jupe frowned, and calculated swiftly. "Approximately four hundred and eighty dollars a pound . . . times seventy . . . or—" Jupe whistled softly "—over thirty thousand dollars! Thirty-three thousand, six hundred dollars, to be exact!"

"Wow!" Bob exclaimed again. "And Shelby said they were taking three hundred bars!"

"I make that amount to be ten million, eighty thousand dollars," Jupe calculated. "Quite a haul."

"That makes us witnesses to a pretty important bank robbery," Bob whispered. "We'd better get out of here, if we want to stay alive!"

Jupe agreed, his voice husky with excitement. "The question is *how*—Mr Shelby is too close to the dragon!"

He walked forward slowly, thinking. Then suddenly he darted to the head of the dragon.

Bob was right behind him, wondering if Jupe had found a new place for them to hide.

Jupe stopped so abruptly, Bob bumped into him.

"Sorry," Bob murmured, "I didn't expect—"

His companion raised a warning finger to his lips.

He leaned forward, his eyes gleaming with excitement.

"Hold tight!" Jupe whispered fiercely. "They've left the ignition key in!"

Bob's jaw gaped. "You mean—you're going to drive it—away? Can you drive it? How will you see? There's no windscreen".

Jupe shrugged. "It's worth a try. I'm sure this runs like an ordinary car, and I know how a car works. There's a foot clutch, brake, gearshift, accelerator. And it'll be on the tracks to the end of the tunnel."

He dropped to the small seat. "Here goes," Jupe called, and turned the ignition key.

The engine whined shrilly.

It whined again. Then it coughed and stopped.

"It coughed, Jupe!" Bob exclaimed. "Then it wasn't Shelby coughing."

Jupe nodded, biting his lip. "It stalled," he said bitterly. He turned the key again, holding it hard in the lock.

The engine whined once more. Suddenly it caught with a loud roar.

Jupe sighed, relieved. He pulled the gearshift into first and slowly eased his foot off the pedal.

The dragon bucked forward in one convulsive leap. Then it coughed and stopped. The engine was quiet.

"Stalled again!" Jupe cried bitterly. "It's the clutch that—"

Then he and Bob whirled. Something heavy was banging on the side of the dragon. They heard something fall against it with a loud thud. Then they heard something more ominous.

The hatch was opening.

"We should have locked it!" Bob whispered.

Jupe nodded, his eyes frightened. "I know. I'm sorry —I wasn't thinking."

to grab the long tail of the dragon. Now he saw them braced, leaning back, holding it still.

Then one of them ran forward.

"Get 'em out of there, Harry!" the other Morgan yelled.

Harry nodded. He leaped for the metal ridges leading to the top of the dragon and the open hatch.

"They got us, Jupe," Bob cried. "What'll we do?"

Jupe sighed. There was nothing else to do. He got up and walked down the narrow aisle.

"Perhaps if we surrender now, they won't hurt us," he said, doubting his words as he said them.

Preceding Bob on the narrow ladder, he held his arms up high.

"We give up, Mr Shelby," he called. "We're coming out now."

He heard Shelby's angry shout. Then another noise filled the cave. It was a roar that echoed and bounced off the thick walls of the tunnel.

"*RR—AAAAAAGHHHHHH!*"

Jupe jerked his head round at the roar and saw the wall ahead of them had closed.

He heard the Morgan brother coming up the side call out, "Watch out, Jack!"

Then, incredulously, he saw the tough faces of the husky men dissolve into astonishment, then into fear. Another frightening roar filled the cave.

Bob grabbed Jupe's arm. "Look!"

Jupe nodded. A huge ant had suddenly appeared on the cave wall. It seemed very far away. Then, with an astonishing leap, it had closed the gap between them, and was almost on them.

Harry Morgan screamed from the top of the dragon. "Monsters! Look out!"

In almost the same breath, he had reached into

his pocket. A gun gleamed in his shaking hand. He fired twice.

The ant on the wall seemed to scream its defiance, and came closer. Another ant followed, sliding up the tunnel wall to gigantic size, almost filling it.

"I hit him and it went right through him!" yelled the first Morgan. He fired again and again.

The ants roared and kept coming. They came in increasing numbers, filling the cave, crowding the walls.

Arthur Shelby had come up and was staring at the walls, a curious expression on his pale, freckled face.

Both Morgans were firing now.

"Giant ants coming out of the walls," the bigger Morgan yelled. "The bullets don't bother them. Get us out of here, Shelby!"

Shelby shrugged and stared at the moving ants on the wall.

The second Morgan grabbed him, brandishing his pistol. "Open the wall, Shelby, or I'll let you have it. We're getting out of here!"

Shelby looked at him coldly. Then, with a shrug, he reached into his pocket. A thin, tubular object appeared in his hands. He put it into his mouth.

Bob and Jupe waited for the shrill sound of a whistle.

They heard nothing. They saw the wall slowly open.

"Come on, Jack!"

The Morgans ran for the opening, firing wildly at the ants on the wall screaming back at them. In another instant they had gone through the huge walls.

"Run, you fools!" Arthur Shelby said mockingly. He looked up at Bob and Jupiter, a curious appraising look on his face.

"Very clever," he said drily. "But a little too clever,

my young friends. You've cost me a fortune, and I don't see how I can decently let you get away with that."

He reached into his other coat pocket. This time he held a more frightening object. His eyes glittered.

"Don't shoot," Bob gasped.

Shelby coldly nodded to them. "Step down, please." And as Jupe came down, followed by Bob, Shelby added, "The next time you try to appropriate a bus-like vehicle, I strongly suggest you learn how to double-declutch when you change gear. Stops stalling you see."

Both boys climbed down. Shelby turned towards the darkest corner of the wall and the cone of light. "And you with that projector," he called. "Shut off that film and come over here, at once! I've a gun in my hand, I warn you!"

The screaming in the cave stopped. The ants flickered on the wall and then disappeared.

"D-don't shoot!" Pete yelled. "I'm coming."

He came up slowly, looking wonderingly at Jupe and Bob standing beside the still dragon

"It's really not real?" he asked Jupe.

Jupe shook his head.

"No more real than your giant ants," Shelby snapped. He looked at the boys and then at the gun in his hand. "I regret this, boys, really I do. But you had no business interfering—"

He halted suddenly, his arm extended and trembling. A loud eerie moan floated through the tunnel.

"*Aaaaaahhhh . . . oooooohh . . . oooo!*"

"Oh, no! Not again!" Shelby cried. Quickly, he reached into his pocket and produced the slender object he had used before. He put it to his lips. Again it made no sound.

The huge walls rustled and closed.

Jupiter, listening intently, smiled. He flicked on his torch.

Caught in his glaring beam, they saw huge, leaping shapes coming at them, their eyes glowing, their jaws open, sharp teeth menacing.

"Look out!" Pete yelled. "Those furry animals—"

Then he gasped and grinned sheepishly. "I mean, dogs," he added. "Wow! What a dope!"

Arthur Shelby groaned too. "Too late," he sighed.

The first animal bounded up to them, barking happily. Its long, brushlike tail swept back and forth in a feverish arc. Its dull reddish coat gleamed.

"Red Rover!" Jupe exclaimed. "He's come back."

The big setter ignored Jupe's outstretched arm and leaped for Shelby. The red-headed man backed off, holding his gun outstretched.

"Go away, Rover," he snapped. "I'm warning you—for the last time—go home!"

The big dog shook its head and whirled round the man. The other dogs came at him, too, backing him up to the wall.

They leaped happily at the man, growling and barking, their tails wagging. Once more, Shelby waved at them with his gun. His face was pale, shining with sweat.

"It's no use, Mr Shelby," Jupe said. "You can't shoot them. You like dogs too much. And they're certainly crazy about you."

The thin, red-headed man regarded the leaping animals and lowered his gun.

"Yeah," he said morosely. "Crazy about me. That's it, all right."

He looked blankly at the slender metal object in his hand, then shrugged and put it back in his pocket.

He put his hand down and almost unconsciously stroked the heads of the happy dogs.

"Now what?" he asked, speaking to himself.

"I've an idea, sir, if you care to listen," Jupe said.

"You have?" The pale eyes stared at the stocky boy.

Jupiter Jones nodded. "Yes, sir. It's based largely on the idea that you're really a practical joker, not a greedy criminal. Would you care to hear it?"

The red-haired man nodded curtly.

"Put everything back. We'll help you, if you like," Jupe said. "You might want to leave the hole you drilled in the wall, just as it is. It will be your joke on them. That you had the chance to take all that gold, and you didn't. We won't tell, and they'll never know who did it—or rather who *nearly* did it!"

20

Alfred Hitchcock Offers a Hand

When Pete, Bob and Jupiter entered Alfred Hitchcock's office two days later, the famous director was seated at his desk, reading a newspaper. He motioned them to his big, comfortable chairs.

"Sit down, boys," he said. "I'll be with you as soon as I finish this interesting article in the papers."

They sat and waited patiently. Finally, the director folded the paper and put it aside on his desk.

"So!" he boomed in his hearty voice. "I suggest a case for you concerning the missing dog of an old friend. And what happens? Not only his, but several others are returned. I also see a column in the Seaside newspaper telling of some bizarre plot to rob a large bank. The heading reads: 'BANK OFFICIALS PUZZLED BY CONTRITE AND CONTRARY CROOKS!' Was this all your doing? I must admit I am puzzled, too."

Jupe cleared his throat. "Yes, sir. It was. They were—I mean, sir—yes, we're kind of responsible for everything."

Mr Hitchcock held up his hand. "Your modesty, lad, is most laudable. Still, I would rather hold my own praise in abeyance until I completely understand how you three solved this unique mystery of the missing dogs."

"Well, sir," Jupe said. "Actually you helped us a great deal in solving the mystery, sir, when you showed us that old film Mr Allen made with the dragon."

"Ah, yes," Mr Hitchcock said. "And, as I recall, there was some talk about you boys actually encountering one of those rather fantastic beasts."

"We sure did," Pete said abruptly. "And we're lucky to be alive to tell about it. Even if it *wasn't* real."

"Incredible!" Mr Hitchcock murmured. "The very real menace of a dragon that wasn't real. I should like very much to hear about it."

Bob Andrews whipped out his note book. He proceeded to tell how the investigation had run into a snag at the very beginning, and then how they had managed to pick up the threads that ultimately led to the solution of their original mystery. Mr Hitchcock listened attentively.

"Your Mr Shelby sounds like a most ingenious and interesting man," he said. "Do I understand you correctly when you say he voluntarily gave up his foolproof plan to steal several million dollars' worth of gold, rather than hurt you and some dogs?"

"Yes, sir," Jupiter said. "He kept the dogs alive and fed them. He had to tranquillize them to keep them quiet and out of his way. He told us he was going to turn them all loose when he left the cave for the last time with the dragon and the gold.

"He could have forced us at gunpoint to help him carry out the gold after the Morgan brothers ran away. He could have taken enough to be wealthy. He didn't need the entire ten million dollars."

Mr Hitchcock drummed his fingers on the desk. "And his original plan was actually to run the dragon underwater at night, in conjunction with those villainous Morgans?"

Jupe nodded. "I thought the dragon was too light, but he had calculated his ballast in advance—the heavy gold bars. He had to test his dragon in the water, at first, by loading it with rocks. As a matter of fact, that's how your friend Mr Allen happened to see the dragon. It was out on a test run, while he was looking for Red Rover."

"And your clue to Shelby's part in it was his cold?"

Jupe smiled weakly. "He had a bad cough when we met him. So I associated him with the coughing of the dragon. Later I found out it coughed when it stalled. That was partly due to wet wiring, from the many experiments in the sea."

"But your mysterious phone call—the ghostly, rasping voice—that was really Shelby?"

Jupe nodded.

Mr Hitchcock shook his head. "This Arthur Shelby doesn't sound like a typical crook at all. How did he happen to tie up with such low characters as the Morgan boys?"

"They had a salvage rig and he knew them as tough men who would do anything. He needed their help for the work in the cave, drilling into the bank vault through the concrete wall of the tunnel, and then getting the gold out. When he offered them a million dollars, they were more than willing."

"And how did they propose to get the gold from the sub into the boat?"

"After he got under way, the Morgans with their underwater gear were to attach a cable from the sub to their tug, and tow it out to sea. When they were far enough out, they were going to surface the sub and unload the gold bars. Then they were going to head for Mexico."

Mr Hitchcock nodded. "Why a dragon, at all?"

"That was from knowing your friend Mr Allen and his film background, using dragons to scare people. You see, at first Shelby just thought it would be a new way to play a practical joke on his neighbour. But when he heard of a large shipment of gold bars to that bank, he decided to carry out a robbery. He figured the dragon could easily be converted into a functioning sub. It suited his kind of offbeat thinking—a funny and perfect way to get the gold from the bank through the old tunnel to the sea. It backfired on him because it was the oddity of the dragon that kept us interested in trying to solve the mystery."

"I should have imagined Mr Shelby to be without sufficient funds to construct something as elaborate as that dragon," Mr Hitchcock said.

Bob was ruffling through his notes. "I left out a page," he explained. "He told us he had friends working at some of the studios. Some of them liked to make gadgets like he did. They told him of a prop dragon that was to be destroyed to make room for other properties needed in storage. He saved them the trouble, went down and took it apart there himself. Then he had it hauled to his place in pieces and put it together later."

Mr Hitchcock frowned. "Did it have wheels?"

"No," Bob said. "That was another bargain he picked up. He found an old abandoned chassis from a float at the Pasadena fairgrounds, left over from the Rose Bowl parade. They let him have it for towing it away. He put the dragon on that."

"Hmmm. Clever," Mr Hitchcock said. "Now, how was it that Shelby knew about the big cave and the tunnel, whereas my friend Allen, who lived almost directly over them, did not?"

"Well, to begin with, Shelby knew about the existence of the tunnel from his days as an engineer for the City Planning Board. But he only found a way into the tunnel by accident.

"A landslide from an earthquake had covered the big cave many years before either he or Mr Allen lived there," Jupe continued. "Shelby was walking along the beach one day and saw a fissure in the rock wall. He dug in and discovered the cave and then the tunnel. He told the Morgans. They helped him build the fake wall inside. It was to fool people who accidentally found their way into the cave, and stop them from going farther into the tunnel."

"I assume they helped him make the fake rocks outside the entrance, too?" Mr Hitchcock said.

"Yes," Jupe said. "That was interesting, and well thought out, too. They had to work from the inside of the cave and not attract attention. It was only when they had it all constructed that they could afford to clear the outside rubble away, at night, and insert their own rock covering."

Mr Hitchcock nodded. "The Morgan brothers—were they responsible for the collapsing staircase on your first adventure there?"

Pete interrupted. "They didn't want anybody around who might spoil their scheme, so they weakened that staircase to scare people off the beach. They spotted us from their boat when we fell down it. And when we didn't leave, they came out of the ocean and pointed their spear guns at us. They figured that should frighten us into not coming back."

"I see," Mr Hitchcock said. "I believe you mentioned they had disappeared in the original cave you entered. Did you solve that mystery?"

Bob was back to his missing page of notes. "They went down the same pit I fell in. It wasn't quicksand. Just a lot of mud and water. With their gear, they were able to work their way through to an underground passage that came out in the other cave near the tunnel. Like cave diving. It was an alternative way into the large cave during the day. They couldn't take a chance of disturbing the big rocks outside too much and possibly attracting attention. Incidentally, after they ran out of the cave that last night, they never came back. I guess they were ashamed of being scared."

"And good riddance, I might add," Mr Hitchcock said. "The thin, reed-like object Shelby blew into, that made no sound but opened and closed the fake cave wall. Am I to assume that was a sonic contrivance?"

Jupe nodded. "It opened and closed the prop rock opening outside, too. It had two varying high-frequency sounds. But it was Mr Shelby's undoing actually."

"Indeed, young Jupiter!" Mr Hitchcock exclaimed. "How was that?"

"It was his experimenting with the silent whistle, his sonic beam, that attracted all the dogs to him in the first place. As you know, sir, dogs can hear a higher frequency wavelength than humans. Mr Allen's setter ran to him the first night it was released from the kennel. He didn't expect that because he thought Mr Allen was still in Europe. That meant he had to move fast. The other neighbourhood dogs had already deserted their owners at night and run to Mr Shelby's sonic whistle. He couldn't get rid of them, and had a lot of work to do, getting the dragon ready, the bank-vault opening drilled and the tunnel tracks cleared to the bank. Rather then destroy the dogs, as the Morgans wanted, he merely put them to sleep by adding tranquillizing agents to their food."

Mr Hitchcock reflected some more. "The dragon roared, you said. Was that your imagination running wild, lads?"

Bob shook his head. "No, sir. That roar and a lot of other things, like a windscreen opening in front were controlled by instruments on the dragon dashboard. Jupe was pressing all the buttons he could find in order to get it going."

"Now, this Mr Carter," Alfred Hitchcock asked, "did he get safely out of the cave after being bowled over by the escaping dogs?"

"Yes," Pete interrupted. "He was gone when we went back there to pick up the equipment we'd left behind."

Mr Hitchcock nodded. "And was he actually the living descendant of the Carter who started the tunnel and lost his fortune at Seaside?"

Jupe smiled. "Yes. But although he knew there was a tunnel, he never did find out exactly where. That's why he knew about the first cave, and the boards leading into the next one. He was constantly snooping round there, and was more of a problem and worry to Shelby and the Morgans than we were. I suppose that's why he always carried his shotgun with him, because he suspected something was going on.

"After the staircase near his house collapsed, he got suspicious again and went down to investigate. That's when he nearly ran into Pete.

"Mr Shelby told us the boards in the first cave had evidently been put in a long time ago by smugglers or pirates. He assumed they had built the moving rock. He found it by accident, just as we did. He added the newer plywood pieces himself when some of the old boards rotted. He was afraid somebody else would discover the moving rock and then the big cave and tunnel. He must have been saving the moving rock for a private emergency exit, because he never told the Morgan brothers about it."

"And you helped Arthur Shelby return the gold bars to the bank vault?" Mr Hitchcock asked.

"No," Bob broke in. "He thanked us for the offer but said it was his own responsibility. He didn't want to get us involved in any kind of criminal activity.

"He managed to get the gold bars back inside, and left them lying around carelessly as another kind of joke. Then he patched up the hole they'd made. I suppose the bank will eventually discover the tunnel underneath their vaults. But we haven't told anybody else, not even Mr Allen."

Mr Hitchcock nodded. "It is all certainly possible, given a man of Shelby's considerable engineering talents. And it all came about because he knew the complete underground history of the city of Seaside."

"Yes, sir," Jupe said. "And the present-day history, too. So he knew exactly what banks were accessible from the tunnel all the time."

"I see. One thing disturbs me. You allege my old friend Allen lied deliberately, saying he saw the dragon enter the cave, when it was impossible."

"I'm sorry about that, sir," Jupe said. "We found out later it was a simple mistake. He had been halfway down the steps that time, but had forgotten it in his distress at losing Red Rover. Is there anything else, sir?"

"No, boys. Though perhaps I should meet this Mr Arthur Shelby. A man ingenious enough to scare you three lads is a man I could use. After all, you must remember, horror is my business, too."

"Thank you, sir!" Jupiter cried, and Bob and Pete echoed the words. The First Investigator leaped to his feet. "We'd better get going. We've taken up enough of Mr Hitchcock's time."

There was a flurry of happy boys, and then they had gone.

"Mmmm," Mr Hitchcock murmured to himself. "I wonder if I should borrow that ingenious dragon Mr Shelby devised. Since I've just purchased that large bus-like trailer for my holidays, perhaps it would be a good idea if I learned how to double-declutch the dragon in the cave first, before I ventured forth on the Los Angeles motorways!"

2

The Mystery of the Death Trap Mine

Text by M. V. Carey

The Mystery of the Death Trap Mine was
first published in the U.K. in a single volume
in hardback in 1977 by William Collins Sons & Co. Ltd,
First published in Armada in 1980

Contents

	A Word from Alfred Hitchcock	169
1	The Invitation	171
2	A Roaring Welcome	181
3	Allie's Mysterious Millionaire	187
4	Shots in the Dark	195
5	The Forbidden Mine	202
6	Death Trap!	209
7	Tracing the Dead Man	217
8	A Prowler in the Night	225
9	The Earth Rumbles	231
10	Is the Glitter Gold?	239
11	The Hungry Thief	247
12	A New Suspect	255
13	The Widow Disappears	261
14	The End of the Trail	269
15	The Silent Watchdog	276
16	Flight!	285
17	Breakdown	290
18	Stranded in the Desert	298
19	The Millionaire's Secret	303
20	Where's the Loot?	311
21	A Souvenir for Mr Hitchcock	316

A Word from Alfred Hitchcock

Greetings, mystery lovers!

Once more I invite you to share in the exploits of The Three Investigators—that trio of adventurous young detectives who specialize in solving mysteries of an unusual, if not bizarre, nature. I hope that those of you who are brave of heart will relish a journey with them to a remote New Mexico mining town where a dead man waits in a dead mine to betray a living scoundrel . . . and where a mysterious woman—but I am getting ahead of myself!

If by chance you are not already acquainted with The Three Investigators, let me state that Jupiter Jones, leader of the group, is a plump lad with an excellent memory and an astounding talent for deduction. Pete Crenshaw is quick and athletic, but in his more cautious moments is apt to deplore Jupiter's penchant for stirring up trouble. Bob Andrews is a studious fellow who is in charge of research and records for the trio. The lads reside in Rocky Beach, California, on the outskirts of Los Angeles, but they are never averse to travelling far afield in search of mystery and intrigue.

So much for the formalities. You may now turn immediately to chapter one and get on with the story.

ALFRED HITCHCOCK

I

The Invitation

"HEY, JUPE! Guess who's looking for you!" said Pete Crenshaw as he pushed open a trap-door in the floor and scrambled into the Headquarters of The Three Investigators.

"I don't need to guess. I know," said Jupiter Jones. He leaned back in his chair, which squeaked under the weight of his chubby frame. "Aunt Mathilda was up at six o'clock this morning," he said, in his precise way. "She cooked a hearty breakfast and sent Uncle Titus off to a garage sale in Oxnard. I deduced at once that she planned a busy day." Jupiter peered at his watch. "It is now exactly one-fifteen. From your question, I now deduce that Uncle Titus has returned, that he has made some purchases in Oxnard, and that Aunt Mathilda wishes me to help unload the truck."

"Jupiter Jones, boy genius!" Bob Andrews chuckled. The slender, bespectacled youth was leaning on a filing cabinet, quietly reading through some notes.

The three boys were in the battered old mobile home trailer that Jupe's aunt and uncle had given them for a clubhouse. It sat in a far corner of The

Jones Salvage Yard, concealed behind stacks of old timber, beams, and scrap iron. The salvage yard was a busy place. Filled with all sorts of ordinary scrap, it also contained a variety of unusual items rescued from houses that were being torn down—antique sundials, old marble bathtubs, carved door-frames, and stained-glass windows. As they were always busy cleaning, sorting, and storing these things—and waiting on people who came from up and down the Pacific Coast looking for hard-to-find objects—Jupiter's uncle and aunt had completely forgotten about the trailer in the corner.

The boys had turned the trailer into a headquarters for their junior detective firm—The Three Investigators. Inside was a tiny lab and darkroom, and an office fitted out with a worn desk, chairs, and a telephone. A large filing cabinet held reports on all the boys' cases, meticulously written up by Bob Andrews. Jupiter, the leader of the trio, spent much of his free time in Headquarters, pondering the firm's cases and exercising his incredible brain.

Jupiter was proud of his uncanny knack for deduction. Now, as Pete and Bob grinned at him, he scowled. "Aunt Mathilda is *not* looking for me?" he asked.

"Don't complain," said Pete. "When Aunt Mathilda's looking for you, you know what it means—work! No. 1 was down at the Rocky Beach Market this morning and I bumped into Allie Jamison."

Jupe sat suddenly upright in his chair. Bob

stopped shuffling papers and stared. Allie Jamison, the daughter of one of the wealthiest families in Rocky Beach, had been their client the summer before. In a case they called *The Mystery of the Singing Serpent*, they had helped her get rid of a sinister house-guest and had exposed a diabolical blackmail plot. But their association with the girl had not been a complete pleasure. She was impulsive, devoted to getting her own way, and not above bending the truth when it suited her.

"Oh, good grief!" said Jupe at last. "I thought that girl was spending the summer with an uncle in New Mexico. The Jamison house is closed up and Mr and Mrs Jamison are in Japan!"

Pete nodded. "I know. But right now Allie is here in Rocky Beach. She told me she and her uncle needed to pick up some stuff from the house, and her uncle had business in town. And something's up with her. She's just busting with some great news and she's going to come tell us about it before she and her uncle leave for New Mexico."

Bob sighed. "And it started out to be such a peaceful summer."

"Never mind," said Jupiter. "She *is* leaving again—soon, one hopes! Pete, how long will Allie be here?"

"Only until tomorrow!" said a voice from behind the curtain that separated the little laboratory section of the trailer from the office. Pete groaned as the curtain was pulled to one side and Allie Jamison stepped out, grinning. She looked like a young rodeo rider in her faded jeans and western shirt. Her face was tanned and her long, tawny hair was sun-streaked. "Aren't you glad to see me?" she asked innocently. But her hazel eyes sparkled with malicious glee.

"How did you get in here?" demanded Pete.

Allie laughed. She went to the desk, pulled herself up on to it, and sat there cross-legged. "I got here ahead of all of you," she said. "There's a painting of the great San Francisco fire on the back fence of this place, and in the painting there's a little dog watching the fire."

Jupe slouched wearily. "And there's a knothole in the dog's eye. You stuck your finger through the knothole, undid a catch on the inside of the fence, and the boards swung open." Jupiter was referring to Red Gate Rover, one of several secret entrances to the salvage yard that the boys had devised.

"You deduced right this time," said Allie. "I watched you guys open that gate at least a dozen times last summer. And I didn't have to be an Einstein to figure out that you had some kind of secret hideout back here."

"Go ahead, Allie," said Pete. "Rub it in. How did you get in here?"

Allie went on with obvious delight. "You guys aren't as smart as you think! There's a sign that says 'Office' on top of a pile of junk right inside that gate. But the arrow on the sign doesn't point to the junkyard office. So I figured it must point to your detective headquarters, And I was right! I just followed the arrow through the junk . . . and ended up in front of that sliding panel." Allie pointed to a panel at the back of the trailer. "That's darn good detective work, if I do say so myself," said Allie.

"We must put a lock on that panel," said Jupe.

"Yeah, and take down that sign!" added Pete.

"Don't bother," snapped Allie. "I *am* leaving tomorrow, and I don't care about your silly secrets anyway." She gave a saucy toss of her head. "Besides, I've got better things to do."

"Such as what?" demanded Pete.

Allie leaned forward intently. "I've got a case of my own," she said. "I'm going to investigate like you guys, and I'm going to keep my Uncle Harry from having the wool pulled over his eyes."

"Oh?" said Jupe. "Is your Uncle Harry incapable of taking care of himself?"

Allie's face was serious. "My Uncle Harry is Harrison Osborne, and he's no dope," she told them. "He made a couple of fortunes in the stock market before he retired and bought that Christmas tree ranch in New Mexico. But when it comes to people, he really can be *dumb*!"

"And you're smarter?" Pete laughed.

"I can spot a phony when I see one," said Allie. "The place my uncle bought once belonged to a mining company. There's a mine on it—Death Trap Mine."

"That's a great name," jeered Pete. "What was in the mine? Dinosaur bones?"

"Silver," said Allie. "The mine's dead now. The silver's all gone. It's called Death Trap Mine because a woman once wandered in there and fell down a shaft and was killed. Some of the old-timers in Twin Lakes—that's the town where

Uncle Harry's got his place—they say the woman's ghost still haunts the mine. Of course, I don't believe a word of that. But there *is* a spook around. He's the guy who bought the mine and a hunk of land around it from my uncle."

An angry spot of colour showed on Allie's tanned face. "He's up to something," she said. "He's playing some kind of game. He was born in Twin Lakes, see?"

"Is that a crime?" asked Bob, puzzled.

"No. But there's something funny about a guy who's born in a town and who leaves when he's practically a baby and then, years and years later, he comes back a millionaire and puts on this big act about how he's so glad to be home. Only he's about as friendly as a rattlesnake. Also, he opened the mine. The entrance was sealed with an iron grille, but he opened it and bought a guard dog to watch it. What is there to guard in a dead mine? The guy potters around the place in brand-new jeans and he's even got a hard hat, like construction workers wear. The get-up doesn't match the rest of him. He's got manicured nails!"

Allie paused. When the boys said nothing she went on with her recital. "He won't let anybody near that mine. I smell a rat. He's pulling some kind of fast one right in my uncle's front yard, and I'm going to figure out what it is."

"Lots of luck!" said Pete.

"Allie!" A man's voice came faintly to them. Bob went to the periscope that Jupe had rigged up and installed in the roof of the trailer so the boys could look out without being seen. He put his eye

having trouble getting help in Twin Lakes. Why don't you three come with Allie and me tomorrow morning and spend a couple of weeks at my ranch?

He turned to Aunt Mathilda. "If you could spare the boys for a while, I'd like to have them. We've got plenty of room, and I'll pay them by the hour, just as I'd pay anybody I got locally."

Aunt Mathilda looked doubtful. "I don't know." she said. "I thought that this week we might clear away that stack of salvage in the far corner of the yard. It's only taking up room."

All three boys started. Aunt Mathilda was planning to remove the heaps of junk that protected Headquarters! Jupe thought quickly. Without the boys, she would never get to this task.

"Aunt Mathilda. I would like very much to go with Allie and her uncle. It would be a new experience."

"And new experiences are good for you!" said Allie, laughing. "Besides, you just might run into some mystery in Twin Lakes, and that would be fun!"

Jupe suddenly realized that in some devious way Allie had put her uncle up to issuing the invitation. She had trapped them into helping her with her case.

"It might be fun at that," said Pete. "I think my folks will let me go."

Bob looked eager. "I *know* I can get leave of absence from my part-time job at the library. It's slow there now."

"Well, all right," said Aunt Mathilda.

Harrison Osborne shook her hand. "I promise not to work the boys too hard."

"I'm not worried about that," said Aunt Mathilda. "It can't be done. They can think of more excuses not to work than a centipede has legs!"

2

A Roaring Welcome

"SUCH AS IT IS, this is Twin Lakes," announced Harrison Osborne.

He slowed the big air-conditioned station wagon that had carried them across the Arizona deserts and up into the hills of south-western New Mexico. The boys, who rode in the back, looked ahead along the tar-macadamed logging road and saw a green valley between two ranges of tree-covered mountains. There were rows of little frame houses on dusty streets that ran back from the main road. Several buildings faced the road—a grocer's store, a drugstore, a newspaper office, and a tiny crumbling hardware store. In the centre of town a faded brick courthouse reared up to an imposing two storeys. There was a filling station and, beyond this, the Twin Lakes Fire Department.

"Fire!" said Pete suddenly, pointing to a place beyond town. Smoke curled up into the clear afternoon air.

"Don't panic," said Allie. She sat next to her uncle in the front seat. "That's just smoke from the furnace at the sawmill."

"Mining used to be the big thing here," Uncle Harry told them. "Now the mines are all played out and the sawmill keeps the town going. Logging is the only thing left. Forty-five years ago Twin Lakes was a rip-roaring place, but no more."

"Last place in the world I'd come to if I wanted to pull a fast one," said Pete.

Harrison Osborne looked away from the road for a second. "A fast one?" he said. "Allie, have you been telling the boys any of your wild tales?"

Allie stared straight ahead.

"*Allie?*" Her uncle stopped the car to let a woman dressed in jeans and a plaid shirt cross the road in front of him.

"I only said that Wesley Thurgood is a phony—and he is, Uncle Harry!"

Uncle Harry made a sound that was halfway between a snort and a laugh. He kept his foot on the brake and turned to face the boys. "I know you three are amateur detectives," he said, "but don't go bothering Wesley Thurgood. He is our neighbour and I don't want any trouble with neighbours. Thurgood's got a fine reputation. He's made a lot of money in real estate, and he came back to Twin Lakes because that's where he started out. He was born here—just before the mine closed down. His family moved away soon after, but he told me he grew up hearing exciting stories of Twin Lakes' boom-town days. He bought Death Trap Mine because his father once worked there. Now that doesn't seem to me like such a far-out thing to do."

"So why'd he open up the mine again?" demanded Allie with all the authority she could muster.

"That's none of our business," said her uncle.

"I do know that it wasn't so kids could prowl around and maybe get hurt. Thurgood's one hundred per-cent aboveboard. I've checked him out and so has my bank. He's a millionaire—his credit rating would make a Vanderbilt look poverty-stricken."

He turned to the boys and smiled. "Allie has a way of going off half-cocked," he said. "She's got it in for Thurgood because she tried to explore the mine one day and he marched her back home by the scruff of the neck. And quite rightly. It's called Death Trap Mine because a woman was killed in there years ago on just that sort of an expedition."

Pete exploded with laughter. "Allie! You didn't tell us you got thrown off Thurgood's place!"

"Oh, shut up!" Allie's voice shook with anger.

Jupe chuckled as he pictured the proud girl being marched out of the mine.

"He's a phony, I tell you!" cried Allie.

"Perhaps he's only eccentric," said Jupe. "Wealthy people sometimes *are* eccentric."

"That's no crime," said Uncle Harry. He released the brake and they were moving again. "I don't want you to bother him again, Allie. And that goes for you, too, boys."

The car turned off the tar-macadamed road and bumped across a wooden bridge that spanned a tiny waterfall between two lakes that were hardly more than ponds. The boys guessed that these gave the town its name. Beyond the road was a dirt track and dust billowed out behind the car. About a mile from the bridge, on the left side of the road, were fields filled with young evergreens and, farther on, an open gate. Across the road from the gate sat several small houses. One was newly painted, but the others looked desolate and abandoned. Uncle Harry slowed and honked the horn at a tall, lean woman who was watering the garden next to the trim little house.

"That's Mrs Macomber," said Allie.

The woman smiled and waved at them. She wore dark slacks, a white shirt, and a massive Indian necklace of silver and turquoise. When she moved back to turn off her hose, the boys could see that although her black hair was streaked with silver and she must have been at least sixty, she moved as easily as a young girl.

"She was born here way back in the boom days," said Allie. "She married the superintendent of the mine. They moved away after the mine closed down. When her husband died she worked in Phoenix to save enough money to come back and buy the house she had lived in as a bride. She owns those other places, too—the little run-down houses—but she doesn't use them for anything."

"So her story's not so different from Wesley Thurgood's, is it?" said Bob.

"That's not the point," snapped Allie. "Mrs Macomber is a nice lady."

"That *is* the point," said Uncle Harry. "Twin Lakes is a great place to live and a perfect place to retire." He stopped the car outside the open gate and pointed ahead to where the road ended and steep mountains edged the western side of the valley. In a hillside towards the left, about a quarter of a mile away, the boys could see an opening—a black timber-framed square.

"That's Death Trap Mine," said Uncle Harry. "The cabin up there is where Mr Thurgood lives. And he also owns that big building behind it. It used to be the mine works."

The boys nodded as Uncle Harry turned left through the gate on to a narrow, rutted drive. Rows of small Christmas trees spread out on both sides. The car bounced past a fenced pasture on the right, where Allie's horse, a handsome Appaloosa named Indian Queen, grazed together with three other horses. Farther down the drive, on the left, a spanking new ranch-house sat in a clearing among the low trees. It was cedar red with immaculate white trim. At the end of the drive was an ancient sagging barn that had not been painted for many years.

Uncle Harry stopped the car in front of the ranch-house, yawned, and stretched. "Home at last," he said.

The boys and Allie tumbled out of the station wagon, and the boys stood for a moment and looked around. A dusty, no-nonsense pick-up truck was parked in front of the barn. On the far side of the house they could see the edge of a fenced enclosure where chickens clucked and scratched.

Uncle Harry got out from behind the steering wheel, moving rather stiffly. "I like my eggs real fresh," he said, pointing towards the hen-yard. "Besides, there's something kind of peaceful about waking up in the morning and hearing them cluck around. And I *do* wake up in the morning because the rooster thinks it's his personal responsibility to start the day."

The words were scarcely spoken before the rooster could be heard from behind the house. He wasn't crowing—he was squawking.

A split second later there was a screeching, fluttering, flapping uproar in the hen-yard. An instant after that the boys heard the thunderous explosion of a gun.

Pete shouted and fell to the ground, instinctively covering his head with his arms. Jupe and Bob ducked behind the car.

A huge dark shape came racing from behind the hen-yard and bounded towards Jupe. Jupe had a confused impression of gleaming white teeth and dark eyes. Then the creature leaped, knocked him to the ground, and bounded over him to disappear westwards into a field of Christmas trees.

3

Allie's Mysterious Millionaire

"WELCOME TO PEACEFUL ACRES!" laughed Allie, as the afternoon stillness settled over the ranch again.

Pete sat up and blinked. "What the heck was that?" he demanded.

"Just Wesley Thurgood's monster of a guard dog having another go at the chickens," Allie explained as Jupiter picked himself up. "He tries to dig his way under the fence into the chicken-yard. The chickens squawk and Magdalena runs out and shoots off her shotgun. If that dog doesn't watch it, she just might stop shooting into the air, and he'll have a tail full of buckshot."

"Magdalena?" said Bob.

"My housekeeper," explained Uncle Harry.

A stout black-haired Mexican woman came round from behind the house. She wore a dress made of course cotton fabric with bright flowers embroidered at the neck and on the sleeves, and she carried a shotgun.

"Senor Osborne!" she cried. "Allie! I am pleased you are back. It is too quiet when you are not here."

Harrison Osborne chuckled. "So you have your

own ways of livening things up," he said.

Magdalena scowled. "That dog, he is a thief!"

"Never mind," said Uncle Harry. "Keep blasting away with that gun and he'll reform. Magdalena, these boys are friends of Allie's. Jupiter Jones, Bob Andrews, and Pete Crenshaw. They're going to stay with us for a couple of weeks."

Magdalena's black eyes sparkled. "Ah, good, good!" she cried. "It is nice to have more young people here. I will get steaks from the freezer. You are hungry after your journey."

She disappeared into the house.

"I hope you *are* hungry after your journey," said Uncle Harry. "Magdalena doesn't have any patience with people who pick at their food."

"Don't worry!" said Jupe heartily.

Uncle Harry began to take suitcases out of the station wagon and set them on the front porch. The boys hurried to help him. In a few minutes they had carried their things into the house and upstairs to a big bunkroom directly above the spacious living room. Allie's room was on the first floor, next to her uncle's. Magdalena had her own little apartment behind the kitchen.

"You'll want to wash up," Uncle Harry called to them as they began to unpack. "Don't take too long. I'd like to show you around the place before dinner."

Pete immediately lost interest in stowing his clothes in the closet. "We can unpack anytime," he said, heading for the bath across the landing from the bunkroom.

Soon the boys, Allie, and Uncle Harry were out

under the blue New Mexico sky. Allie ran down the drive, two lumps of sugar in her hand. "Here, Queenie," she called. Her Appaloosa snorted and galloped to the fence. The girl hugged the horse's neck and it tossed its head, whinnying joyfully.

"Getting Allie off that horse's back, even for a couple of days, was quite a job," said Harrison Osborne, "C'mon. I want to show you the machetes we use for pruning."

"Machetes?" said Pete. "Aren't they big knives?"

Uncle Harry nodded. "In adventure stories, the heroes use them to hack a path through the jungle." He led the boys past the pick-up truck and opened the door of the dilapidated barn. The boys smelled hay and saw bales piled high in one corner. Coils of hose hung from pegs in the wall. Spades, shears, trowels, and hoes were neatly stacked beside a workbench which had a grindstone fastened to it. Over the workbench was a rack with five, huge, deadly-looking knives.

"We always use shears when we prune at home," said Pete.

"With thousands of Christmas trees to be done, shears are too slow," Uncle Harry told him. "Besides, you can really get a good sweep with a machete." He took down one of the great knives, stepped away from the boys, and demonstrated. "The trees don't grow to be a perfect Christmas-tree shape naturally," he said. "When I bought this place three years ago. I thought all I'd have to do was stick little trees into the ground and wait for them to get big. There's more to it. You've got to irrigate and kill weeds, and you have to prune. You look at a tree and picture it the way a Christmas tree should look—nice and tapering, full at the bottom and small at the top. Then you take aim and bring the machete down like this—"

The blade flashed and the air swooshed as Uncle Harry's arm came down in a slanting motion. "You cut off anything that's going to interfere with that nice shape. But be careful, because if you make a mistake with a machete you can open a king-sized gash in your leg. I prune in the summer and by the time my trees are ready to be harvested in November, the new growth has come out to cover the cuts and the trees are fuller. Got it?"

"Right," said Pete.

Uncle Harry carefully put the machete back in its place and pointed to a dusty old automobile that stood on solid rubber tyres in the far side of the barn. "One of these days I'm going to build a new barn," he said, "and that car is another thing I'm going to do something about."

Jupe went to the car and peered through a half-opened window. He saw seats covered with cracked black leather, and bare wooden floorboards. "It's a Model T Ford, isn't it?" he asked.

"It is," said Uncle Harry. "I got it as kind of a bonus when I bought this place. It was standing right there, half-covered with hay. I got as far as getting the hay off, and then I had to forget it. I've been too busy. But when I can, I'm going to restore it. Model T's are collectors' items today."

Allie appeared at the open door. "Wesley Thurgood's coming down the drive," she announced.

"Okay, Allie. You behave yourself," warned Uncle Harry. "No smart talk, you hear?"

Allie didn't answer. The boys heard footsteps outside and a voice called. "Mr Osborne?"

"In here," said Uncle Harry.

A thin fortyish man with blond wavy hair came into the barn. He wore jeans that were so new they were stiff, and boots that were gleaming and unscuffed. His western shirt looked as if it had been taken out of the box that afternoon. Jupe watched him shake hands with Uncle Harry, then listened as he apologized for the intrusion of his watchdog. Jupe felt that in at least one of her accusations Allie had been right. Thurgood *did* look like a person who was playing a part—an actor who had costumed himself for a role. But then Jupe reflected. What else would anyone wear in a place like Twin Lakes but jeans and boots and a western shirt? And if Wesley Thurgood didn't have old jeans, what would be more natural than to buy new ones?

"I've chained the dog up," said Thurgood. "He won't be down here to bother you again."

"It's no big deal," said Uncle Harry. "So long as he doesn't actually get any of the chickens, and I don't think he will with Magdalena around."

Uncle Harry then introduced the boys. Allie ignored Thurgood and stared into space. He glanced at her briefly, and his clear blue eyes became hard for a second. Then he seemed to look right through her to the Model T. "Say, that's quite a rare car you've got there," he said.

"I was just telling the boys I'm going to fix it

up one of these days," said Uncle Harry.

Wesley Thurgood stepped over to touch the car, and suddenly Pete straightened.

"Wesley Thurgood!" he exclaimed. "I thought I'd heard that name before!"

"Eh?" said Thurgood.

"My father does special effects for the movies," said Pete. "He was talking about you at dinner a while back, Mr Thurgood. He said the props department at his studio needed an old Reo for a picture they were making, and they got it from you. You're an old car buff."

"Oh? Oh, yes, that's right," said Thurgood.

"Dad was telling us about your collection of old cars," said Pete. "He said you've got a private garage where you keep them and a full-time mechanic who doesn't do anything except make sure they're in running condition."

"Yes," said Thurgood. "Well, why not? They don't make them like they used to, do they?"

"Wasn't it your Silver Cloud that was used in the movie *The Fortune Hunters?*" Pete asked.

"Silver Cloud? Why, yes. I did let one of the studios borrow that not . . . not long ago."

"A Silver Cloud?" said Uncle Harry. "Guess my Model T looks pretty humble."

"I started small, too," said Thurgood. "Once you really get the old car bug, you'll probably start buying. You'll have to enlarge your barn."

"You mean I'll have to build a new one," said Uncle Harry, and he and Thurgood strolled out of the place with Uncle Harry talking excitedly of his plans for his ranch.

"Well?" said Allie, when the two men were gone. "Have you ever seen such a phony?"

"So his clothes are new," said Pete. "So what? I didn't remember the name Wesley Thurgood until he got so interested in the Model T, but my dad talked a lot about him and his car collection. He's got piles of dough and he's kind of a recluse—has a big house in Mandeville Canyon with ten-foot walls around it."

Jupiter cleared his throat. "He did not, however, lend a Silver Cloud to be used in the filming of *The Fortune Hunters*," said Jupe, in the somewhat stuffy manner he used when imparting information. "There was an article in *Film Fun* about that car. It didn't belong to Thurgood. It belonged to Jonathan Carrington, the financier. Also, *The Fortune Hunters* was not filmed recently. That picture has been out for several years."

No one contradicted Jupe, who prided himself on his knowledge of motion pictures and the theatre. But Allie Jamison crowed in triumph. "What did I tell you? A phony! He lied!"

Jupe smiled. "Not necessarily, Allie. You're jumping to conclusions again. Wesley Thurgood is a very wealthy man, and if he owns a fleet of antique automobiles and has a man whose exclusive duty is to take care of them, he would hardly be bothered with details. He might not remember whether he loaned a certain car to a studio at a certain time. No doubt some employee takes care of the negotiations and the mechanic delivers the car to the studio."

"Ha!" said Allie, since there seemed to be

nothing more clever to say in reply.

There was a rather stiff silence in the barn until Magdalena could be heard calling the four young people for dinner.

4

Shots in the Dark

"HAVE MORE STRAWBERRY SHORTCAKE," said Magdalena from her end of the long table in the big kitchen. Jupe had just finished the last crumb of his dessert.

"No thanks," he said. "It was delicious, but I'm trying to take off some weight."

Magdalena frowned, "You young people—always you worry about weight. Allie, she eats like a sparrow, so she is skinny like a little stick. This summer I try to make her plump like a pigeon."

"You've got it all wrong, Magdalena," said Allie. "The American Medical Association says skinny is the thing to be. Baby Fatso here," and she nodded towards Jupe, "should pay attention."

Jupe reddened. He hated to be reminded of the time when he had been a child star, distinctly on the plump side, and known from coast to coast as Baby Fatso.

"I diet all the time," said Jupe.

"You mean when you're not actually eating." Allie stood up and carried her dishes to the sink.

"Allie, you are a rotten hostess and if you were a little younger than you are I'd turn you over my knee and paddle you," her uncle told her.

Allie didn't answer. She rinsed her dishes and put them into the dishwater.

Magdalena got up from the table. "Go and talk with your friends. I will do those."

"We can help, Magdalena," Bob offered.

"No, no! I do not like a crowd in my kitchen. Besides, there is the dishwasher and it does the work."

Uncle Harry, Allie, and the boys retreated to the living room, where Uncle Harry promptly fell asleep in front of the television set. Soon the boys were yawning.

"Deadheads!" jeered Allie. "It's not even nine o'clock."

"We were up at five this morning," Bob reminded her.

"So was I," said Allie. "Tell you what. I'll get out the chessboard and . . ."

"No thanks!" Jupe interrupted. "I have decided that according to my own official clock, which is inside my head, it is ten-thirty. I am going to bed."

"Me, too." Pete started for the stairs.

Bob yawned and went after him.

"Spoilsports!" Allie taunted.

"That Allie can be a pain in the neck," Pete complained, when the boys were upstairs and getting into bed. "She never runs out of steam."

Jupe stretched out and put his hands behind his head. "I'm not so sure," he said. "Listen."

Bob and Pete were silent. They heard the muted sound of the television being turned off. Harrison

Osborne's voice came to them, low and sleepy. A door closed and water ran in a shower. Then another door closed.

"Allie's going to bed, too," said Jupe.

He turned over on his side and turned off the bedside lamp. The room was dark, except for the moonlight which came through the open windows and threw cold squares of light on the floor.

Jupiter closed his eyes. In a second he was asleep. He slept deeply, not stirring, until he was jarred awake by a noise that came from outside—a muffled roar that echoed and rumbled and then died away.

Instantly alert, Jupe sat up. He concentrated, listening for a repetition of the sound.

In his bunk, Pete groaned. "Magdalena," he mumbled. "Shooting at the dog again."

"No." Jupe got out of bed and went to the window. "It sounded like a shot, but it wasn't Magdalena. Too far away."

Jupiter looked out over the moonlit fields of Christmas trees stretching away from the house. To his right, he could see Mrs Macomber's house and the abandoned dwellings that made up her little domain. Straight ahead, Wesley Thurgood's property was fully visible on the rising slope of land. A small, square-shaped truck was parked near the mine entrance. A shadow moved next to Thurgood's cabin, and the guard dog prowled to the end of his chain, lifted his head, and howled.

A light went on in the little house across from Uncle Harry's gate. A door opened and Jupe saw Mrs Macomber come out in a dressing gown. She stood on the porch and looked up towards Thurgood's place.

There were voices in the living room below. Uncle Harry was up, and so was Magdalena.

"It was not me," the boys heard the housekeeper say. "I did not shoot the gun."

Bare feet thudded on the stairway, and there was a pounding at the door. "Hey, you guys!" It was Allie. "Did you hear that?"

The Three Investigators got into their dressing gowns and went out on the landing. Allie was kneeling at the window there with her elbows on the sill. "It's Thurgood!" whispered Allie. "I'm sure that shot came from Thurgood's place. And look!"

Pete went to the window. "What is it?" he asked.

Allie pointed across to Mrs Macomber's house. The woman on the porch turned, went inside, and shut the door.

"The sound woke Mrs Macomber," Allie pointed out. "And it woke the dog. He barked. And it woke us. But it didn't wake Thurgood. At least he didn't put on any lights and he didn't go out to calm the dog down. I'll bet it was him shooting!"

"Allie!" Harrison Osborne's voice came from below. "What are you doing up there?"

"Just seeing what I can see," called Allie. She got up and went to the top of the staircase. "Uncle Harry, I'm sure that was Wesley Thurgood shooting,"

"Allie," said her uncle wearily, "you're getting to be a nut about Thurgood. It was probably somebody out hunting jack rabbits or coyotes."

"Who?" demanded Allie. "From here I can see all the way to the hills. There isn't anybody out. Besides, if there's a coyote around, wouldn't he be trying to get at our chickens?"

"Not if somebody shot at him first," said Uncle Harry. "Now you come down here and go back to bed, and let the boys get their sleep."

"Oh, blast!" exclaimed Allie.

She had started down the stairs when Jupe suddenly called her back to the window.

Thurgood had appeared in the clearing near his cabin. A shotgun was cradled in his arms. The boys saw him gaze at the hills across the road from his property. Then he put the gun to his shoulder, took aim, and fired.

Again the sound of a shot broke the night stillness. Again the dog howled. Thurgood went to him and patted him on the head. The dog stopped barking, and Thurgood disappeared into his cabin.

"You were right about one thing, Allie," said Pete. "It was Thurgood."

"And it looks like your uncle was right about another," Bob pointed out. "He must have been firing at a coyote."

Allie made an indignant noise and flounced down the stairs.

"Allie sure has it in for Thurgood," said Bob, as he padded back into the bunkroom. "No matter what he does, she decides he's up to no good."

Jupiter got into bed. "I think that if I owned a mine, I would escort Allie Jamison on an inspection tour so that she could satisfy her curiosity," he said. "It would be so much easier than making an enemy of her."

Bob and Pete climbed into bed, and in a few minutes their steady breathing told Jupe that they were asleep. But Jupiter found himself oddly wakeful. The First Investigator lay in the darkness and listened to the wind rustle the Christmas trees.

Finally Jupe sat up. "Where was Thurgood when he fired that first shot?" he said aloud.

"Hm?" Pete turned over in bed.

"Wha . . . what?" said Bob.

"Where was Thurgood when he fired the first shot?"

"The first shot?" said Pete "In his house, I suppose."

"Did you see him come out?" Jupe asked. "Did you see him come into the yard before that second shot?"

"No. I guess not. I was watching Allie."

"So was I," said Jupe. "Bob, did you see where Thurgood came from before he fired again?"

"No, I didn't," said Bob.

"So he could have been anyplace," Jupe concluded. "I don't think he was in his house. The first shot was muffled, so much so that I wasn't even sure it *was* a shot. The second one was clearer and it sounded nearer. I think Thurgood was in the mine when he fired that first shot."

"So what?" asked Pete.

"Nothing, perhaps," said Jupe, "except that I don't think there was a coyote. The dog would have barked at a coyote, and we would have heard him. But the dog didn't bark until after the shot. What if Thurgood shot at something in the mine and then came out and found that the noise had roused the neighbours. Suppose he didn't want anyone to know he was shooting in the mine. What would he do?"

The other two boys didn't answer.

"Wouldn't he stand out in the open and shoot again?" asked Jupe. "Wouldn't he want it to appear that he *was* shooting at a coyote?"

"You're getting as bad as Allie," said Bob.

"That may be," Jupe admitted. "But it is also possible that there is something a bit odd about Mr Thurgood. Perhaps Allie *does* have a case after all!"

5

The Forbidden Mine

WHEN JUPE WOKE to see sunshine, his suspicions of the night before seemed ridiculous. He dressed and went down to the kitchen, where Bob and Pete were already eating. Uncle Harry sat at the head of the table, and Magdalena was at the stove pouring pancake batter on to a griddle.

Pete lifted a hand in greeting. "Allie's out riding and we were about to come up and wake you," he said, "Today we get to do our stuff with the machetes."

"That will be a change," said Jupe.

"A change from what?" asked Uncle Harry.

"From moving junk around The Jones Salvage Yard!" Jupe told him.

"I hope you enjoy it." Uncle Harry smiled. "I do. It's kind of creative to think that you're carving a Christmas tree. Don't work like slaves the first day though. Just go at it for an hour or so at a time, then rest."

After breakfast Uncle Harry took down three of the great knives that hung over the workbench in the barn. The boys followed him to a field between the ranch-house and the road. They watched as he pruned a tree, bringing the machete down in quick slanting strokes to cut away branches that grew out in odd places. "Don't get too close to the tree," he warned. "Stand back away from the machete, and always swing the knife off and to one side. I don't want any accidents."

Uncle Harry watched while each of the boys pruned a tree. When he was satisfied that they had the hang of it, he left them in the field and went back to the house. A few minutes later he drove off in the station wagon with Magdalena.

The boys worked in silence until they heard the hoofbeats of Allie's Appaloosa pounding in the fields between the drive and Wesley Thurgood's property. As the boys looked up, Allie rode on into the pasture, unsaddled the mare, and rubbed it down with handfuls of straw. Then she disappeared into the ranch-house.

Before long the boys heard the sound of a car starting. They looked towards the barn. "Oh, wow!" Pete said, "What next?" Allie had climbed behind the steering wheel of her uncle's pick-up truck. Gears clashed and Allie and the truck came lurching down the drive.

"Allie, you nut!" yelled Pete. "What are you doing?"

Allie came abreast of the boys and stepped on the brake. The engine coughed and died. "It's okay," said Allie cheerfully. "I can drive it, so long as I don't take it off the ranch."

"You're too young!" protested Bob.

"I'm too young to get a licence," said Allie. "But as long as I can reach the pedals, I'm not too young to drive Uncle Harry's pick-up truck."

She tried to start the truck again and failed. "Need more practice, I guess," said Allie.

"Does your uncle know you do that?" asked Pete.

"Sure!" Allie answered. "He thinks girls should know how to do everything guys can do."

"I'll bet," said Pete. "That's why you waited until he and Magdalena left."

Allie leaned out of the cab. Her eyes were dancing. "They've gone to the store and they won't be back for a while. And Wesley Thurgood isn't home either, and the dog is chained up."

"I know what you're thinking," said Pete. "You want to explore that mine. Well, you're on your own."

Jupe stood holding a machete. He remembered the sound of the shot in the night—a muffled sound that might have come from a tunnel in the mountainside.

"Stick-in-the-muds!" jeered Allie. "Okay! Stay there and forget about the mystery." The truck engine ground again, and this time it caught.

"Wait a second!" shouted Jupe. "I'll go with you!"

"Good!" Allie laughed. "Bring your machete along. If Thurgood comes back, we'll run back to the truck and pretend to be pruning in the field near his place. What about you, Pete? And Bob?"

Pete looked doubtfully at Jupiter. The tallest and most athletic of the Investigators, Pete enjoyed physical adventures—but he hated walking into trouble. Jupe, on the other hand, could not resist investigating any mystery, no matter how slight, no matter what the danger. And once he had decided to act, he couldn't be stopped. Shrugging, Pete climbed into the cab next to Allie. Bob, too, realized that Jupiter was on the trail of something, and followed him into the back of the truck.

Allie got the pick-up started again, and they went bouncing off through the fields on a rough dirt track that had been bulldozed across Harrison Osborne's property.

"This is a great truck," Allie exclaimed. She was so busy trying to control it that she seemed to be in action from the top of her head to the soles of her feet. She had to slouch low every time she put the clutch in, and push mightily on the gear-shift lever. Her hand flashed out to touch a second lever next to the gear shift. "That's to convert it to four-wheel drive, in case you go up into the hills and need the extra power," she said. "And there's a winch on the front in case you get stuck or go into a ditch. And it's got four, forward speeds. The diagram for the gear shift is on the lever. You push it up there for first and then pull it towards you for second and . . ."

". . . And I only hope we get it back to the barn in one piece!" said Pete as the truck lurched forwards.

"You worry too much," said Allie. She stopped the truck at the edge of the field that bordered Wesley Thurgood's property. The boys climbed out of the vehicle and stood looking around.

Across a bare stretch of ground they saw the mountainside jut up abruptly. The mine entrance was a dark, threatening hole at the base of it. They could see a few feet into the mine, past the timbers that framed the entrance. There was dry white sand and some gravel on the floor of the mine tunnel. The tunnel itself seemed to slope downwards away from the entrance. To the right of the mine was the decaying cabin where Thurgood lived.

"Crummy, huh?" Allie said, pointing.

"He'll probably fix it up sooner or later," said Bob. "How long has he been here?"

"Almost a month," Allie told him. "He moved in with a bedroll and some pots and pans, and I think that's all he's got now. He's really roughing it. That big building behind his cabin used to be the mine works. That's where they took the ore from the mine and separated out the silver."

A chain rattled and the guard dog came around the corner of the cabin. He was not as enormous as the boys had thought at first, but he was a very large dog. Jupe guessed that he was part Labrador retriever and part German shepherd. When he saw Allie and the boys, he gave a low growl.

"You sure that chain he's got on is attached to something real solid?" said Pete.

Allie laughed. "Don't worry. I threw a stick at him before, when I rode past on Queenie. He can't get at us."

"I like the way you make friends with dumb animals, Allie," said Bob. "Suppose he'd gotten loose?"

"Then Queenie and I would have outrun him," declared Allie. She took a flashlight from the glove compartment of the pick-up. "Come on."

They started across the clearing to the mine entrance. The dog went into a frenzy, flinging himself at them, trying with all his might to break his chain. Allie ignored him, and The Three Investigators followed her into the brooding gloom of the mine.

When they were a few feet past the entrance, Allie snapped on the light. Its beam darted along the floor of the tunnel, which slanted downwards. Side passages went off at intervals. The walls were braced with timbers as big as railway sleepers, and huge crossbeams helped support the rocky ceiling.

Apart from the sound of the dog barking outside, the mine was perfectly quiet. Yet somehow there was a faint air of menace all round. Allie and the boys moved slowly along the tunnel, picking their way on the rocky, uneven floor. Jupe kept his eyes fixed on the beam of light as it probed the waiting darkness ahead.

About fifty yards into the mountain, the tunnel branched out and became two tunnels, one leading off to the right and one extending at a slight angle to the left. They hesitated. Then Allie started towards the left. The boys followed and the feeble light from the mine entrance was gone. Except for the flashlight, they were in total darkness. Their footsteps echoed eerily in the tunnel.

"I wonder where the lady fell," said Allie. "The one who was killed in here."

In spite of herself, she shivered.

"Wait a minute, Allie," said Jupe. He had glimpsed something on the floor of the tunnel. "Shine the light over here a second, would you?" he asked.

Allie flashed the beam of light on a little heap of loose rock and pebbles. They seemed to have fallen from the wall of the tunnel. As Jupe bent to pick up a small stone, Allie and the light abruptly moved away.

"Hey!" shouted Pete. "Come back with that flash!"

Allie kept going, the flashlight bobbing and glowing ever more faintly from a side corridor that she had dodged into.

"Allie!" called Bob.

Suddenly there was a light in the tunnel behind them—a very powerful light that caught the boys and held them in its glare. "Exactly what do you kids think you're doing?" demanded an angry voice—the voice of Wesley Thurgood.

"Uh-oh!" said Pete.

Then The Three Investigators heard Allie drop her flashlight. It clattered against some rocks and they heard glass breaking.

At the end of that darkened corridor, Allie let out a blood-curdling scream.

She screamed and screamed and screamed.

6

Death Trap!

"ALLIE! WHAT IS IT?" shouted Jupe.

The screams went on, high and hysterical.

"Blast that brat!" Thurgood dashed past the boys and plunged into the side corridor. The boys stumbled after him.

Allie was there, standing stiffly at the edge of a pit that gaped in the floor of the mine. She stared down into the darkness at her feet and she screamed.

"Stop that!" Thurgood seized her arm and pulled her back away from the pit.

Allie trembled and pointed towards the pit. "D-d-d-down there!"

The boys went cautiously to the edge of the shaft and Thurgood shone his light down. The pit was not deep—only ten or twelve feet—but the walls were sheer, straight up and down.

At the bottom of the hole was something that looked like a heap of old clothes. But then, in the light of the torch, they could all see what had once been a hand—a human hand. There was a body inside the clothes, a body that lay strangely twisted on the rocky floor of the shaft. They saw hollow eyes and a dusty, matted tangle of hair.

"Dead!" cried Allie. "He's . . . it's dead! Dead!"

"Stop that!" snapped Thurgood again.

Allie gulped and was quiet.

"Now get out!" ordered Thurgood. "All of you!"

Jupiter and Bob grabbed Allie's arms. With Pete stumbling behind them and Thurgood herding them along with his flashlight, they made their way back to the main mine tunnel and then out through the entrance into the sunlight. The dog barked, but it seemed to Jupe that the sound was unreal—part of a nightmare. In his mind Jupe kept seeing the crumple of clothing at the bottom of the shaft, the head with the staring eyes, and the skinny, leathery hand.

"You kids get home!" said Thurgood. "Get home and stay there, all of you. If I ever catch you in my mine again, I'll . . . I'll . . ."

He walked quickly to his cabin and slammed the door closed. Allie and the boys moved off slowly, past Thurgood's shiny red Chevy Suburban "truck," which was now parked near the mine, past Uncle Harry's pick-up, which they left standing in the field.

By the time they reached the ranch-house, colour had come back to Allie's face. "We'll call the sheriff," she said. "That Thurgood! I knew there was something spooky about him!"

"I am sure he has already called the sheriff," Jupe told her. "I am also sure that you'd better not accuse him of anything."

"Why not?" said Allie. "There's a dead man in his mine!"

"And at the moment we have no idea how that dead man got there," Jupe pointed out.

A cloud of dust soon appeared on the road to town. A second later a tan sedan sped past. The word "Sheriff" was stencilled on the door panel. The boys glimpsed the driver, a big man wearing a stetson. The car turned in towards Thurgood's cabin and halted.

Jupe smiled. "You see?" he said to Allie.

Allie smiled back, but her smile was malicious. "I wonder what Thurgood's going to tell the sheriff."

"What are you going to tell your uncle?" Jupe nodded towards the road. The station wagon was approaching, with Uncle Harry and Magdalena in the front seat. Uncle Harry turned in at the gate, and Jupe could see that he looked concerned.

"Allie!" he called. The car came to a stop in the drive and Uncle Harry leaned out the window. "Sheriff Tait passed me on the road. Is anything wrong?"

"There's a body in Thurgood's mine," said Allie smugly.

"A body? In the mine?"

Allie nodded.

"*Madre de Dios!*" Magdalena got out of the station wagon. "Allie, how do you know this?"

There was an uncomfortable silence. Harrison Osborne looked at his niece. "Allie, were you in that mine again?"

Jupe took a step forward and answered Uncle Harry's question. "Yes, we all were, Mr Osborne. I was curious about those shots last night, and . . ."

"I don't want to hear any explanations!" said Uncle Harry. "I want you all to go into the house and stay there, do you understand?"

Uncle Harry stamped away across the fields, heading for Thurgood's property. As he went he was joined by Mrs Macomber, who had come out of her house when the sheriff's car passed.

The Three Investigators and Allie prowled from window to window on the second floor of the ranch-house, trying to catch a glimpse of any action. After a time an ambulance drove up to Thurgood's property and backed up to the mine entrance. It was more than an hour before it left and disappeared towards town. In the meantime several other cars arrived. One of them belonged to the highway patrol. At three, Harrison Osborne returned to the ranch-house in his pick-up truck.

"Well?" said Allie. "Did they arrest Thurgood?"

"Certainly not," said Uncle Harry. "Why should they arrest him? Whoever that was in the mine, he's been dead for a long, long time. The coroner's going to do an autopsy, but it looks as if the dead man got in there years ago, fell down that shaft, and broke his neck. It's got nothing to do with Thurgood. It must have happened before the mine entrance was sealed."

"Five years ago," said Magdalena, who had come in from the kitchen. "The poor soul. For five years he has been there, and no one to know it!"

"Is that when the mine was sealed?" asked Pete. "I thought it closed down forty years ago."

"You are right, Pete," said Magdalena. "The mine closed down long ago, but people could still get inside. *Si*. It was five years ago—in the springtime—they shut it with an iron grille. I remember it."

Jupe sat on the floor, absent-mindedly tossing a pebble into the air.

"What is that?" Allie asked him.

Jupe caught the pebble. "I picked it up in the mine this morning, before you went off with the flashlight." He wet one finger on his tongue and rubbed the pebble. "You told me Death Trap is a played-out silver mine," he said. "Was there gold in it, too?"

"Not that I ever heard of," said Uncle Harry.

Jupe held the pebble towards the light. "It has a small bright streak," he said. "Probably just iron pyrite. They call it fool's gold."

"I don't care about iron pyrite," said Allie. "What I want to know is why Wesley Thurgood didn't report that body in the mine. We had to go in and find it before he was forced to call the sheriff. I mean, once we'd seen the corpse, what else could he do?"

Uncle Harry was losing his patience. "Wesley Thurgood did not *know* the body was in the mine," he said. "He removed the iron grille from the entrance only last week, and he hasn't had time to explore the mine thoroughly. Allie, he had no reason to conceal that body. If you don't stop making wild accusations you'll force me to lock you in the cellar and tie a sack over your head!"

A car pulled up in the drive outside, and the

sheriff came across the porch. Magdalena had the door open for him before he could knock. Uncle Harry stood up, but the sheriff looked at Allie. His gaze was stern. "Allie, you know why they call that mine a death trap?"

Allie nodded.

"People can get killed there, can't they?"

Again Allie nodded. "I know, Sheriff Tait."

"If you ever go in there again, I'll arrest you and take you down to the courthouse and your uncle will have to come and get you. That goes for you, too, boys."

Sheriff Tait took a chair across from Uncle Harry.

"Did you find out who that man was?" Harrison Osborne asked.

Tait nodded. "I think so. There was a wallet in the hip pocket with an identification card that had a San Francisco address. We telephoned San Francisco to see if the police there had a missing-persons report on a Gilbert Morgan who might have disappeared five years ago, or perhaps even longer ago than that. They sure did. In January, more than five years ago. Gilbert Morgan, who has also used the names George Milling, Glenn Mercer, and George Martins, was released from San Quentin after serving six years of a fifteen-year sentence for armed robbery. He reported twice to his parole officer in San Francisco, and then disappeared. He's been on the wanted list ever since. We're going to have to verify his identity by checking dental charts, but the general description matches. The body isn't too badly decomposed. The climate here's so dry, it just kind of mummified."

"Poor Mr Thurgood," said Allie, in a nasty-nice voice. "I don't suppose he even knew the body was there."

"Of course he didn't know. He'd have called me right away if he'd known." The sheriff stood up to go. "Remember what I told you about that mine, young lady."

He and Uncle Harry went out and stood in the drive, talking quietly together.

"It *is* odd that Thurgood didn't explore his mine the moment he removed the grille from the entrance," said Jupe. "I certainly would if I purchased a mine."

"I told you he was a spook!" said Allie.

"Five years ago," said Jupiter. "Five years ago, in January, a thief named Gilbert Morgan was released from prison. He reported to his parole officer in San Francisco, then disappeared. Sometime between January and the time the mine was sealed in the spring, he came to Twin Lakes, got into the mine, and was killed. I wonder where he was in the meantime. Magdalena, could he have been here in town?"

Magdalena shook her head. "Twin Lakes is a small place. A stranger would be noticed."

Jupe nodded. "True. And if the man was a fugitive, he would not have wanted attention. He would have gone to a place where he could be part of a crowd and thus not be noticed. Yet he was here."

"I wonder what else happened in Twin Lakes

five years ago," said Allie. "The mine was sealed with the crook inside. Was anybody else in town who might be interesting? Like Wesley Thurgood, for instance?"

"I'd be very surprised if we found that he was." Bob had been leafing through a pile of newspapers that were stacked on the coffee table. "If it'll make you feel better, though, we can check."

"How?" asked Allie.

"The local paper," said Bob. He held up a tabloid-size sheet of newsprint. "The *Twin Lakes Gazette.* It has stories on absolutely everything that happens in town, including who is having guests and where the guests come from. If we could go through the files, we might find some clue in the back issues about what brought the crook named Gilbert Morgan to Twin Lakes."

"Great idea!" exclaimed Allie. "Let's go! I know the editor—he interviewed me when I came here. I'll keep him busy while you guys go through the back files."

"You think your uncle will let us out of the house?" asked Pete.

"I think he'll let us go anyplace," declared Allie, "so long as it isn't near that mine!"

7

Tracing the Dead Man

UNCLE HARRY FLATLY refused to permit Allie and the boys to leave the ranch that afternoon. Instead, he sent them out to prune Christmas trees until dinner-time. Allie sulked for hours.

By the next morning, however, Uncle Harry's mood had softened. When Allie told him she'd like to take The Three Investigators into town, he only said, "Don't be gone all day."

"We couldn't possibly be gone all day," Allie pointed out. "There isn't that much to Twin Lakes!"

Allie and the boys set out on foot for the mile-long hike down the dusty road. As they walked several cars passed them, going slowly up towards Thurgood's. One stopped as it came abreast of them and a man leaned out.

"This the road to Death Trap Mine?" called the man.

"Yes, it is," said Allie.

"Good!" The man started to drive on, then suddenly stopped again. "You wouldn't be the kids who found the body, would you?" he asked.

"Come on, Allie. Let's go." Bob took her arm and started to hurry her along.

"Hey, wait a second!" The man climbed out of his car with a camera in his hand. "Hey, I want to take your picture, okay?"

"No, it's not okay," said Pete.

The boys and Allie walked off as rapidly as they could without actually running. Another car passed them and they were aware of curious eyes staring at them.

"I guess it's to be expected," said Jupe. "The Death Trap Mine *did* make the news on television last night, and people *are* curious."

"But you'd better not pose for any pictures," Pete warned Allie. "I have a feeling your uncle wouldn't like it."

"I *know* he wouldn't like it," said Allie.

The main street in town was humming with activity. Cars cruised along and sightseers scanned the sidewalks. A little knot of men and women clustered outside the courthouse, where Sheriff Tait, looking red-faced and harassed, gestured as he talked with them.

"Reporters, following up on the story," said Bob.

The office of the *Twin Lakes Gazette* was in what had once been a store. A plate-glass window faced the street, and inside there were two battered desks. One was piled high with bills and notices, and newspapers from other parts of the West. At the second desk sat a string bean of a man with sparse, reddish hair and sharp features. He looked wildly excited, and he was pounding madly on a typewriter.

"Allie!" he shouted, when she came through the

door. "Just the girl I wanted to see! Been talkin' to Ben Tait, and he tells me you're the one found that body up at the mine."

Allie grinned. "Mr Kingsley, so far you're the only one who's happy about it. Mr Thurgood wants to knock my block off, Sheriff Tait says he'll put me in jail if I ever go near the mine again, and Uncle Harry's so mad at me . . ."

"I know. He'll get over it, don't you worry. Only you'd better stay out of mines from now on. Hate to have to write your obituary." The man squinted at The Three Investigators. "These your friends from Los Angeles?"

"Mr Kingsley, this is Jupiter Jones," said Allie. "That's Pete Crenshaw over by the door, and Bob Andrews is the one with the glasses—his dad works for the *Los Angeles Times*."

"Well, now," said Kingsley. "That's some newspaper!"

"Yes, sir," Bob agreed. He was edging towards a partition that separated the office from a huge dim room in the back of the building. He could see a small rotary press and a linotype machine. The place was old and dusty, and smelled of printer's ink.

"Want to look around?" asked Kingsley.

"I'd like to very much," said Bob. "I'm interested in newspapers. Do you run the linotype yourself?"

"I do everything," Kingsley told him. "Most weeks that doesn't amount to much. This week'll be different. This week we've got news. Now Allie, you just sit right there and tell me about looking down that shaft and seeing that body, make yourselves at home. Turn on the lights back there. Look at the press if you want."

The Three Investigators went back past the partition. Jupe touched a light switch and fluorescent fixtures in the ceiling filled the place with glare. Bob pointed to shelves along one wall. There were rows of file boxes, each one marked with dates.

"Those must be the old issues," Bob said.

"We want the ones for five years ago," murmured Jupe.

Bob nodded, and the three boys began to remove file boxes from the shelves. The papers for the year when the mine was sealed took up six file boxes.

"Go through every issue," said Jupe. "Scan the headlines. We don't want to miss anything that might possibly be a clue."

The three seated themselves on the floor, and each one opened a box, took out stacks of newspapers and began to work through them. They could hear Allie in the front office, her voice clear and excited, as she described to Kingsley what he doubtless already knew—that it was both thrilling and disturbing to find a dead body.

At first the old newspapers were disappointing. There were accounts of two small fires in the town. There was the report of the purchase of a new car by the sheriff's department. There were stories about visitors who had come to stay for a few days with relatives in Twin Lakes. There was nothing that could relate to Gilbert Morgan. But then, as he went through the issue for the week of 29th April, Jupe said, "This may be something."

"What is it?" asked Bob.

Jupe was silent for a minute, reading a news item to himself. Then he looked up. "A five-year-old girl wandered away from her home near town and was missing for three hours. She was found by a search party in Death Trap Mine. It seems that the entrance had once been boarded up, but over the years vandals and curiosity seekers had managed to remove some of the old boards. The little girl got into the mine and fell asleep. Her parents wanted to start a fund to raise money and have the mine sealed permanently. They said she could have been killed if she had gone further into the mine—and we know that indeed she could have."

Jupe looked around. "Where's the issue for May sixth?"

"Here," Bob held up a paper he had been reading. "There's a front-page story about the mine. The owner of the Twin Lakes Market put an empty five-gallon water jug next to his cash register and asked the citizens to donate to a fund for closing the mine. In two days they had raised enough for an iron grille to seal the mine entrance. The grille was ordered from Lordsburg, and they planned to seal the mine on May fourteenth."

There were further details about the planned sealing of the mine in the paper dated 13th May, and the issue for 20th May carried a story of the simple safety measure that had caused tremendous excitement in the little town. There had been a parade before the mine was sealed, then a ceremony as the grille was actually cemented into place.

"They made a big thing out of it," Pete observed.

"You heard what Mr Kingsley said," Bob reminded him. "There isn't much news here. Sealing the mine would be an event."

He turned the pages of the newspaper, looking at pictures of the residents of Twin Lakes parading down the village street. Suddenly he said, "Hey! Here's something. On the fourth page. When the people went out to put the grille in place at the mine entrance, they found a car abandoned on the mine property. It was a Chevrolet sedan, and it was identified as a car that had been stolen from the parking lot of a supermarket in Lordsburg three days before. Sheriff Tait is even quoted in the article. He guessed that the car had been swiped by Twin Lakes teenagers who wanted a ride home from Lordsburg. And he warned that if he caught any kids joyriding, he'd see to it that they wound up in jail."

Bob looked up. Jupe was pulling at his lower lip, as he often did when he was thinking intensely.

"A car stolen from Lordsburg, then found near the mine on the day the mine was sealed," he said. "And inside the mine was a convicted thief. I don't think we would be making a wild guess if we assumed that the car was stolen by the dead man. He drove it to Twin Lakes and left it near the mine. Then he went into the mine for some reason and . . . and he did not come out again."

"Okay," said Pete. "But that leaves us about where we were before, except that we can guess he went from San Francisco to Lordsburg and from Lordsburg to Twin Lakes. But why? What brought him here?"

Jupe shrugged.

Bob continued to look through old papers. There was nothing else that seemed remotely related to their mystery. Wesley Thurgood was not mentioned. In an issue for October of that year, Mrs Macomber's return to Twin Lakes was announced. Two follow-up stories told of her purchase of some of the property that had once belonged to Death Trap Mine.

"I wonder how long Gilbert Morgan was in Lordsburg after he left San Francisco?" said Jupiter.

Pete leaned against the linotype machine. "Who knows? He was a parole-breaker. He'd have laid low. And it all happened five years ago. The trail is cold by now."

"True," said Jupiter. "And he seems to have been here for no reason. Yet he was here, in a mine that was subsequently puchased by Wesley Thurgood. How could Thurgood not have known about that body? Could there be a connection between Thurgood, a successful real estate tycoon, and Morgan, a loser, a paroled convict? There is one thing we can do right now."

"What?" asked Pete.

"We can try to take a step backwards into Morgan's past. If he stayed in Lordsburg at all, he must have stayed somewhere. I know it's almost hopeless after all this time, but we can try to trace him. We can check the newspapers and old telephone directories. It's the only thing we *can* do."

8

A Prowler in the Night

ALLIE AND THE BOYS arrived back at the Christmas tree ranch in the early afternoon. Uncle Harry was standing on the porch, his ruddy face flushed with impatience. There were three cars in the drive, and several people were clustered near the porch, trying to argue with Uncle Harry.

"My niece cannot possibly talk with anyone," Uncle Harry was saying. "She's a sensitive young girl, and she's far too upset after . . ."

He broke off short when he saw Allie and the boys. "Allie—into the house!" He jumped off the porch, took Allie by the elbow, and propelled her through the door. Jupiter, Pete, and Bob hurried after her, and when they were inside, Uncle Harry slammed the door behind them.

"Those people are reporters and I do not want you talking to them," said Uncle Harry.

"Why not?" asked Allie. "I'm news, aren't I?"

"Because if your mother should find out what you've been up to, she'd have my head, that's why not," said Uncle Harry.

"Well, it's too late to worry about newspapers," said Allie. "I just talked to Mr Kingsley."

"Kingsley's different," Uncle Harry said. "Your

folks aren't likely to pick up a copy of the *Twin Lakes Gazette* anywhere in the Far East. Now I want you to stay inside for the rest of today. You, too, boys. And stick close by tomorrow, too, if those people are still around."

"Mr Osborne," said Jupe, "we had hoped to go to Lordsburg tomorrow."

"What for?" asked Uncle Harry.

Jupe put his hand into his pocket and took out the pebble he had found in the mine. "I wanted to show this to a jeweller. It's the pebble I found yesterday in Death Trap Mine."

Harrison Osborne smiled. "I suppose you think it's a gold nugget. Well, it isn't. There's no gold here. But I do have to go into Lordsburg later this week. You and Allie can come with me. As a matter of fact all of you can come along. I wouldn't think of leaving you at home. I'm afraid of what you'd get up to."

Uncle Harry went outside to get rid of the reporters. The Three Investigators and Allie spent the rest of the day reading and playing Monopoly. From time to time Allie ran upstairs to stand on the landing outside the bunkroom and look out towards Wesley Thurgood's property. She reported gleefully that Thurgood was standing guard over his domain with a shotgun, and that the dog, exhausted with barking at curiosity seekers, had stretched out and gone to sleep.

That evening the boys went up to the bunkroom early. From their windows they could see a light on in Thurgood's cabin. But even before they got into bed, Thurgood put out his light.

Soon the lights went out in Mrs Macomber's house across the road.

"Guess everybody's tired tonight," said Pete. He rolled into his bunk. "I know I am, but I'm darned if I know why."

"Some kind of delayed reaction," said Bob. "It was spooky, seeing that guy in the mine yesterday. I know he was a crook and all, but that was a nasty way to go."

"I wonder what he was doing here," said Jupe aloud. He had wondered it to himself many times that day. "Perhaps we'll find some trace of him in Lordsburg."

"You really going to show that pebble to a jeweller?" asked Bob.

"It can't hurt," said Jupiter, "and it will give us an excuse to go off by ourselves while we're there. I'm sure Uncle Harry doesn't want us to concern ourselves with the dead hold-up man in any way—but we *are* concerned."

"Allie isn't," said Bob as he put out the light. "She's just concerned with Wesley Thurgood, and I don't think we're going to find any connection between Thurgood and the crook."

"Maybe not, but I'm bothered by the fact that Thurgood didn't find the body himself," Jupe replied. "He wasn't even curious enough to explore his own mine, which is very strange indeed."

The boys dozed off, each thinking of the man in the mine, each wondering how he had come to be there and exactly how he had met his death.

It was very late when Pete woke up. He frowned in the darkness and listened intently. Something had moved outside, beyond the open windows. He lifted himself on one elbow when the sound came to him again—a lurching, sticky squeak.

"Jupe!" He kept his voice low. "Bob! Listen!"

"Huh?" Bob turned over. "What is it?"

"Someone just opened the barn door." Pete was up and crossing to the window in his bare feet. He leaned on the window-sill and looked out. Bob and Jupe joined him.

"The door's closed now," said Bob.

Then the boys saw a light moving inside the barn, dancing on the dusty, side windows of the place. The light flickered and went out, and then flared up again.

"Someone's lighting matches!" said Jupe. "Come on."

It took only seconds for the Investigators to pull on shirts and jeans and stick their bare feet into sandshoes. They crept down the stairs and opened the front door without a sound.

The moon had set when they came out on to the drive. They groped towards the barn with Jupe in the lead. They had almost reached the barn when Bob put his foot down on a rock in the drive, turned his ankle, and let out a barely audible cry as he crumpled to the ground.

The light in the barn had flickered again. Now the barn went dark.

"Blast!" breathed Pete.

Bob sat on the ground rubbing his ankle and looking towards the barn. After a moment he got up and the three boys again crept towards the old building. Jupe put his hand out and touched the door-latch, which rattled slightly.

Suddenly the barn door swung out, catching Jupe in the chest and knocking him to the ground. Pete leaped to one side as a burly figure dashed into the open, pounded past them, and disappeared among the Christmas trees beside the drive.

"What's that?" came a roar from the house. "Who's out there?"

Jupe picked himself up. "There was a prowler in the barn," he called.

"Oh, good grief!" said Uncle Harry, "I'll call the sheriff."

Pete pointed towards Thurgood's place. "He went that way."

The boys listened, but there was no sound. The fields of trees were dark and still. "He can't be far," said Jupe.

Pete swallowed and slowly stepped in among the trees. He strained his ears, listening for some sound, alert for some movement in the fields. For a few minutes he was aware of Bob and Jupe coming up behind him. Then Jupe went off quietly to the left and Bob slipped away towards the right. Pete crept forward alone, one careful footstep after another, avoiding the tree branches that might catch at his legs.

Then Pete stopped. He could hear the blood rushing in his own ears, and he could hear something else—a gasping, rasping sound; the sound of laboured breathing. Someone was quite close to him, fighting for breath as if he had been running for a long distance.

Pete froze where he was, listening, and the

harsh breathing went on. The unknown person seemed to be only a few feet from Pete, just beyond an evergreen that Pete could touch with his hands. Pete opened his mouth to call out for Jupe and Bob, then hesitated. His cry would only send the prowler off again.

When Pete heard a car on the road from town, he grinned. That would be the sheriff coming in answer to Uncle Harry's call—and Pete had the intruder pinned down.

But as the car turned in at the gate and the headlights swept across the fields, the prowler dashed from the shelter of a bushy tree. Pete leaped after him. But then he saw, against the night sky, an upraised arm—and something that made him throw himself to the ground. As he went down a murderous blade flashed through the air, slicing the top off a small tree! Then the stranger was gone again, gasping and stumbling as he crashed off across the fields.

Pete got to his knees, shaking.

Jupe was suddenly beside him.

"A machete!" said Pete. "He had a machete! And he almost took my head off!"

9

The Earth Rumbles

SHERIFF TAIT HAD A deputy with him—a young man named Blythe. When the two men heard of the intruder in the barn, and of his slashing attack with the machete, they took powerful flashlights and started across the fields. They picked up the trail of the prowler next to the tree where Pete had been standing. Footprints went away from the tree, and the sheriff followed them until they were lost among a jumble of prints on the road near Thurgood's place.

The boys and Allie watched from the upstairs windows of the ranch house. The sheriff and his deputy continued to search. They roused Thurgood and entered his cabin while his guard dog barked ferociously. They went into the mine. Mrs Macomber was up and her lights were on. They went into her house and then into each of the abandoned houses she owned. More than an hour later they returned to the ranch house.

"Whoever it was," the sheriff told Uncle Harry, "he must have gone up the mountainside. We'll never trail him up there in the dark. Not much point, anyway. It's probably one of those weirdos who came from Lordsburg or Silver City when they heard about the body in the mine. You get crackpots whenever anything unusual happens. But I wish he hadn't panicked and taken that machete."

Sheriff Tait and Deputy Blythe went back to town, and Uncle Harry locked the front door and closed all the windows on the ground floor.

In the morning, the boys were wakened by hearty laughter from below. They went down to find Allie perched on a stool in the kitchen, watching with obvious pleasure as Mrs Macomber sat at the table, drinking coffee and talking with great animation to Magdalena. The widow's tanned face was alive with excitement.

"Sorry if we disturbed you last night," said Jupe, when he and the others had been introduced.

"I'm not." Mrs Macomber laughed. "It reminded me of the old days. Forty-five years ago Twin Lakes was quite a town! The sheriff had to break up fights every Saturday night."

"Say," said Allie, "speaking of the old days, do you remember Wesley Thurgood?"

Mrs Macomber laughed. "How could I forget him? I see him every day."

"No," said Allie. "I mean, do you remember when he was a little kid? He says he was born here."

"And so he was," said Mrs Macomber. "His folks lived in the little green house down by the court-house and his father was foreman on the night shift. He was a real mining man. Wesley was the last boy born in town before I left here. That was at the end of the boom days and people had started to move away. Wesley was only a toddler when the mine shut down and he and his folks left. I keep meaning to ask him about his parents—what they did after they left Twin Lakes—but I never get a chance. He's so darned busy driving around in that fancy red truck of his, lugging stuff in, pottering around the mine. He was out at dawn this morning. I saw him go by wearing that ridiculous hard hat, which he needs the way I need another head."

The group in the kitchen heard a car pass by on the road. Allie ran upstairs to the window on the landing. She was back shortly with the news that Thurgood had returned and that he had two men with him. "They looked like Mexicans," she reported. "Now what's he up to?"

"Why don't you ask him?" prompted Mrs Macomber.

"Because he isn't speaking to me," said Allie, "and if I bother him again, Uncle Harry swore he'd lock me up."

"I doubt that," Mrs Macomber told her. She took her leave and returned to her own house across the road.

In the days that followed The Three Investigators finished pruning the largest field of Christmas trees and started work on another. Allie pruned, too, but she also spent a great deal of time riding Queenie in the field near Wesley Thurgood's place. She saw that the two dark-haired, dark-eyed labourers seemed to be living in the big building that had once housed the mine works. A shiny new padlock had been put on a little wooden shed that stood near the mine entrance. Thurgood continued to drive out on his mysterious errands. The second day after the labourers arrived, a truck delivered sacks of cement, dozens of steel fence posts, and great rolls of chain-link fencing. Under Thurgood's direction, the two men set to work putting up an eight-foot fence around Thurgood's property.

At lunch that day, Allie said, "He's going to a lot of trouble to protect a worthless mine. Who cares about the mine, anyway?"

"You do," said her uncle. "You'd give your eye-teeth to get in there and he knows it. To say nothing of those creeps who came swarming in when that body was found. I don't blame him for fencing his place. If people were as interested in Christmas trees as they are in mines, I'd fence this property."

Uncle Harry left after lunch to spray weeds in the field near the road. Jupe leaned back in his chair and frowned. "No one *is* interested in Christmas trees," he said. "So why was there a prowler in the barn the other night? What is there in the barn that would interest even the most avid curiosity seeker?"

The others couldn't answer him. When the dishes had been cleared away they all trooped out to the barn to look around again.

"Nothing," said Pete. "A lot of hay for the horses, some tools and hoses, and an old car that doesn't run."

"Maybe the prowler just wanted a machete," said Allie.

"That's a gruesome idea," said Bob. "A machete is an ugly weapon. And if someone wanted a weapon, why a machete? A gun would be better and lots of people around here must have guns."

They left the barn in time to see Thurgood's red Chevy Suburban pass the gate. It was headed towards the mine. A man sat in the front seat with Thurgood—a dignified-looking gentleman who wore a light summer suit and a white hat. Allie and the boys raced into the ranch-house and up to the landing outside the bunkroom, where they could have a better view of Thurgood's property and his visitor.

The two labourers were not working on the fence. Instead, the watchers saw one of them emerge from the mine. He was staring straight ahead in a stolid manner as he pushed a wheelbarrow loaded with dirt and rocks. He came abreast of Thurgood and his companion. Thurgood stopped him, picked a handful of earth out of the barrow, and showed it to his guest. Then he spoke to the labourer, who went on with the wheelbarrow, trundled it up a ramp made of two stout planks, and disappeared through an open door in the side of the big mine works. Thurgood and his visitor went into the mine.

A minute later Allie and the boys heard the sound of a muffled explosion. It rumbled on for a few seconds and then died away.

"He's shooting again!" cried Allie.

"That didn't sound like a gun," said Jupiter. "It sounded like something much more powerful. An explosive of some kind!"

Across the road, Mrs Macomber came out on her porch and looked towards the mine.

Thurgood and his visitor appeared in the mine entrance. They were accompanied by the second labourer. He, too, trudged into the mine works pushing a loaded wheelbarrow. Thurgood and his guest stood in the clearing talking for a few minutes. Then they got into the red truck and Thurgood drove down the road. He ignored Mrs Macomber, who was still on her porch. When he had gone, she crossed the road and came up Uncle Harry's drive, trying impatiently to reclasp a large Indian bracelet.

The Three Investigators and Allie went downstairs and met Mrs Macomber at the door. "How about that?" she cried. "Wesley Thurgood is working the mine!"

Magdalena came out of the kitchen. "But no, Senora Macomber!" she protested. "In that mine there is nothing. You have said so yourself. All of the silver is gone."

"But he's working it anyway," insisted Mrs Macomber. "He's blasting. Didn't you hear it? I couldn't be mistaken about that sound. I've heard it too many times."

"He's playing games," said Pete. "Or maybe he's going to make the mine into a tourist attraction. You know, like the people who buy old ghost towns and fix them up."

Mrs Macomber looked upset. "He'll ruin the placc! Tourists mean traffic jams and litter."

"Well it *is* his property," said Allie, mimicking her uncle.

Mrs Macomber made an impatient noise and walked out. Jupe rocked on his heels, considering the situation. "I doubt that Wesley Thurgood is going to open the mine to tourists," he decided. "Twin Lakes is too far off the beaten track."

"Then what is he doing?" demanded Pete.

Jupe smiled. "We could try asking his Mexican labourers," he said. "Thurgood and his guest are gone. Let's go up and see what the men have to say."

A few minutes later The Three Investigators and Allie stood by the fence around Thurgood's property and called to the two men. They tried addressing them in English and got no answer. They tried a few words of Spanish, but that brought no reply either. The two Mexicans simply eyed them suspiciously.

Frustrated, they returned to the house to enlist Magdalena's help.

"You speak their language, Magdalena," said Pete. "They'd trust you, don't you think?"

Magdalena went towards Thurgood's place willingly enough, but she was soon back to report failure. The men had ignored her. She had got close enough, before the dog saw her and barked, to overhear them talking quietly together, but she had caught only one word: *oro*.

"Oro?" echoed Jupe. "That means gold! Could Thurgood be working the mine for gold?"

"But it is a silver mine!" protested Magdalena.

"Gold and silver are often found near each other," said Jupe. He took out the pebble with the odd little shiny streak. "Allie, when did your uncle say he was going into Lordsburg?"

"He's going tomorrow," reported Allie.

"And we're going with him. We'll see exactly what's in this pebble."

10

Is the Glitter Gold?

UNCLE HARRY PARKED the station wagon beside the express office in Lordsburg. "I ordered three loads of young trees from San Jose," he said. "After I pick them up I have to go to the builder's supply company for some things I need. I'll meet you boys back here at one o'clock, and we'll have some lunch before we start back to the ranch."

"I'm going with Jupe and Pete and Bob," Allie announced.

"Okay. Just stay out of trouble," said Uncle Harry. "Though I don't know why I should worry. There's no mine here for you to get into."

He left them and went into the express office.

"What's first?" demanded Allie eagerly.

"We check out Jupe's pebble, huh?" said Pete. "That shouldn't take long. Do we tell the jeweller where we found it when we show it to him?"

"I think not," said Jupiter. "We don't want any more prowlers, and if the streak in the pebble *is* gold, that might bring them swarming. Leave it to me. I'll think of something to say."

Two blocks from the express office they found a small shop with a display of watches and pendants in the window. A sign indicated that the proprietor, J. B. Atkinson, bought old gold and silver.

"Exactly what we need." Jupiter Jones opened the door and they went in.

A plump, rosy-faced man sat on a stool behind a glass partition. He had a jeweller's lens in one eye and was repairing a watch. They saw a case with some worn but beautiful silver pieces on display and several handsome old gold pins and rings.

"Mr Atkinson?" said Jupiter.

The man behind the partition put down a tiny screwdriver, took the lens from his eye, and smiled.

Jupe took out his pebble. "We've been staying with friends near Silver City," he told the man. "We were out hiking in the hills yesterday, and we met an old prospector."

Atkinson nodded. "There are still some around."

"He said he needed money," Jupiter went on. "He said he'd been carrying this for a long time, but he'd sell it to us." Jupe handed the pebble to Atkinson.

Atkinson looked at the pebble, squinted, and rubbed it with his finger. His smile did not change. "How much did you pay for it?" he asked.

"Five dollars," said Jupiter.

"Is it real?" asked Allie.

"It's a real pebble, right enough," said Atkinson. "Whether the stuff in it is gold or not, we'll see. He opened a drawer and took out a small bottle of liquid and a little file. He cut a tiny notch in the shiny streak of the pebble with the file, then put a drop of the liquid on to the notch. "This stuff is nitric acid," he said. "'Most any metal *except* gold will react with it." After a moment he nodded. "Yep. I'd say you've got gold here."

"Does pure gold often exist in nature?" asked Jupe.

"It's usually combined with other metals," said the jeweller. "This looks to be pretty fine stuff. Wonder where your prospector pal got it."

"He didn't say," Jupe replied.

"I doubt if it matters." Atkinson handed the pebble back to Jupe. "I'd guess it's from some worked-out mine, probably in California. Prospectors can still make enough to keep themselves in beans by panning the streams near the old mines."

Jupe put the pebble in his pocket. "You say gold is usually combined with other metals. Do you think there's any silver in this gold?" he asked.

"No. it's reddish, which might mean some copper. Silver gives gold a greenish colour." He opened one of the cases and took out a pin which looked very old. It was made of gold which had a greenish cast, and it was formed in the shape of a leaf. "This is what we call green gold. It's about twenty-five per cent silver, which means it's eighteen-carat gold. Those little finger rings there in the case are even finer. They're baby rings. People used to buy them for children for christening presents. They're more than twenty-carat gold, and that's why some of them are worn through. They're quite soft. I sell one now and then, just as a curiosity. And that's what you've got there in your pebble. A curiosity. A hunk of the old gold rush days."

"Worth five dollars?" asked Pete.

"I reckon so," said Atkinson. "You pay can more than that for a hunk of something plastic these days. Hang on to it. If you ever feel like having it made into a tie clasp or anything, come back and see me."

They thanked him and went out to the street.

"The real McCoy!" exclaimed Pete. "There's gold in that mine!"

"And copper, too," said Jupe thoughtfully. "But the gold in our pebble isn't mixed with silver. Odd, since Death Trap Mine was a silver mine in the old days. I know that gold and silver can often be found in the same mine, but gold and silver *and* copper!"

"Interesting, isn't it?" said Allie. "That creep Thurgood has found a vein of ore that nobody even suspected was there. His father worked in the mine. Maybe his father knew something and told it to Thurgood. So Thurgood made up that cockeyed story about how he wanted to return to his old hometown, and he bought the Death Trap and now he's working it."

Jupe frowned. "If that's true—that there was a family legend about a secret vein of gold—then why would Thurgood wait so long to come here? He's at least forty. He could have investigated the mine anytime in the last twenty years, and bought it cheaply. Maybe he had no interest in it when he was a young man, but he should have had some interest a few years ago, when the price of gold went up. Why didn't Thurgood show up then?"

"How do we know he didn't?" Allie insisted.

"How do we know he wasn't here five years ago, when Gilbert Morgan fell down the shaft? Maybe they were confederates. Maybe they got to fighting and Thurgood shoved Morgan."

"Allie, that's wild!" protested Bob. "Why should a super-successful real estate man get all heated up about an old mine? There wouldn't be any reason. And if there is gold and he knew it, he wouldn't need a confederate. Nobody asked any questions when he just bought the property, did they? But speaking of that crook . . . hadn't we better start tracing him?"

Bob took out his notebook and read: "Gilbert Morgan, parole violator. Also used the names George Milling, Glenn Mercer, and George Martins. Released from San Quentin and disappeared from San Francisco five years ago. Probably left San Francisco late in January or early in February. Probably reached Twin Lakes sometime in May of that year, using a car stolen in Lordsburg."

"A good summary, Records," said Jupiter.

"He always used the initials G. M., no matter what his alias," said Bob. "That is all we have to go on. If he was in Lordsburg for any length of time, he may have left some trace. Shall we try the public library?" he asked. "They'll have phone books, city directories, and back issues of the local newspaper."

Allie led the way to the library, where a librarian listened to Jupe explain that he was vacationing in the area and was trying to locate a long-lost uncle. "He sent my mother a postcard from Lordsburg five years ago," said Jupe. "We wrote to him, but the letters came back because we didn't have a real address. I promised my mother I'd try to find him."

The librarian, impressed by Jupe's earnest manner, produced telephone books and city directories for the last five years. Allie and the boys sat at a long table and started checking the five-year-old directories. "Look for a name with the initials G. M.," said Jupe. "A name that only appears in one directory or one telephone book—the one for five years ago."

It did not take long. In ten minutes they had checked the names of sixteen persons with the initials G. M. against the directories for the following year. All but one had remained in Lordsburg. The one odd name, Gilbert Maynard, was missing from several directories, but appeared in the current telephone book. "He must be someone who moved away and then returned," said Jupe. "He took up residence at the same address."

"So he can't be our crook," said Pete. "Okay. Morgan passed through town without doing any of the ordinary things, like having a telephone or a job, or getting himself listed as a resident."

"He was only here a few months, if he stayed at all," Bob pointed out.

"Any luck?" called the librarian.

"No. No, it looks as if my uncle didn't stay here," confessed Jupe. He then managed to look very much embarrassed. "Uncle Geoffrey did have a way of . . . ah . . . attracting attention. Maybe the newspapers for that year . . . ?"

"Oh, he was that sort, was he?" The librarian shook her head, but she showed the way to the room where periodicals were on file, and left them to go through bound volumes of the Lordsburg newspapers. There was nothing—nothing that could be remotely connected with the deceased hold-up man—until they came to the issue for 10th May, five years before. "Death Trap Mine to Be Sealed," Bob read from a headline. "So it *was* announced in the paper here in Lordsburg. Could that have had anything to do with our guy's death?"

Jupe shrugged. "Who knows? He could have seen the story in the paper and decided for some reason to go to Twin Lakes and explore the mine. What day was the car stolen from the supermarket parking lot?"

Bob consulted his notes. "May eleventh," he said. "That's one day after the sealing of the mine was announced in the Lordsburg newspaper and three days before the mine actually was closed up. There could be a connection."

"But what, for Pete's sake?" cried Allie. "The crook sees the story about the mine being sealed and he's in such a sweat to get there that he swipes a car and drives it to Twin Lakes, where he dashes into the mine, falls down a shaft, breaks his neck, and is not heard of again for five years! That doesn't make sense. Now suppose he and Thurgood had a meeting set up . . ."

"Allie!" snapped Pete. "Can't you forget about Wesley Thurgood for just a minute?"

"We're about where we started," said Bob. "We know that Gilbert Morgan could have been in Lordsburg and he could have stolen a car and driven to Twin Lakes, but we can't prove it. It was a long chance, but we had to check it out."

"The morning isn't completely wasted," said Jupiter. "We are sure of one thing." He took out his pebble. "We know that there was at least this much gold in Death Trap Mine on the day Morgan's body was found. I'm not sure how much that means, but I'm sure it means something!"

11

The Hungry Thief

IT WAS MID-AFTERNOON when they arrived back at the Christmas tree ranch. The boys helped Uncle Harry unload the station wagon, putting the loads of tiny trees out near the barn and watering them with a hose. When Uncle Harry went into the house, Jupe looked across at Mrs Macomber's place.

"I imagine your neighbour knows more about the Death Trap Mine than almost anyone in town," said Jupe.

"Mrs Macomber? She sure does," said Allie.

"Let's pay her a call," Jupe suggested.

The others were more than willing. They went down the drive and across the road and knocked on Mrs Macomber's door. The widow called to them to come in. Allie opened the door and they walked directly into the neat little kitchen.

"Busy?" Allie asked Mrs Macomber.

She smiled, and the wrinkles at the corners of her eyes deepened. "Don't have all that much to be busy about these days," she said. "But I sure would appreciate it if one of you boys would step out to my truck and bring in the carton that's in the back. I've got to put away my groceries in the fridge or the frozen stuff will melt."

"I'll do it," said Pete. Mrs Macomber's small pick-up truck stood in a dirt driveway beside the house. There was a large cardboard carton jammed with brown paper bags in the back of the truck. Pete brought it into the kitchen and put it down on a counter.

"Much obliged," said Mrs Macomber. "I just can't seem to do all the things I used to," She began to take out vegetables, bread, and packages of frozen foods and pile them on the counter.

Suddenly there was a dull booming sound. Mrs Macomber went to a window. "Wesley Thurgood's playing miner again," she announced. "I've been kind of expecting that. I saw him drive in half an hour ago with one of his city visitors."

"He seems to be actually working the mine," said Jupiter.

"Sounds that way," agreed Mrs Macomber. "He's setting off explosives in the mine, that's for sure. I was born here and I know that sound. I lived in this very house when my husband was superintendent here. You can't mistake dynamite going off in a mine tunnel. But Thurgood isn't working the mine full-time. He does his blasting only when he's got company. Showing off for his rich friends from Los Angeles, I suppose."

"It's a weird hobby," said Bob.

"I've known of stranger ones." Mrs Macomber smiled. "I once heard of a man who bought an old railroad locomotive. He had three hundred yards of track put down in a field behind his house and he ran his locomotive back and forth on that. He wore a conductor's uniform whenever he played with his big toy, and he had a ball. Lots of money'll do that to folks. Maybe Wesley Thurgood's got some fuzzy notions of the old days when his dad was a miner, and he's trying to go back to that time. It's harmless."

"You make him sound so innocent," said Allie.

"Take my advice and don't complicate things if you don't have to," warned Mrs Macomber. "The truth of the matter is—you've got it in for Thurgood because he's sore at you. I don't suppose I blame you. He isn't very friendly and I'm glad he's finally got a fence around his place. I didn't like that dog of his running loose. But then, I don't have the right to tell him how chatty he's supposed to be or what kind of a dog he can own."

The booming sounded again from the mine.

"Mrs Macomber," said Jupe, "is there any possibility that Thurgood is working the mine for profit?"

She shook her head. "The Death Trap Mine is dead, dead, dead. The silver was played out forty years ago. I ought to know. My husband and I had a rough time after the mine closed. We had to leave here. You think we'd have gone if there was any chance of staying? Then after Henry died—he had a heart attack twenty-two years back—I took the insurance money and opened a shop in Phoenix. Sold Indian jewellery and moccasins to the tourists, but I lost everything. I'm no businesswoman. I had to sell out and I wound up working in the same place I'd owned, scraping and saving and standing on my feet all day." Her expression had become bleak. Suddenly her look softened. "I wanted to retire here," she went on. "I wanted to get back to the place where I'd been happy, and I'm glad I did. Maybe that's what Thurgood wants. I remember when he was a dirty-faced kid, toddling around Twin Lakes licking a lollipop. There was something peculiar about that boy even then . . . but I just can't remember . . ."

"But the mine . . ." insisted Allie.

"Well, the mine made Twin Lakes what it was," said Mrs Macomber. "But I don't feel I have to own it to bring back the good memories. Maybe Wesley Thurgood does. Maybe he's got to play the role all the way and really be a miner, like his father."

"And there's no chance he's taking anything out of the mine?" Jupe persisted.

"No chance. There's nothing left to take."

"Even if the silver is gone," said Jupe, "could there be gold? Silver and gold are often found together."

"Not at Death Trap."

"Copper?" suggested Jupe.

"No. There was silver and the silver is gone." She shook herself, as if to get rid of an unpleasant thought. "Now that's enough of that. When the mine was open Twin Lakes was a boom town and we had some good times. And today I own a hunk of what used to be that boom town. If we ever have another wave of prosperity around here, I can fix up my five houses and rent them and make a fortune in my old age. C'mon. I'll show you boys my little estate."

Mrs Macomber led Allie and the boys outside. "I thought about putting padlocks on the doors when I moved in here," she said. "But I'd have to put a trail of silver dollars from the highway to this place to get even a hobo up here—or at least I felt that way until Allie found the hold-up man in the mine. There were plenty of strangers around here after that. Did they ever find your uncle's missing machete, Allie?"

"No, they didn't," said Allie.

"It'll probably turn up all rusty someplace on the mountain," said Mrs Macomber. She walked to an old frame house that stood to the north of her own residence. "This place belonged to the McKestries," she told them. "He was a paymaster at the mine."

Mrs Macomber pushed on the door and it opened with squealing protest. Allie and the boys followed her inside. They saw long-unused furnishings, cracked plaster, and cupboards with doors that sagged open to show odd pieces of chipped pottery. "Lots of people left things behind," said Mrs Macomber. "I guess they figured some stuff wasn't worth taking."

"You'd have to do a lot of clearing out and fixing up before you could rent this place," Allie told her.

"Of course I would. I had to do a lot to my house before I could move back into it. But it was fun."

As they went from one place to another in Mrs Macomber's domain they sniffed air that was heavy with dust and dry rot. In some of the houses the roofs had let in the rain, and ceilings were splotched and stained. In one, a heap of yellowed newspapers was piled near a rusted wood-burning stove.

Bob crouched and flipped through the old newspapers. "Were these here when you bought your property, Mrs Macomber?" he asked. "I mean, when you came back five years ago?"

"I suppose so," said Mrs Macomber. "Well, of course, they must have been. How else would they get here?"

"Interesting," said Bob. "Could I have them?"

"What on earth do you want with a pile of old newspapers?" asked Mrs Macomber

"He's a newspaper nut!" Allie laughed "But he sure helped us find out a lot about what was going on here five years ago. After we discovered that body in the mine, we went down to the *Twin Lakes Gazette* to see if we could figure out what Gilbert Morgan might have been doing here. We found out a whole bunch of stuff, but—"

Jupe shot Allie a menacing glance as Bob interrupted her. "My dad's a newspaperman," said Bob. "He's got me interested in old papers. Could I take these?"

Mrs Macomber seemed puzzled for a moment. "Well, I guess you can have them," she said.

Bob carefully picked up the stack of newspapers and held them at his side, and they all went out into the late-afternoon sun.

"Say, would you kids like something to drink or will that spoil your dinner?" Mrs Macomber asked.

"*Nothing* can spoil Jupe's dinner!" Allie laughed.

"Good, I've got some orange soda."

They returned to Mrs Macomber's snug little house, but there was no soda in the refrigerator or in the cupboard or in the pantry that opened off the kitchen. "What on earth?" Mrs Macomber exclaimed. "I'm sure I had some orange soda. I know I didn't drink it all myself."

Jupe, with his eye for detail, stared at the groceries still piled on the counter. "You also had a loaf of bread," he said. "And some canned tuna. They're gone!"

Mrs Macomber looked at Jupe as though she didn't understand. Then she gasped. She charged out on to the porch and peered up and down the road, as if expecting to see someone walking off with her supplies.

Bob put down his newspapers. He removed a soggy cigarette butt from the gleaming kitchen sink and held it up between two fingers. "Mrs Macomber," he said "You don't smoke, do you?"

Mrs Macomber stared at Bob's find.

"No, I certainly don't," she said. By now Mrs Macomber seemed to have recovered from her shock. "I can't understand why anyone would steal from me," she said. "If someone wanted some food, all he had to do was ask me!"

"Well, he didn't," said Pete. "Maybe he wanted more than food. We'd better check the rest of the house."

Mrs Macomber shrugged and led the way out of the kitchen. They went through every room and closet of the immaculate little house. No intruder lurked under the furniture, and not one of the widow's many knick-knacks and mementoes seemed out of position.

"I don't have any valuables," said Mrs Macomber. "And nothing else is missing."

"I suggest you get those padlocks after all, Mrs Macomber," said Jupiter. "And lock this house when you go out."

"But no one around here locks up," protested Mrs Macomber.

"There have been strangers around lately," Jupe pointed out. "Morbid people drawn here by the finding of the hold-up man's body in the mine. If one of them helped himself to your food—he might just come back!"

12

A New Suspect

A FEW MINUTES LATER The Three Investigators and Allie crossed the road to Harrison Osborne's property. Bob was lugging his stack of newspapers.

"What's with those?" Pete asked, indicating the papers. "They of great historical interest or something?"

"And why did you guys shut me up back there?" said Allie.

Bob shifted the pile of papers so that his companions could see the one on top. "Most of these are copies of the *Twin Lakes Gazette*," he said. "They're more than forty years old. They must have been left in the house by whoever lived there before the mine closed. But the paper on top is a Phoenix paper, and the date is five years ago—May ninth. Look at that headline!"

"Hm!" said Jupiter. "I suggest that we find a private place and read that article with care."

The Three Investigators and Allie hurried past Uncle Harry's house and into the barn, where Bob put the papers down in a pile near the old Model T. They knelt on the floor and Bob unfolded the Phoenix newspaper with its bold headline.

ARMOURED CAR HELD UP

MASKED MEN ESCAPE WITH $250,000!

Today at 3 P.M. an armoured truck belonging to the Securities Transport Corporation was robbed outside the Phoenician Savings and Loan Company on North Indian Head Road. Three men wearing ski masks and armed with sawn-off shotguns forced driver Thomas Serrano and guard Joseph Ardmore into the rear of their truck. After binding and gagging Serrano and Ardmore, the hold-up men escaped with an undisclosed amount in negotiable securities, and cash estimated at approximately $250,000.

According to a witness who asked that his name be withheld, the thieves got into a white Chrysler sedan that was parked near the armoured truck. They crouched on the floor. A woman then emerged from a nearby card shop, took the wheel of the Chrysler, and sped away from the bank, heading north on Indian Head Road. No complete description of the hold-up men could be obtained, but the woman was described as between 55 and 60 years of age, slender, with slightly greying hair and tanned skin. She is said to be approximately 5 feet 7 inches tall, weighs about 130 pounds and was clad in dark slacks and a white turtleneck shirt. The witness reported that she wore an unusually large Indian necklace of turquoise and silver.

"Wow!" said Pete. "They got a quarter of a million bucks!"

Jupe mused, "May ninth. That paper is five years old and it's dated May ninth. Bob, wasn't that the day before the sealing of Death Trap Mine was announced in the Lordsburg newspaper?"

"Right," said Bob. "And on May eleventh, five years ago, a car was stolen from Lordsburg."

"At that time," said Jupiter, "all of Mrs Macomber's houses were empty—she didn't come back to Twin Lakes and purchase her property until October. But *someone* who had been in Phoenix on May ninth was here and left that paper in one of the houses that she now owns."

"Gilbert Morgan, the dead hold-up guy!" cried Pete.

"It seems possible," agreed Jupe. "Phoenix is not far from Lordsburg. A quarter of a million dollars stolen only days before Death Trap Mine was sealed. . . . Then a car stolen in Lordsburg and driven to Twin Lakes, and five years later the body of a known hold-up man is found in the closed mine. . . . Yes, it's conceivable that Morgan was in Phoenix on the ninth of May—holding up an armoured car—and that he went immediately to Lordsburg and then came to Twin Lakes. And I think we can figure out what he was doing here."

"He was hiding out!" declared Pete.

"No," said Jupiter. "No one would hide out in a place like Twin Lakes. A stranger in this town would be too obvious. But suppose that Morgan took part in that robbery and was looking for a safe place to hide his share of the loot. What could be safer than a mine that was about to be sealed?"

Allie looked bewildered. "But if he put it in a sealed mine, how would he get it out again?"

"I don't think a little iron grille would be much problem for a determined crook," Bob pointed out.

"Then Thurgood's got the dough!" cried Allie. "If it was hidden in the mine, Thurgood's got it! No wonder he didn't let on that the body was there. He probably planned to get rid of it so no one could ever guess he found the money. But we got there first!"

"That is possible," said Jupiter. "But let's not worry about who has the loot just yet. There's another reason why Gilbert Morgan might have chosen to come to Twin Lakes."

"What's that?" asked Bob.

"Suppose that Gilbert Morgan knew more about Death Trap Mine than what he read in the Lordsburg newspaper. Suppose he knew someone who told him all about the played-out mine—and the abandoned mine property. Suppose that person was one of his accomplices!"

"What are you getting at?" demanded Allie.

"After years of working in a little shop in Phoenix, Mrs Macomber returned to Twin Lakes—several months after the robbery. She had enough money to buy a sizeable piece of property. Perhaps *she* was an accomplice of Morgan's!"

"You're nuts!" cried Allie.

"Oh, I don't think so," said Jupe airily. "Records, give us that description of the driver of the getaway car again."

"Golly!" exclaimed Bob. "It was a woman, between fifty-five and sixty years of age, with slightly greying hair and tanned skin. Approximately five feet seven inches tall, and weighing about a hundred and thirty pounds. And she was wearing Indian jewellery!"

"Does that sound like anyone we know?" asked Jupiter.

"But . . . but there must be millions of people who look like that," Allie declared. "And Mrs Macomber's such a nice lady."

"Nice is not the point. She was living in Phoenix at the time of the robbery. She had lost her nest egg and was working at a job that couldn't have paid very much. Yet somehow she had enough money to buy the property here, soon after the robbery, and now she lives comfortably without working at all. She's vigorous, calm, and self-reliant, which one would have to be to take part in a daring robbery. And she fits the description of the getaway driver perfectly!"

"So what!" snapped Allie. "Jupiter, you haven't got one shred of real evidence against Mrs Macomber!"

"No, I don't," admitted Jupe. "But I see a lot of strange coincidences, and we can hunt for evidence." He looked slyly at Allie. "There's still another possibility we must consider. If Mrs Macomber *was* in on the robbery of the armoured truck . . . ." Jupe paused dramatically.

"Go on, go on," Allie ordered.

"Then it's quite possible that Gilbert Morgan did not come to Twin Lakes alone. Perhaps . . . perhaps he never had a chance to hide his money. . ."

"You mean Mrs Macomber shoved Morgan down that pit?" screamed Allie. "You're out of your mind, Jupiter Jones! I won't listen to another word you say!" Allie jumped up and stormed out of the barn.

Bob looked at Jupiter. "You don't really think Mrs Macomber murdered Morgan and stole his share of the loot, do you?"

"No," said Jupiter. "I simply couldn't resist suggesting it to Allie. But I wouldn't be surprised to find that Mrs Macomber did have some connection with the robbery!"

13

The Widow Disappears

AT THE END OF BREAKFAST the next day, Allie and The Three Investigators were sitting alone in the kitchen. Jupiter had devoured his food almost absent-mindedly. When he finished, he stared at his plate for a moment, then said to Allie, "What was the name of the shop in Phoenix where Mrs Macomber said she worked? Do you know?"

"Not that it's any of your business," replied Allie, "but the shop was called the Teepee. Mrs Macomber told me a lot about it. Some woman named Mrs Harvard bought it from her and kept her on as a saleslady. Mrs Harvard was a real miser —Mrs Macomber once said she'd have paid her help with Confederate money if she'd had any."

"Oh?" said Jupe. "That makes it even more curious that Mrs Macomber was able to amass enough to buy her property. Well, that part of her history we can check."

"Jupiter Jones! Don't you dare go snooping into Mrs Macomber's business!" cried Allie. "She's okay! I like her!"

"And you *don't* like Wesley Thurgood," said Jupe. "That doesn't mean that Wesley Thurgood is a criminal or that Mrs Macomber is not. As a matter of fact, I like Mrs Macomber myself. But as a detective, I can't let my personal feelings influence my judgment."

"Oh, come off it!" said Allie. "Your judgment is screwy, period. The *idea* that Mrs Macomber could be a robber!"

Jupe sighed. "Look, Allie. I don't know that Mrs Macomber has done a thing. But I do know that she was living in Phoenix when a woman remarkably like her took part in a robbery. And a hold-up man *was* found dead in a mine that she knew all about. Coincidences like that have to be investigated—they might not *be* coincidences. For a start, we can at least verify that Mrs Macomber worked all those years in that shop."

"Why don't you call Phoenix?" dared Allie. "You'll find out that she was telling the truth and you won't be any further ahead."

"That may be," conceded Jupe. Trailed by the others, he went to the telephone in the living room and got the number for the Teepee shop from Phoenix information. He dialled it and put on his deepest, most sincere, grown-up voice.

"Teepee? . . . May I speak to Mrs Harvard, if you please?"

There was a brief pause. "Mrs Harvard? said Jupe. "This is Emerson Foster of the Bon Ton Department Store in Lordsburg, New Mexico. We have an application for employment here—a Mrs Henry Macomber. She has given your name as a reference. I understand that she left the Teepee approximately five years ago. Mrs Macomber tells us that she resigned and—"

Jupe paused. The telephone made noises which the others could not understand.

"After fifteen years?" said Jupe finally.

"I told you so," whispered Allie. "She's on the level."

But Jupe was listening to the voice on the telephone, and he looked very serious. "That's . . . that's hard to believe!" he said. "Yes. Yes, well thank you for being so frank. Believe me, we appreciate it."

He hung up the telephone.

"What did she say?" asked Pete.

"Mrs Macomber worked at the Teepee for fifteen years," Jupe told them. "She left there in the spring, five years ago. Mrs Harvard said it was in April or May. She didn't remember exactly. But Mrs Macomber did not resign."

"So she was fired," said Allie. "So what?"

"She *wasn't* fired," said Jupe. "She simply didn't come to work one morning. She didn't even telephone, and when one of the women in the shop went to her apartment to see what was the matter, she was gone. She'd moved out, and left no forwarding address."

Allie looked blank.

Bob had been slouched on the sofa. Now he leaned forward. "Five years ago in the spring," he said. "That would be about the time the armoured car was held up. Jupe, you could be right. She may have driven that getaway car, and then run for it. I wonder where she was in the months between the time she left the Teepee and the time she came back to Twin Lakes."

"Lying low?" suggested Pete.

"Let's not leap to any conclusions," said Jupe. "There could be some explanation. Why don't we go across the road and see her? Perhaps we could persuade her to talk more about Phoenix and what took place that year."

"Subtle questioning," said Pete. "Jupe, you're good at that. Let's go!"

"I think you all stink!" cried Allie.

"Okay. Don't come with us," said Pete.

"Oh, I'll come all right. I want to see you fall flat on your faces when you find out you're wrong."

But when Allie and The Three Investigators crossed the road, they discovered that there would be no subtle questioning. Mrs Macomber's truck was gone and there was no answer when they knocked at her door.

"She's probably in town," said Allie. "Let's get this settled. I'll leave a note on her kitchen table and ask her to come to lunch. Magdalena won't mind."

She opened the door and went into the kitchen, followed by the boys.

"Mrs Macomber?" called Allie. When no answer came, she went on into the living room, looking for a scrap of paper. The Investigators waited in the kitchen, which was not nearly as neat as it had been the day before. There were unwashed pots on the stove, and the kitchen sink was filled with dirty dishes that looked as if they had been left overnight.

"Hey, I think Mrs Macomber is going on a trip." called Allie.

"What makes you think that?" asked Jupe, walking into the living room.

Allie pointed through the open door to Mrs Macomber's bedroom. A small suitcase lay on the bed, with some articles of clothing strewn beside it. Jupe moved forward to the bedroom door. "I think she's already left!" he said after studying the room a minute.

"Hunh?" Pete had come up behind him.

Jupe indicated the bedroom closet, which stood open. "All her clothes have been cleaned out of the closet. And look at those drawers hanging out of the bureau—they're empty. Fellows, she's gone—and I think she left quickly!"

"What do you mean?" demanded Allie.

"That all the signs indicate a very hasty departure," replied Jupe. "You saw this house yesterday. It was neat as a pin. Is Mrs Macomber the type to go away leaving bureau drawers open, extra clothes and a suitcase lying around, and dirty dishes in the sink? Never—not unless she were in a great hurry or had no choice!"

"She's been kidnapped!" cried Allie. "That guy who took her groceries yesterday . . . maybe she got a look at him and so he . . ."

"So he kidnapped her, thoughtfully packing her clothes before he took her away?" said Jupe. "That is hardly likely."

"Maybe she's away on vacation," suggested Pete.

"Doubtful," said Jupe. "She wouldn't have left the house a mess before going on vacation. And she didn't say anything yesterday about taking a holiday."

Bob said, "Maybe some family emergency came up. She might have had a call after we left."

Jupe pulled at his lower lip and frowned. "That's the best suggestion yet, Bob! But there's another possibility. She may have decided to leave because you found that Phoenix newspaper."

"But she didn't know what was in the paper," said Allie. "She said it was there when she bought this place."

"Maybe it was," conceded Jupe. "But if she took part in that robbery, and caught a glimpse of that headline yesterday, she'd know what was in the paper. And then she'd know that she was in trouble, because *you*, Allie, had to go and tell her that we were digging into the story of the dead hold-up man! She wouldn't have to think very long to realize that we might put two and two together—and might start asking her some difficult questions. And you know what she'd do then?"

"She'd run for it!" declared Pete.

"If you think that, you should put your money where your mouth is," said Allie. "Call the sheriff."

"And report what?" asked Jupiter. "That Mrs Macomber has gone away? She has every right to do that. We have no proof that she had any connection with Morgan or with the robbery. It's all conjecture."

Jupe went out and walked down the short dirt driveway to the road. He stopped, bent, and examined the tyre tracks in the dust. The others went to him, and he pointed to the most recent tracks which overlaid the traces of other vehicles. They indicated that a truck had backed out of Mrs Macomber's drive, then headed towards Wesley Thurgood's property.

"Odd," said Jupiter Jones. "She didn't drive towards town. She went the other way."

"If those marks were made by her truck," said Allie.

"They match all the tracks in her driveway," said Jupe.

Allie and The Three Investigators followed the tracks in the dusty road. Mrs Macomber's truck had been driven past Wesley Thurgood's gate. When the boys and Allie passed Thurgood's enclosure, the huge dog leaped against the fence and barked wickedly. Now that the fence was finished, the dog was no longer kept on the chain. Thurgood and his Mexican labourers were nowhere in sight.

A few hundred yards beyond Thurgood's property, they could see where the truck had turned off on to a rutted trail that was barely recognizable as a road. It went up the mountain in a series of hairpin turns.

"Why ... why she took the old Hambone Road," said Allie.

"Hambone?" questioned Jupe.

Allie pointed. "Way up there, on the top of the ridge, there's a real ghost town. It's called Hambone. There was a mine there, too, but its played out just like the Death Trap. There wasn't any sawmill to save the town, so it died. I've never been up there myself. The road is too bad. You need a four-wheel-drive jeep or truck to get up there."

"Mrs Macomber had a four-wheel-drive truck," said Jupiter, "and she certainly went that way."

Pete looked excited. "Why don't we? We can follow her trail and see what she's up to. Allie, your uncle has a four-wheel-drive truck and . . ."

"And I can only drive it on the ranch," Allie reminded him. Suddenly she brightened. "We can take the horses," she cried. "The horses could get up there. We really ought to. If Mrs Macomber had an accident on the road, or if her truck broke down she might be in bad trouble. We can pack a picnic lunch and tell Uncle Harry that we want to explore a real ghost town."

"You tell him, Allie," said Pete. "You can make up stories better than the three of us put together!"

14

The End of the Trail

MAGDALENA PREPARED a large picnic lunch for Allie and the Investigators, which they packed into saddle-bags.

"Be careful with the fire when you roast the hot dogs," Magdalena warned from the porch. "You do not wish to burn down the mountain." She waved to them as they set out.

Allie was mounted on Indian Queen, her handsome Appaloosa. Jupe, sweating slightly, was astride a stout mare. Pete sat easily on a rawboned gelding, and Bob rode the third of Uncle Harry's horses, a dappled steed. They passed Thurgood's gate at a trot, sending the dog into an outburst of barking, and drawing stares from the two Mexicans. The men were now painting Thurgood's cabin.

Allie was in the lead when they started up the mountainside. Jupe tagged close behind on the mare, who was much more interested in nibbling the grass beside the path than in getting to the top of the slope. Once Allie wheeled Queenie round and seized the reins of Jupe's horse. "You've got to hold her head up!" Allie scolded. "Come on. Get with it!"

Jupe's face went red. He tugged at the reins and

the mare quickened her pace, then she slowed and again ambled on, one plodding step after another.

"It'll take us all day to get there!" cried Allie.

"Giddap!" Jupe kicked his chubby legs against the mare's sides, but the mare kept to her stolid pace.

"No one will ever mistake you for the Lone Ranger!" said Bob. But he rode stiffly, looking down at the rugged hillside from time to time. "I'd hate to have a fall here," he muttered.

They rode on, now and then glimpsing the marks of Mrs Macomber's tyres in sandy places on the trail. Pine trees on either side blocked their view of the mountainside. It was after one when at last they reached the bare crest of the hills and found themselves ambling down the dusty main street of Hambone. All round them were tinder-dry houses with broken windows and warped, paintless boards pulling away from uprights. Rusted bedsprings lay in the street with old tin cans, battered furniture, and shards of jagged glass.

Allie dismounted and tied her Appaloosa to the railing of a porch in front of what had once been the Hambone General Store. The boys got down, moving stiffly, and secured their mounts.

"It's pretty bleak." Pete looked round as if he expected the ghost town to contain an actual ghost.

"Uncle Harry says a real ghost town gets this way," said Allie. "Vandals come in and break things and throw things out the windows." She pointed down the street to a big building very much like the one on Wesley Thurgood's property. The walls and roof were of rusted corrugated iron, and gaping holes opened on to blackness within. "That must be the mine works," Allie said.

They started towards the huge shed. "Be careful where you step," warned Allie. "And don't pick up any of those sheets of iron. The rattlesnakes like to get under things to keep out of the sun, and if you scare a rattler . . ."

"We *know* what happens if you scare a rattler!" said Pete. "Don't worry. We're not about to poke around in the junk."

They reached the doorway of the mine works and stopped. The door had long since fallen away, and Allie and the boys looked into a gloomy building.

"Wonder if that floor would hold us," said Bob. "Or is it rotten?"

"That's of no interest to us," said Jupiter. "The truck is not here. We didn't come simply to tour an abandoned town." He went to the middle of the street to examine a set of tyre tracks. "Mrs Macomber certainly reached the top of the crest," he announced. "If she hadn't, we would have found her on the trail." He went on, not stepping on the tracks, until he reached the corner of the mine works. "Aha!" he said loudly.

"What is it?" Allie darted to join him, and Pete and Bob followed her.

There, behind the ruined building, stood Mrs Macomber's truck.

"Mrs Macomber!" shouted Allie. She ran towards the truck. "Mrs Macomber! It's me! Allie!"

She had almost reached the truck when there was a nasty whirring sound.

"Allie! Stand still!" shouted Jupe.

Allie tried to throw herself backwards. Her feet slipped from under her and she went down. A deadly, sinister shape seemed to fly from beneath the truck. Allie flung herself to one side, and a wicked head with fearful wide jaws and lethal fangs struck at the spot where, an instant before, she had been.

Allie didn't move.

The rattler lay stretched to its full length for just a second, then once more sounded its hideous warning and began to pull its body into coils.

"Keep still!" whispered Pete. He picked up a large stone, took careful aim, and hurled it at the rattler.

"Bull's-eye!" cried Bob. "Right on the head! Boy that was close."

Allie scrambled to her feet and looked with horror at the struggling, writhing snake. "Thanks," was all she said to Pete, but she was very pale and shaking.

"Nothing any well-trained boy scout wouldn't do," said Pete. He crouched and peered under the truck, making sure he kept a safe distance. "Guess that was the only rattler there," he said.

Allie and the boys stepped round the dying snake and began to examine Mrs Macomber's truck. It was empty. There was no luggage of any kind, and there were no keys in the ignition.

"If she was called away on a family emergency, she wouldn't have left the truck here," said Bob.

"I don't get it," said Allie. "Where'd she go, and where is her stuff?"

"Could she be hiding someplace?" wondered Pete.

They searched the town, peering through windows, opening doors that moved on rusty hinges. They found nothing but broken furniture and heaped-up rubbish. Here and there they found footprints. But they saw no trace of Mrs Macomber.

"There *have* been people here," said Jupe. "A number of people." They returned to the truck and stared at the ground. There were footprints—some been made by Allie and the boys, but some had not. Twenty yards from the truck there were the marks of a second set of tyres.

"Someone else came here in a jeep or a truck," said Pete. They followed the tyre tracks along the street to the edge of the abandoned town. There, leading down the far side of the mountain, was a road—a narrow road, but one that was still in fair condition.

Jupiter was quiet for a moment. "She could have arranged to meet someone here," he said. "Yes . . . that's it. She drove up from Twin Lakes, transferred her belongings to another vehicle, abandoned her truck, and left. Allie, where does this road go?"

"I'm not sure," Allie admitted. "I've never been here before. But I know there's a lot of desert on the other side of the mountains."

A cloud of dust billowed above the trees on the slope below them, and they heard the sound of a motor labouring up the grade.

"She's coming back!" exclaimed Pete.

But it was not Mrs Macomber returning. Instead, a jeep appeared, bouncing slightly and skidding on loose gravel. At the wheel was an elderly man who wore a wide-brimmed straw hat. A woman in a printed cotton dress sat beside him.

"Hi there!" The man grinned and stopped his jeep.

"Hi!" said Pete.

"You youngsters here by yourselves?" the man asked.

Pete nodded.

"Bottle hunting, I suppose?" said the man.

"Bottle hunting?" asked Bob.

"That's what we come for," the woman told them. "We drove all the way from Casa Verde to these old towns in the hills. If you're lucky you can find some wonderful old bottles in these places. Got to watch it, though. Don't touch anything with your hands. If you want to move something, use a stick. Snakes around here."

"We know," said Jupiter. "Have . . . are there lots of people who drive up here?"

"I suppose," said the man. "The road up here to Hambone wasn't bad. Even if you don't find any bottles, these old places are interesting. I found a kerosene lantern in one ghost town last week. It was good as new."

He drove the jeep on and parked near the store.

"So much for the other tyre tracks," said Bob. "Those could have been made by someone who came to meet Mrs Macomber or they could have belonged to any antique hunter."

Jupiter sighed. "It doesn't really matter, does it? Mrs Macomber was here, but she isn't here now. We've reached the end of the trail."

15

The Silent Watchdog

AFTER ROASTING THEIR HOT DOGS, Allie and the Investigators got back on their mounts. The return journey to Twin Lakes was slow, with the horses sticking close together and picking their way cautiously down the steep slope from Hambone.

"I wouldn't have believed it," said Jupe. "Mrs. Macomber appeared to be a self-possessed woman, yet she seems to have panicked and run."

"You're just guessing," Allie told him. "We don't know everything that happens with Mrs Macomber. There might be another explanation."

"There seems to be only one," said Jupiter. "When she realized that we had been investigating what went on here five years ago, she got frightened and fled. Perhaps one of her confederates met her in Hambone. It is even possible that another member of the hold-up gang has been lurking around Twin Lakes for the last few days. We still do not have any explanation for the prowler who took the machete from the barn."

Pete brightened. "Hey! He could have been part of the hold-up gang. Mrs Macomber could have hidden him when the sheriff searched for him that night."

"And what about the groceries . . . and the cigarette butt?" added Bob.

"What about them?" Allie asked.

"Just listen for a minute," said Bob. "Suppose Mrs Macomber was hiding the prowler—let's just say he was part of the gang. He could have been somewhere nearby when we went to see her yesterday. He might have gotten hungry and decided to grab a snack while we were going through her houses. Remember, it wasn't Mrs Macomber who first missed the food. It was Jupe who noticed that the things were gone."

"Good thinking, Bob," said Jupe.

"You're all nuts!" said Allie.

"Don't get upset, Allie," said Jupe. "Remember, we *are* only guessing. At this point we have a number of odd things going on. We have found the five-year-old corpse of a man who may or may not have been involved in a hold-up five years ago. We also have a widow who just might have been involved—and who has mysteriously disappeared. We have a prowler who stole a machete and who may or may not have been a confederate of the widow, or of the dead man in the mine. We also have the mine—a played-out silver mine that is seemingly being worked by a wealthy real estate man from Los Angeles. And we have a gold pebble from that mine. According to Mrs Macomber, the mine never contained an ounce of gold."

"Mrs Macomber might have lied," said Pete.

"Whatever her connection with the dead man, there would be no reason for her to lie about the gold," Jupe pointed out. "She seems to have no connection whatsoever with Wesley Thurgood, except that she remembers his birth here in Twin Lakes."

"Don't forget the loot from the robbery," Pete said. "If it was ever here, did Thurgood get it? Or did Mrs Macomber get it five years ago?"

The four were silent for the rest of the trip down the mountain. By the time they reached the bottom it was late afternoon. As Thurgood's compound came into view, they saw that his red passenger truck was gone. There were buckets of paint near Thurgood's cabin, but the job had not been finished, and the Mexican labourers were nowhere to be seen. The huge watchdog was stretched out, sleeping in the sun.

The horses clip-clopped past Thurgood's closed, padlocked gate. The dog slept on.

"That's strange," said Jupe. "He's usually trying to tear the fence down to get at us."

When they reached Harrison Osborne's pasture they unsaddled the horses. The front door of the house was open and there was a note on the kitchen table: "Magdalena's sister needs her. I am driving her to Silver City and we'll be back late tonight. Take cold cuts for dinner and *keep out of trouble!* Love, Uncle Harry."

"How nice!" Jupiter's solemn face brightened.

"I don't think it's nice—what if Magdalena's sister is sick? What's the matter with you, Jupiter Jones?" asked Allie.

"Let us hope that Magdalena's sister is not ill," said Jupe. "What's nice is that no one is here. Mrs Macomber is gone. Thurgood's truck is missing, and his two labourers are not about. Your uncle and Magdalena are away. The coast is clear—and we're free to investigate the one mysterious event that we haven't yet looked into: the appearance of a bit of gold in a played-out silver mine."

Jupe took the pebble from his pocket, tossed it into the air, then looked eagerly at his companions. "Let's go—while we have a chance! We've got to find out what's happening in that mine."

"You forgot the watchdog," said Pete. "The dog is there, and he isn't chained up, either."

"Don't worry about the dog!" Allie flew to the refrigerator, and yanked out the remains of the leg of lamb they had had for dinner the night before. "Plenty of meat on this, and a nice bone to chew. It should keep old Fido busy for a spell."

A few minutes later The Three Investigators and Allie were hurrying across the Christmas-tree field towards the mine. When they reached the edge of Uncle Harry's land, they looked through the fence into Thurgood's enclosure. The dog still slept.

"Hey!" Pete shouted. "Hey, Rex! Rover! Yahoo, Rover!"

"Come and get it, pooch!" Allie brandished the leg of lamb.

The dog did not stir.

Pete called to the dog once more. When he did not move, the tall investigator took hold of the fence, scrambled to the top, and jumped down into Thurgood's clearing.

"Watch it," warned Bob.

"Toss the bone over," said Pete. "If the dog

wakes up, I'll throw it to him."

Allie threw the bone to Pete. He stood watching the dog. "You'd almost think he was dead," he said.

"Let's just take advantage of the situation," said Allie. And she, too, climbed to the top of the eight-foot fence and then down to the ground. Bob followed her example, and Jupe—with some huffing and puffing—managed to push his bulk over.

The four warily approached the dog. Allie kept talking to the animal. "There, boy. Easy there!" she crooned.

"Careful!" whispered Jupiter.

She leaned over and touched the dog. He twitched and whimpered as if he were dreaming.

"Well, he's only sleeping," said Allie. "But how come he doesn't wake up?"

Jupe spied a tin pan near the fence. He picked it up and sniffed at a few scraps of raw meat that remained on it. "I can't smell anything, but the dog may have been drugged," he announced. "Perhaps someone wanted him out of the way!"

The others looked around apprehensively, but no other person could be seen.

"I wonder where the Mexican men are—the ones who work for Thurgood." Without realizing it, Bob had lowered his voice to a whisper.

"Hello!" shouted Pete. "Is anybody here?"

The cry echoed and re-echoed from the hillside.

"Pipe down!" snapped Allie. "So somebody drugged the dog and no one's here." She pulled out the flashlight she had stuck in her back pocket. "Let's move fast before somebody does show up."

She started towards the mine entrance, which lay in deep shadow now that the sun had disappeared behind the mountain. It would be dusk soon.

Just inside the mine were several shovels and a wheelbarrow. Allie flashed her light on the tunnel walls and up over the timbers that supported the ceiling. "What have they been doing here?" she said. "I don't see where anybody's been blasting."

"We haven't gone in far enough yet," said Jupe. "The sound of those explosions were muffled. Let's go on to the place where I found the pebble."

He took the light and led the way to the spot where the tunnel branched out to the right and the left. He turned left without hesitation. "It was about fifty feet from here," he said, and he paced forward.

Now there was a bigger pile of loose rock and pebbles on the floor of the mine. Above the heap of rubble was a wide hole that had been blasted in one wall. Something glittered at the edge of the cavity.

"Look!" cried Pete. "Gold!"

Jupe stepped forward and held the light close to the tunnel wall. Bright specks glinted under the torch's beam. "Amazing!" said Jupe. With his finger-nails he dug a bit of shining yellow metal out of the hard earth. He turned the light full on his prize and stared at it.

"So Mrs Macomber was wrong!" said Allie. "There *is* gold in the mine!"

Suddenly all four of them froze.

Very faintly, from somewhere outside the mine, came the sound of what could have been a shot, or perhaps a car backfiring.

"Someone's coming!" whispered Pete.

"We'd better scram!" said Allie. "I don't want to get caught in here again!"

Jupe put the bit of gold into his pocket and they hurried towards the main tunnel. The timbered entrance now showed only as a faint square of light. When they glimpsed it, Jupe snapped off the flashlight and they groped towards the fresh air, stumbling up the slanting floor of the tunnel. At the mine entrance, Jupe stopped them.

The dog still lay in the clearing, almost invisible in the gathering dusk. A car screeched to a halt outside the fence. Allie and the boys watched two men get out of the car.

"Okay, Gasper," said one of the men. "Grab a rock or something and we'll get that padlock off the gate."

"No sweat, Manny," said the second, in a rasping wheeze. "I'll shoot it off!"

"You crazy?" said the first man. "Somebody hears you and that fat-cat sheriff will be up here. Get a rock."

Even from where they stood, yards from the gate, Allie and the boys could hear the laboured breathing of the man called Gasper.

"Jupe!" Pete whispered. "That sound. It's the prowler who was in the barn! The one who took a whack at me with the machete! He breathed like that!"

They shrank back into the darkness of the mine tunnel.

"What are we going to do?" whispered Allie. "If we try to make a run for it, those creeps are sure to see us—and I don't think they're here on a friendly visit! There's not a soul up here tonight—*or* back at the ranch!"

They could hear the man called Gasper pounding at the padlock on Thurgood's gate. The lock dropped to the ground and the gate was pushed open.

"If it's still here, it's probably in the house," croaked Gasper.

The two men crossed the clearing to Thurgood's cabin. "Might not be here at all," said his partner. "He's had plenty of time to stash it someplace else."

"If we don't find it here, we can check out the mine," said Gasper.

"And if we don't find it there," Manny replied, "we wait for that crumb to come back and we *force* him to tell us what he did with it!"

The two men laughed as they went into Thurgood's cabin.

Allie almost squealed. "They're going to catch us in here," she cried. "We've got to try and make it to the ranch. We can call the sheriff from there."

"Are you crazy, Allie?" whispered Pete. "Those guys are armed!"

"But she's right," said Bob. "We've got to do something!"

Jupe crawled to the entrance of the mine and looked out. A bucket of liquid stood nearby, next to the rickety shack that Thurgood had padlocked some days before. Jupe crept forward and sniffed the bucket, then looked at the tinder-dry wood of the shack.

He slipped back to the entrance of the tunnel. "The Mexicans left a bucket of paint thinner next to Thurgood's shack," he reported. "If we set fire to the shack someone in town is sure to see it and alert the fire department. We'll get the fire truck and probably the sheriff up here in no time—and those thugs will be trapped. Pete, you took matches to Hambone today. Do you still have them?"

Pete took a book of matches out of his pocket and he and Jupe crept outside. Jupe picked up the bucket and sloshed its contents over the shack. Pete struck a match and tossed it. Instantly a sheet of flame engulfed the old wood. The shed was burning fiercely.

"Beautiful!" said Pete. "That ought to do it."

Suddenly Jupe gasped and shouted: "It sure will! Quick! Get into the mine. I think I know what Thurgood was storing in that shack!"

They dodged into the mine entrance and the four scrambled down the slanting floor.

"Get down!" yelled Jupe.

They all hit the ground—and the shack exploded with a roar that shook the earth!

16

Flight!

THE EXPLOSION WENT ON AND ON, thunderous and deafening. When at last it stopped, echoes of the blast rumbled back from the hills. Allie and the boys stumbled out of the mine. The remains of the shed blazed beside the mine entrance, and bits of burning debris were strewn over the ground.

Pete gaped. "All we wanted was a little fire!"

"I should have guessed that Thurgood was keeping his dynamite in that shack!" said Jupiter.

As the shock of the explosion wore off, things started happening with frightening speed. The door of the old mine works building sprang open and the two Mexicans rushed out. They scrambled over the fence and disappeared among the rocks on the slope above the mine. Manny and Gasper staggered out of the cabin just as Thurgood's red truck careered into the clearing through the open gate.

"Hey, Mr Thurgood!" yelled Pete as he ran forward. "Watch out! Those guys broke into your house, and they're armed!"

As Gasper turned threateningly to Pete, Thurgood jumped out of his truck, pulling a shotgun after him. "Hold it right there," he yelled. "If you take another step, you're finished."

But Gasper was too fast for him. Before Thurgood could raise his gun barrel, the thug lunged at Pete and grabbed the boy's shoulder. Pete stumbled and felt something press into the small of his back.

"Drop your gun," Gasper told Thurgood, "or I'll blow the kid in half!"

Thurgood lowered his gun slowly, then let it fall to the ground. Manny ran forward and picked it up. A nasty grin spread over his flat features. His eyes darted to the other kids near the mouth of the mine. "You girl!" he called. "Get over here!"

"No, wait!" Bob tried to step in front of Allie.

"Out of the way, kid!" ordered Manny. Brandishing the shotgun, he ran over and grabbed Allie, twisting her arm behind her back. "Now march!"

Suddenly they heard the wail of a siren. It was the fire engine coming from Twin Lakes.

Manny and Gasper looked at each other, and tightened their hold on the hostages.

"That road . . ." Manny nodded towards the rutted track up to Hambone, faintly visible in the failing light. "Where's it go, girlie?"

"Just . . . just to an old ghost town," said Allie.

"What's on the other side of them mountains?"

"Only the desert." Allie looked frightened, but she held her chin high.

Gasper nodded towards Thurgood's truck. "We can make it in that. It's got four-wheel drive."

"You'll never get away with this!" cried Allie.

"Shut up!" croaked Gasper.

They could hear the distant rumble of the fire engine now. Again the siren sounded.

"Hurry up! Into the truck!" Manny shoved Allie in front of him, thrust her into the back seat of Thurgood's truck, and climbed in after her. Pete ended up in the front seat next to Gasper. Jupe, Bob and Thurgood stood by helplessly. The truck lurched out of the clearing and, with a clash of gears, started up the slope of the Hambone road.

Jupe and Bob ran to the gate after the departing truck. Gasper was driving without lights, and the truck was soon lost from sight among the pine trees on the mountainside. In the other direction, the red lights of the approaching fire engine showed beyond Uncle Harry's gate. Siren screaming, it pulled into Thurgood's clearing a few minutes later. The sheriff's car raced in after it and braked abruptly.

Sheriff Tait got out and glanced at the wreck of the shack, which was now a glowing heap. "Looks like the emergency's over, Sam," said the sheriff to the man at the wheel of the fire engine. Then Tait came towards Wesley Thurgood. "What happened?" he demanded. "Sounded in town like the whole mountain fell on you."

Jupiter stepped forward quickly. "I set fire to the shack," he said. "There were two men breaking into Mr Thurgood's cabin and I wanted to attract some attention—but that's not important now! Those men have Allie Jamison and Peter Crenshaw with them! They took Mr Thurgood's truck up the Hambone road. They're armed . . .

and they seem desperate men to me!"

Sheriff Tait stared off into the darkness that now shrouded the mountains. "Somebody took Allie?"

"And our friend Pete Crenshaw," insisted Jupiter. "At gunpoint!"

The sheriff rubbed a big hand across his chin. He scowled. "How long have they been gone?"

"Just a few minutes. You can catch up with them if you hurry. They're driving without lights, so they can't be going very fast."

"They'll go fast enough if they see me behind them. Might well run off the road. Chasing them is mighty risky when they've got those kids along."

"Then wait for them on the other side of the mountain," urged Jupe. "When they reach Hambone, they'll certainly keep going. If the road is blocked on the far side of the ridge . . ."

"Which road?" said the sheriff.

Jupiter gaped. "There's more than one road?"

"Son, if they make it to Hambone. They've got a dozen different routes they can take. There's lots of little dirt roads on the other side of the hills. They branch off from the main Hambone road and run to little cabins and some old mines. Then they meander on down to the desert. Those guys can stay hidden in the hills for weeks if they want to."

"But they *can't*," shouted Bob. "They've got Allie and Pete!"

The sheriff went to his car and reached in to take the speaker from his two-way radio. "I can have a helicopter from the highway patrol here in less than half an hour," he said. "And I'll tell them to cover the foothills on the far side by car. Let's just pray those bandits don't decide they can move faster if they get rid of a couple of hostages!"

17

Breakdown

JIM HOOVER, THE HELICOPTER PILOT, grinned and nodded when Jupe and Bob begged to go along on the search for the fleeing thugs.

"I don't like it," Sheriff Tait complained. "It could be dangerous." But he stood aside so the boys could squeeze into the helicopter and kneel behind the seats for pilot and passenger. The sheriff climbed into the passenger seat and laid a rifle with a telescopic sight across his knees.

"All set?" said Hoover. He lifted the chopper off the road near Thurgood's mine. Except for the pale light of a crescent moon, it was now pitch dark. As soon as they were airborne Hoover flipped a switch. The blue-white beam of a searchlight stabbed the night. "You can control the light from there," said Hoover to Sheriff Tait. He indicated a lever in front of the sheriff's seat.

Sheriff Tait leaned forward. "They must still be running without lights." The sheriff manipulated the handle and the searchlight swept across the slope below. They could see rocks and huge boulders that cast grotesque shadows. They could see parts of the narrow, twisting ribbon of road that led from Twin Lakes to Hambone. It appeared almost white among the dark evergreen trees that crowded close to it on either side.

"Unless they ditch the truck, they've got to stick to that road at least as far as Hambone," said Hoover.

The helicopter veered towards the mountain and Jupe felt his stomach lurch. He gasped.

"Take it easy, kid," said Hoover. "Make believe you're riding in an elevator that goes sideways instead of just up and down."

"I'm fine!" declared Jupe. "Perfectly fine!"

The helicopter covered every inch of the road between Twin Lakes and Hambone. There was no truck.

"Man, they were making time to get over the ridge this fast," said the sheriff as they skimmed above the crest of the mountain. "And without lights!"

Bob wondered. Had Manny and Gasper really managed to get to the top of the rise and beyond? Or had Gasper run the truck off the road in the darkness? Were Pete and Allie all right? Or were they lying below, caught in the wreckage of the truck, possibly hurt?

Bob hunched his shoulders. Sheriff Tait must have sensed his fear. "Don't worry, son," he said kindly "My deputy and another guy will come up the road in a jeep. If anything happened to that truck, they'll find it."

Jim Hoover took his craft low over the roofs of Hambone, and the searchlight probed the open areas between the rotting old buildings.

"What's that?" cried the sheriff. "There's a

truck down there . . . behind the old Hambone mine works!"

Jupiter leaned forward. "That's Mrs Macomber's pick-up," he said. "We found it abandoned there this afternoon. And we don't know *where* Mrs Macomber is."

"What is going on around here?" demanded Sheriff Tait.

"I think I can explain it all later," said Jupe. "Right now we've got to find Allie and Pete."

"Well, if they got past Hambone they're somewhere on the west slope, down on one of those little roads," said the sheriff. "But I'm blessed if I know which one I'd take if I were on the lam with a couple of kids."

"There's only one way to find out," said Jim Hoover. The helicopter clattered on towards the west, leaving Hambone to its echoes and its ghosts.

Allie and Pete sat in the truck with Manny and Gasper and listened to the helicopter as it hovered above them. The searchlight on the craft swept the treetops and touched the empty road that led up to the ruined town. For an instant it touched the evergreen trees under which Gasper had driven the truck.

Allie Jamison held her breath. With all her might she willed the searchers in the helicopter to spot them. "Please see us!" she pleaded in her mind. "Please! We're right down here! Can't you see us?"

The sound of the helicopter grew fainter, then faded away. Gasper chuckled. "C'mon. Let's move. He put the truck into gear, and it roared and shuddered as it lumbered out of the gully by the side of the road. Then, still without lights, they started slowly up to Hambone again.

"If we get away clean, I'm never coming back." Gasper's voice was morose. "Wouldn't get us anything, anyway. If that Thurgood creep hasn't found the stuff yet, he'll sure start looking now. Don't take no genius to figure out we were after something big."

"How big *was* Gilbert Morgan's share of that quarter of a million dollars?" said Allie.

Gasper stamped on the brake and the truck screeched to a stop. "Who said anything about a quarter of a million dollars?" he demanded. When Allie didn't answer he fumbled a cigarette out of his pocket and lit it. "We ought to dump these two some place," he told Manny. "Some place where nobody will ever find them."

Allie coughed loudly and waved cigarette smoke away from her face. "A terrible habit, smoking," she said. "Ruins your wind—in case you haven't noticed—and it does horrible things to your voice. And it wouldn't do you any good to get rid of us. We know about the robbery in Phoenix five years ago. There were four crooks—three men and a woman. Gilbert Morgan was one of the men, wasn't he? And you're the other two. We know, and so do Bob and Jupe."

Manny groaned. "The other two kids. And we left them behind!"

"Stupid of you, wasn't it?" said Allie.

Manny held up the shotgun, and Allie was silent.

Soon they reached Hambone and started down the other side of the mountain. Gasper let the truck roll, holding it in check with the low gear. After a time they came to a place where the main road curved off to the right, and a narrower, rougher way opened to the left. Gasper crushed a cigarette stub in the already overflowing ashtray and pointed to the main road. "Where's that go?" he asked Allie.

"I don't know," said Allie, waving smoke away from her face. "Down to the desert, I suppose."

"Take the side road," ordered Manny. "I've got a hunch that by this time there are about a hundred cops waiting for us at the bottom of the main road."

Gasper grunted and turned the truck on to the narrower road. It was barely more than a pair of tyre tracks winding among the trees. The truck lurched and rocked, but Gasper fought the wheel and kept going. The thug tossed a newly lit cigarette out the window and held on to the wheel with both hands.

"If you set the mountain on fire the whole highway patrol will find us in a minute!" said Allie snidely. Gasper was too busy controlling the truck to reply.

It seemed to Pete and Allie that they travelled through the hills for eternities. Sometimes they saw cabins, dark and secret, nestled under the trees. Once they came upon a settlement that was smaller than Hambone and even more ruined. A coyote loped away, keeping to the shadows. Several times they again saw the searchlight of an approaching helicopter, and Gasper pulled off the road and waited until it disappeared. Pete and Allie tried to doze, but the lurching of the truck kept waking them up.

For a while they seemed to be climbing higher and higher. But at last the road became a series of switchbacks that zigzagged down the slope. "I think we've got it made." Gasper's hands were tight on the wheel. The moon had set and only the faint light from the stars that powdered the sky showed the way. The rutted track widened and levelled off, and they were at the foot of the hills. A paved highway ran across their path in front of them. On the other side of the highway was the open emptiness of the desert.

Gasper stopped the truck and looked cautiously to the left and the right. Manny chuckled. "No cops," he said. "Like I figured, they're all back at the main drag waiting for us."

"They could be anyplace." Gasper took a deep rasping breath and coughed. "We don't want that road," he decided, nodding towards the paved highway. He put the truck into first and it rolled out from beneath the trees, crossed the highway, and bounced on to the desert floor.

"Ouch!" cried Allie as the truck hit a chuckhole and she was thrown forward. "This truck will never make it!"

"Shut up!" snarled Gasper, nervously crushing out the cigarette he had just lit. "We're bound to pick up another road if we keep going straight ahead long enough—and we need one the cops aren't watching."

The last stars faded. Pete looked back to see a faint glow behind the mountains. When at last the sun came up above the hills, the highway was far behind them and out of sight.

"There's got to be another road soon," muttered Gasper. "One that doesn't connect—"

He broke off as the truck hit a large chuckhole and they were all jerked violently to one side. There was a loud hissing sound, and steam and fumes from the fluid in the radiator filled their nostrils.

"Blast!" Gasper killed the engine, jumped out, and ran to the front of the truck. He stood and glared at the wheels as a puddle of rusty-coloured water darkened the white dust beneath the truck.

"What is it?" demanded Manny.

"The radiator's busted," said Gasper. "And the axle broke!"

Manny groaned. "You stupid idiot!"

Gasper came to the side of the truck and pointed his gun at Allie and Pete. "Okay, out! We'll hike for it!"

"You're crazy!" cried Allie.

"Shut up and move!" snarled Gasper.

Allie and Pete got out. So did Manny, who stood and looked across the flat wasteland. "That way," he decided, pointing ahead. "We'll walk that way and keep the mountains behind us. Sooner or later we'll come to something."

"No!" said Allie. "You can walk for miles and

miles out here and not come to anything. And once the sun is really up, it'll be over a hundred degrees out in the open desert—way over a hundred. We've got to stay with the truck."

"If we stay with the truck, we're dead," said Manny.

"We're dead if we leave it," Allie insisted.

"Knock that off and move!" shouted Gasper.

"No." Allie sat down on the ground. "You can shoot me if you want to, but I'm staying here. I'd rather be shot than die of the heat, or go off my rocker from thirst!" She glared at Manny and Gasper defiantly.

Pete hesitated. Then he, too, sat down beside the truck.

Gasper gave them a menacing look. His fingers tightened on the handle of his gun. Then Manny abruptly turned and stomped off across the desert.

Gasper looked from Pete and Allie to the determined figure of his crony. Then he followed Manny.

Allie and Pete watched until the two gunmen were tiny wavering shapes in the distance. The sun was climbing fast, and heat waves were beginning to shimmer on the desert floor.

"Suppose they've stopped looking for us?" Pete said. His voice was hoarse with anxiety. "We could die of thirst right here!"

18

Stranded in the Desert

HIGH IN THE AIR, Bob and Jupiter watched the mountains turn pink in the dawn light. Sheriff Tait clicked off the helicopter's searchlight and yawned. After a night of searching the hills, their eyes were red-rimmed and sore. Jim Hoover, the pilot, shifted his weight and made still another turn over the mountains.

"I don't know how they got over the ridge and off the mountain without us spotting them," said Sheriff Tait. "But I'll be darned if they're still in these hills. We've combed every inch of them."

"But where else could they be?" asked Bob. "If they'd come down on the main road the patrol cars would have caught them. And that other 'copter pilot radioed that he'd checked out the highway."

"Maybe they *will* stay in the hills," said Jupe. "There are all kinds of abandoned towns down there, and plenty of trees to hide the truck under."

"You could be right, Jupiter," said the sheriff. "But my bet is they've come down on one of the unused roads and set out across the desert. After all, they don't have any supplies, and they can't go too long without food."

"Could we find them if they're in the desert?" asked Bob.

"Sure, if we look long enough," the sheriff replied. "The desert's big, but at least it's open. Let's try there."

Jim Hoover nodded and turned west. The helicopter left the hills and flew out over the desert.

Allie fished a bandanna out of her jeans pocket and mopped her forehead. The sun beat down with white-hot intensity. She was dead tired, but too anxious to sleep. She walked around the truck for the fifth time that morning, then plopped down next to Pete, who sat in the vanishing shade of the truck. "It's getting late," she said. "It must be close to noon. Why haven't they found us yet?"

Pete nodded glumly. "And we haven't eaten since yesterday's picnic in Hambone. I'm starved."

"How can you think about food?" snapped Allie. "My mouth's so dry it feels like a cactus!"

"If the radiator hadn't cracked we could drink what was in there," said Pete.

"Ugh!" said Allie, and she hunched her shoulders. Then suddenly she shouted, "Oh my gosh! What's the matter with me?"

"What do you mean?" said Pete, startled.

Allie jumped to her feet and took the keys from the truck's ignition. She opened the large glove compartment, rummaged around, and pulled out a first-aid kit. Inside it she found a pair of surgical scissors.

"What are you going to do with those?" asked Pete as Allie waved the scissors triumphantly.

She pointed to a barrel cactus nearby. "We can cut a couple of chunks out of that cactus over there," she said. "There's *always* water stored in cactus. They sop it up when it rains and hold it so they can live through the dry spells. I don't know why I didn't think of it before!"

"Better late than never!" said Pete. "Boy, I could sure use a taste of something wet." He took the scissors and ran over to the cactus. He whacked at the tough-skinned plant until he had cut out two chunks of moist pulp. Then he handed one to Allie and bit into the other. They both screwed up their faces.

"I don't know what's worse," said Pete. "Dying of thirst . . . or this!"

Allie slowly chewed all the moisture from the cactus, then she spit out the pulp. Now the sun was almost directly overhead. "We can take cover under the truck," said Allie. "If the helicopter is still looking, they'll be able to spot it."

The two crawled into the shade beneath the truck. "It really is cooler under here," said Pete, as he stretched out and prepared to wait.

Feeling somewhat better, Allie and Pete grew more alert. They heard the faint call of a desert bird, and saw a kangaroo rat stick its head out of the ground, then scurry back out of sight. Several lizards crawled by the truck in search of food. All around, the flat expanse of wasteland shimmered in the hot sun. After what seemed like hours Pete lifted his head. Then Allie perked up. "I heard it too!" she said. Far away, they could hear the unmistakable clatter of a helicopter.

"They're coming!" Allie cried. She and Pete scrambled out from beneath the truck and ran out into the open. But the faint chattering noise died away. They searched the sky, but they could see nothing but blue. "I *know* I heard a helicopter," said Allie.

They both listened again, but they no longer heard a sound.

"Oh, why don't they come?" Allie cried. "We're as good as dead if they don't get here soon."

"Stop that, Allie," said Pete. "They'll find us—I'm sure of it." But his voice didn't sound as hopeful as his words.

Then they heard the sound again. A chopper was flying in the distance. Pete and Allie jumped up and down, waving their arms and yelling wildly. "We're here!" screamed Allie. "Down here."

Now the helicopter had spotted them. It swerved and flew in their direction. As it settled slowly to the ground, Pete and Allie ran forward, bending to avoid the whirling blades.

Sheriff Tait scrambled out of the chopper. "Are you kids all right?" he demanded.

"We're fine," said Allie. "Really!"

Pete pointed across the desert. "The crooks went that way—on foot!" he said.

"They decided to hike for it after they wrecked the truck," Allie added.

The sheriff laughed. "Reckon they're sorry now."

Jupiter and Bob were bursting to get out of the helicopter and grab their friends. But the sheriff climbed quickly back into the front seat and said something to Jim Hoover. The pilot nodded and spoke into his radio. Then he leaned out of his window and shouted to Pete and Allie above the roar of the chopper's engine, "We don't have enough room to get you two in here. But I've called for one of the other helicopters. It'll be here in five minutes. We're going after your kidnappers!" With that, he handed a canteen out to Pete, lifted the helicopter up, and headed west in search of Manny and Gasper.

Pete and Allie grinned at each other.

"I'll bet those creeps didn't get very far," said Allie with satisfaction.

19

The Millionaire's Secret

ALLIE WAS RIGHT. An hour later Manny and Gasper were brought into Twin Lakes and deposited in the clearing near Wesley Thurgood's cabin by a helicopter pilot and a deputy. The disgruntled crooks were sunburned, blistered, and exhausted. They had managed to walk only a few miles through the desert before collapsing from the heat. Allie and Pete, who had been airlifted back to Twin Lakes earlier, smiled with glee as the handcuffed thugs were led out of the helicopter.

A moment later, Sheriff Tait arrived with Jupe and Bob. The boys jubilantly greeted their friends, and said hello to a relieved Uncle Harry. Magdalena was there, busily passing sandwiches round and fussing over the two Mexican labourers. They had returned to the mine compound during the night and now sat on the steps of Thurgood's cabin, subdued and frightened and refusing to speak to anyone. Thurgood's dog lay chained beside the cabin, panting quietly. Thurgood himself stood nearby, looking strained and bewildered.

"Now that everyone is back," he said, "would someone please tell me who those men are—" he nodded to the manacled crooks "—and what's been going on here?"

Ignoring Thurgood, Allie turned to Jupe and exclaimed, "We guessed right about Gilbert Morgan! He was in on that armoured car hold-up in Phoenix five years ago—and those two guys were in it with him! They admitted it last night, when we were driving over the mountain."

"We didn't say a thing," declared Manny.

"Yes, you did," said Allie. "When I told you that we knew about the robbery, you said you ought to dump us. Knock us off, I guess. That's just the same as admitting it!"

Jupiter Jones smiled like a contented cherub. "So we *were* correct in our reconstruction," he said. "Everything's beginning to fall into place."

"What *are* you talking about?" demanded Sheriff Tait.

"Maybe you'd like to clue us in, Jupiter," said Uncle Harry. "I'm as much in the dark as anyone."

"I can try," said Jupe with obvious relish. He wolfed down the last of a sandwich and took a deep breath.

"When the dead man in the mine was identified as a wanted parole-jumper—a convicted hold-up artist—we wondered what such a person had been doing in such a remote place as Twin Lakes. What had drawn him to Death Trap Mine? So we checked the back issues of the *Twin Lakes Gazette* and found that several interesting events took place here five years ago.

"We knew that five years ago Gilbert Morgan's body was sealed in the mine. On the same day that the mine was sealed, a car stolen from Lordsburg was found near the mine. We could only guess that Morgan came here in that car. So we tried to trace Morgan to Lordsburg, but all we found there was an announcement in the Lordsburg newspaper of the sealing of the Death Trap Mine.

"Five years ago Mrs Macomber returned to Twin Lakes and purchased her property. In one of her abandoned houses we found a five-year-old Phoenix newspaper that contained the story of a robbery there—a robbery that netted three men and a woman at least a quarter of a million dollars. That newspaper was dated just days before the sealing of the mine—which was several months before Mrs Macomber took possession of her property. It seemed quite possible that Gilbert Morgan brought the paper here—that he was in the house before he entered the mine. We guessed that Morgan was one of the hold-up men. We now know that he was—and that you are the other two." Jupiter smiled at Manny and Gasper.

"When that body was found in the mine last week, this place was overrun with curiosity seekers. You, Gasper, came here at the same time—when you heard the news of the discovery of Morgan's corpse. You got into Harrison Osborne's barn, and when we surprised you, you attacked Pete with a machete. But you were looking for something. You had to stay on. So you hung round here, perhaps on Mrs Macomber's place. I'm sure you were the one who stole food from her kitchen and left a cigarette butt in her sink. Or did she give you food willingly?"

Gasper didn't answer.

"No matter," said Jupe. "Manny must have been round somewhere, too, but we never saw a trace of him. I guess you, Gasper, were the look-out. Yesterday afternoon the coast was clear. Everyone in the neighbourhood seemed to be away. So you drugged Thurgood's dog with some doctored meat, went and got Manny, and came to look for Morgan's share of the robbery loot."

Jupe turned to Wesley Thurgood. "You did find that money in the mine, didn't you, Mr Thurgood?"

Thurgood shook his head. "Sorry, kid, but you're on the wrong track. I admit I didn't examine the mine completely when I first opened it. But the sheriff went through it after the hood's body was found. There is nothing in that mine."

"Nothing, Mr Thurgood?" said Jupiter. He took a pebble out of his pocket and tossed it into the air. "Not even . . . not even gold?"

Thurgood looked startled.

"Gold?" said Sheriff Tait. "There was never any gold in the old Death Trap."

"There is gold now," said Jupiter. "I picked this pebble up in the mine the day Allie found Morgan's body. I showed it to a jeweller in Lordsburg. He said that the bit of shiny reddish metal in it is gold—gold with a high percentage of copper."

The sheriff looked stunned. "But . . . but if there is gold in the Death Trap Mine why didn't anyone find it before?"

Jupe dug into his pocket again and took out a second bit of gleaming metal. He handed it to the sheriff. "Because it was not there when Mr Thurgood bought the mine," said Jupiter. "When we were in the mine yesterday evening, I found this lodged in a wall, along with a number of other bits of metal. If you will examine it closely, you will see that it is greenish gold—probably gold with a high percentage of silver." Jupe rocked back on his heels.

"As we searched the hills for Pete and Allie last night, I started thinking about those two bits of gold. I knew that gold is often found alloyed with other metals—such as copper or silver—but I doubted that two completely different alloys would be found so close together. I also began to think about the shot we heard in the mine . . . and all the blasting. So I took a closer look at that bit of greenish gold. If you do that, Sheriff Tait, you will see that it was not always lodged in the wall of Death Trap Mine."

The sheriff held up the bit of metal and squinted at it. "It's . . . it's got a design on it!" he exclaimed.

Jupiter Jones nodded triumphantly. "A pattern of orange blossoms. That gold was once part of a wedding ring!"

Thurgood stepped forward. "Where did you get that?" he demanded. "Where did you really get it? And don't tell me you found it in the mine!"

"I don't need to tell you," said Jupe. "I'm sure that if you were careless enough to use pieces of old jewellery in your confidence game, there are other bits in the mine wall that can be identified. The sheriff has only to go and look at them."

He turned to the sheriff. "Mr Thurgood has been pulling a very old swindle," said Jupe. "He has been ‘salting’ his mine. He loaded a shotgun with bits of gold, fired the particles into the wall of the mine then brought in prospective investors to show them his ‘strike’. He had his Mexican labourers set off dynamite whenever he brought in visitors, so that it would appear that the mine was actually being worked. I assume that the suckers flew to Lordsburg, where they were met by Thurgood. He then drove them to the Death Trap Mine and persuaded them to invest in the mine.”

“Something doesn’t make sense,” Uncle Harry broke in. “Wesley Thurgood had already made a fortune in real estate. Why would he get involved in a crooked scheme like mine salting?”

Thurgood sneered. “That’s simple. I wouldn’t. The very idea is ridiculous.”

“But when we go into the mine, we will see . . .” Jupe began.

“You will go nowhere!” shouted Thurgood. His face was now flushed and angry. His eyes darted to the entrance of the mine. “I am going to call my lawyer. In the meantime, anyone who sets foot in my mine had better have a search warrant, or they will be prosecuted.”

“You can call your lawyer from jail,” said Sheriff Tait. His eyes were cold. “I’ve got enough evidence to hold you on suspicion—and to get a search warrant.”

“Are you going to believe that crazy kid?” cried Thurgood.

“He doesn’t seem crazy to me,” said the sheriff.

“Thank you, Sheriff Tait,” said Jupe. “And now

there is one more thing I'd like to get cleared up."

He turned to Manny and Gasper.

"Where is Mrs Macomber?" demanded Jupiter. "Is she waiting to meet you somewhere?"

"Mrs Macomber?" said Manny, his face blank.

"The old dame who owns the houses across the way," Gasper explained. "Her name's Macomber."

A look of complete astonishment appeared on Jupe's face. "You mean . . . you mean you don't know her? You really don't know her?"

Manny shrugged.

Jupiter pulled hard at his bottom lip. "We suspected that Mrs Macomber was the fourth member of that Phoenix hold-up gang. But we had no real evidence to connect her with the robbery, except that she fits the description of the driver of the getaway car. She fits it perfectly. And she disappeared from Phoenix about the same time as the robbery. Then, after she learned we were investigating Morgan, she disappeared again."

Thurgood shouted, "I told you that kid was nuts. Who could ever suspect Mrs Macomber of being involved with those hoodlums!" Again Thurgood's eyes darted unconsciously to the entrance of the mine.

"If I'm nuts, why are you sweating, Thurgood?" demanded Jupe.

Suddenly Jupiter struck his forehead with the palm of his hand. "I'm an idiot!" he cried. "I thought Mrs Macomber disappeared because she was involved in that hold-up. But that wasn't it at all, was it, Thurgood? She disappeared because she knew *you!* She knew something about you that you didn't want known. What happened to her, Thurgood? Where is Mrs Macomber?"

Thurgood swallowed. "How should I know?" He began to edge towards the mine. Jupe spun round, darted into the sheriff's car, and grabbed a powerful flashlight. He raced for the mine entrance.

The sheriff pointed at Thurgood. "Watch this man!" he roared to his deputy. Then he and Allie, Uncle Harry, Pete, and Bob followed Jupe into Death Trap Mine.

Jupe was well ahead, and the others stumbled after him as he sped down the mine tunnel and turned into the corridor that ran left. He passed the place where golden flecks showed briefly in the light.

Bob and Pete were close behind when Jupe ducked into the passageway that branched off to one side—the passageway that had led Allie to the dead thief. At the end of the tunnel, they stopped and looked down into the pit. There—tied and gagged but struggling mightily—was the missing lady.

20

Where's the Loot?

WHEN MRS MACOMBER saw the group above her, her eyes sparkled. Sheriff Tait quickly brought a ladder and climbed down into the pit after her.

"High time," she said as soon as he removed the gag. "I thought no one would ever come."

When she was untied, she calmly stood up, brushed herself off, and climbed up the ladder without help. The sheriff followed, carrying the suitcase that had been lying in the pit with her.

"Where is that scoundrel?" she demanded.

"Wesley Thurgood?" asked Jupe.

"He is *not* Wesley Thurgood!" said Mrs Macomber. "I finally remembered what was so unusual about that Thurgood baby. When he was born he had brown eyes. Hardly any babies are *born* with brown eyes. Most babies' eyes are blue, and if they're going to have brown eyes the colour changes after a while. But little Wesley Thurgood had brown eyes, and they don't change! That man's got blue eyes—he's an out-and-out impostor!"

"I suppose you told him that!" said Jupiter.

"Well, I asked him what he was up to. The next thing I knew, he was covering me with a shotgun. He made me get down in that hole and he threw my suitcase down after me. Where is he?"

"Outside," said the sheriff. "And he will shortly be in jail."

"Jail's too good for him!" declared Mrs Macomber.

"I agree, but it's the best we can do at the moment."

And, very shortly, the sheriff drove off with Wesley Thurgood as well as Manny and Gasper.

Sheriff Tait returned to the Christmas tree ranch late that afternoon. Uncle Harry and Magdalena had driven to Hambone to retrieve Mrs Macomber's truck. The widow herself sat in the Osborne living room having a cup of tea.

"Well?" she said, when she saw the sheriff.

The sheriff grinned at her, and at Allie and The Three Investigators. "You kids were right," he said. "Those two hoods confessed to the robbery of the armoured car five years ago. Not that it matters a lot. They're already wanted in four states for other stick-ups, and we'll charge them with kidnapping. Like you figured, Gilbert Morgan was one of the gang."

"But what about that rascal Thurgood?" demanded Mrs Macomber.

"He's waiting for a lawyer and he'll need one. We've got his fingerprints on the wire to Washington. My guess is that he's a professional con artist and he's probably got a record. They all do, no matter how slick they are. Of course he isn't Thurgood. I've been in touch with Los Angeles and I talked to the real Wesley Thurgood."

"I knew he was a phony from the beginning!"

crowed Allie. "You guys should have listened to me—especially after he lied and said that his antique car was used in *The Fortune Hunters.*"

"Never mind about that," said Sheriff Tait. "I've got a search warrant and I'm going to go all through his place."

"You're looking for more evidence?" asked Bob.

"Yes, and I am looking for a quarter of a million dollars!" said the sheriff.

He paused to let this sink in, then went on. "According to Manny Ellis and Gasper—whose real name is Charlie Lambert—Gilbert Morgan and a woman named Hannah Troy were also involved in the Phoenix robbery. The woman drove the getaway car. She's in prison right now or she'd probably be here with Ellis and Lambert. They all went directly to Lordsburg and hid in a motel on the edge of town. But the next day Morgan gave them the slip and got away with the entire haul—$250,000! Ellis and Lambert never heard another thing about Morgan until his body turned up in the mine. They came, figuring the loot was still here, and I figure it's still here, too."

"But how do you know Thurgood didn't find it and stash it away somewhere?" asked Pete.

"That's not likely," answered Jupe. "If he found the money, why would he stay here and take the chances he took to pull off his mine swindle? Just consider it. After Morgan's body was found, the place was overrun with sightseers. Sheriff Tait was in and out. Yet Thurgood hired his Mexican labourers and brought in his investors and set off dynamite explosions in the mine. If I had found $250,000, I would simply have taken it and left."

"I would, too," said the sheriff. "That's why I figure the money is still up here someplace. The problem is, where? I know it's not in the mine because I searched all through there after Morgan's body was found. But maybe Morgan hid the loot in one of the old mine buildings—they were empty at the time."

"Hey, he could have put it in one of Mrs Macomber's houses," said Allie.

"Wow, let's start looking!" cried Pete. "A quarter of a million bucks!"

The group set to work right away. First they searched all of Mrs Macomber's houses. In one of them they found Harrison Osborne's missing machete hidden under a sofa, but there was no money. They pried into every corner of the cavernous old mine works and Thurgood's cabin. They combed through Wesley Thurgood's possessions. Although they found precise records of bank accounts and lists of names and addresses—probably of Thurgood's duped investors—they found nothing that would point to a hidden cache amounting to a quarter of a million dollars.

"There's one more chance." Jupe pointed across the fields to Uncle Harry's barn. "That's the only other building that was here five years ago when Gilbert Morgan came. Gasper tried to search it himself, but we scared him off. Morgan may have hidden the money someplace else, or buried it in the ground, but let's at least try the barn."

At first the barn seemed to offer few opportunities for a hiding place. The walls were simply wooden planks, held in place by uprights. The floor was hard bare earth, and the loft was empty except for dust and spiderwebs. Allie climbed into the old Model T and poked around without much enthusiasm. "Maybe Morgan didn't even have the money with him when he came to Twin Lakes," she said.

She sat down in the car, then looked surprised and wriggled slightly. "Seat's loose."

"Loose?" exclaimed Jupe. "Allie, get out."

"Migosh!" She leaped from the car.

Pete and Jupe quickly lifted the car seat and tumbled it into the back of the old auto.

"And there it is!" said Jupe triumphantly.

Sheriff Tait stepped to the car. In the space under the seat there were dozens of plastic-wrapped packages. The sheriff picked up one and opened it—and stared at a sheaf of twenty-dollar bills. They still looked new, crisp, and untouched.

"I wonder how long it takes to count to $250,000!" said Pete.

"I think it will take quite a while," said the sheriff. "I plan to count very slowly!"

21

A Souvenir for Mr Hitchcock

WHEN THE THREE INVESTIGATORS entered Alfred Hitchcock's office several days after their return to California, the famous motion-picture director regarded them with wry amusement. "On the telephone you announced that you had been in New Mexico pruning Christmas trees," he said. "Since you wished to see me as soon as possible, I assume that you managed to turn a prosaic summer job into an adventure among the evergreens."

Bob smiled and handed a file folder to the director.

"Aha!" said Mr Hitchcock, and he began to peruse the notes that Bob had made on the events connected with Death Trap Mine. When he finished reading he shot a reproachful look at Jupiter Jones.

"I trust that you are thoroughly ashamed of yourself," said Mr Hitchcock. "Entertaining such foul suspicions about Mrs Macomber! Where was the blameless widow, by the way, between the time she left that shop in Phoenix and the time she appeared in Twin Lakes? And where did she get the money to purchase her property?"

"She inherited the money," said Jupe. "She had an aged aunt who was suddenly taken ill and who sent for her. She left the shop without notice because the matter was extremely urgent, and also because she did not like the woman who owned the shop and didn't want to bother explaining things to her. Between May and September she was in El Paso nursing her aunt. The aunt died eventually—she was very old—leaving everything she owned to Mrs Macomber."

Mr Hitchcock nodded. "It is heartwarming when virtue is rewarded. Mrs Macomber sounds like a charming and rather unflappable woman. Certainly she recovered quickly after being imprisoned in that mine. I trust that the man who called himself Thurgood will be brought to justice?"

"On a number of counts," said Jupiter. "As the sheriff suspected, he is an experienced con man. His real name is John Manchester and he specializes in stock swindles. A number of his Death Trap Mine victims were wealthy men from Dallas. Manchester met them in a country club there, passed himself off as Thurgood, and convinced them that he had discovered a fabulously rich vein of gold in the old Death Trap Mine. He used forged documents to establish his false identity with Uncle Harry and a bank in Lordsburg, and he peddled forged stock certificates to the dupes who came to inspect his mine.

"Manchester's investment in the Death Trap Mine was small. He paid Harrison Osborne a thousand dollars down on the property and signed a note for twenty-five thousand dollars to be paid in instalments. He never intended to make any payments on that note. He was going to take the money he got from his victims, clean out his bank account, and disappear. That was his pattern; he had done it many times before."

Bob picked up the story from there. "But this time Mrs Macomber got in his way," he said. "After she accused Manchester of being a fake, he forced her into the pit and took her truck to Hambone. He abandoned it there and hiked back to Twin Lakes. He wanted people to think she had gone on vacation. That's why he packed her suitcase, too. We don't think he planned to leave her in the mine very long, or to hurt her. He just needed a little more time to finish his mine swindle. But things started happening so fast he never got a chance. Manny and Gasper saw to that!"

"What about the Mexicans?" asked Mr Hitchcock. "Surely they weren't in on the scheme."

"No, they weren't," Jupe replied. "Manchester needed workmen to make it look as if he were taking ore from the mine. He had them build the fence and start painting the house so everyone would think he was going to stay in Twin Lakes. The men were in this country illegally. So they were afraid to speak to anyone, and that's the way Manchester wanted it."

"Their story has a happy ending," said Bob. "Uncle Harry made arrangements with the authorities and they will remain in Twin Lakes legally and will prune his Christmas trees. And Magdalena has adopted the dog. She fed him until his sides bulged and now he's as tame as a puppy and he sleeps at the foot of her bed."

"I am delighted," said Mr Hitchcock. The motion-picture director leaned back in his desk chair. "A most interesting case," he mused. "How provoking that it will never be completely solved."

"What do you mean?" demanded Pete. "We solved it!"

"In all important respects, yes," replied Mr Hitchcock. "But I don't suppose anyone will ever know exactly what took place when Gilbert Morgan came to Twin Lakes five years ago, and why he hid the robbery proceeds in the old Ford."

"No," agreed Jupiter. "Morgan may have regarded the old car as a temporary hiding place for the money, then gone into the mine looking for a safer one. Was he still alive when the mine was sealed, or was he already dead? We will never know. Incidentally, we are quite sure Manchester found the body as soon as he opened the mine. He probably planned to blast that shaft closed—he wouldn't want to draw attention to himself by reporting the body. No wonder he was furious when he caught Allie in the Death Trap Mine.

"And since the Death Trap turned out to be such an unusual mine, we have brought you a souvenir of the place."

Jupe handed a small stone to the director, who took it and examined it with interest. "A nugget!" said Mr Hitchcock. "Thank you. I shall treasure it. Not everyone has a genuine gold nugget with orange blossoms engraved on it."

"Allie's got one," said Pete.

"I would say she deserves one," declared Mr Hitchcock.

"I guess so. She's an okay kid and she's got good instincts. I mean, she does kind of know about people. But she's so darned . . . darned . . ." said Pete.

"Energetic?" said Mr Hitchcock.

"You could say that." said Jupe. "You could also say she's about as comfortable to be with as—well, as a sockful of ants!"

3
The Mystery of the Magic Circle

Text by M. V. Carey

The Mystery of the Magic Circle was
first published in the U.K. in a single volume
in hardback in 1979 by William Collins Sons & Co. Ltd,
First published in Armada in 1981

Contents

	A Word from Alfred Hitchcock	327
1	Fire!	329
2	The Bleeding Man	342
3	The Double Disaster	348
4	A Case of Witchcraft?	355
5	The Haunted Grove	362
6	The Magic Circle	371
7	The Creature in the Dark	378
8	Murder by Magic?	384
9	The Crime Fighter	392
10	The Witch's Curse	400
11	Friends and Enemies	407
12	The Man from Arson	413
13	The Deadly Trunk	421
14	The Mysterious Second Man	426
15	The Vanishing Suspects	433
16	The Sleeping Beauty	439
17	Conspiracy!	446
18	The Search	452
19	Setting the Trap	457
20	The Surprise Party	462
21	Crash!	469
22	Mr Hitchcock Declines an Invitation	475

A Word from Alfred Hitchcock

Greetings, mystery lovers.

Again it is my privilege to introduce to you The Three Investigators, those young detectives whose specialty is mystery—and the more unusual, the better. In this adventure, the intrepid sleuths encounter a witch who hides from the world, performing secret rites and brooding on an accident that happened long ago. Or was it an accident? It may have been murder done in a magical fashion!

If you have not already met The Three Investigators, you will wish to know that Jupiter Jones, the leader of the group, is a stocky boy with an astonishing talent for deduction. Pete Crenshaw, the second investigator, is quick and athletic, while Bob Andrews, a studious fellow, uses his talent for research to help solve the problems the youths encounter. The boys live in Rocky Beach, California, not far from Hollywood.

So much for the formalities. You may now turn to Chapter One and proceed with the adventure.

ALFRED HITCHCOCK

1

Fire!

"EXACTLY WHAT are you boys up to?" demanded Horace Tremayne. He stood in the doorway of the mail room of Amigos Press and scowled at Jupiter Jones, Bob Andrews, and Pete Crenshaw.

"Up to?" said Pete. "We're . . . we're just sorting the mail."

"Don't give me that!" snapped Tremayne. His face, which was usually quite pleasant, looked threatening. "You've got some nerve, pretending to be mail clerks when you're really private detectives!"

With that, Tremayne—the young man who was publisher at Amigos Press, and who was called Beefy by everyone on the staff—relaxed and began to chuckle. "You *are* private detectives, aren't you?" he said.

"Hey," said Pete, "you really scared me!"

Bob Andrews smiled. "The private detective business is slow this summer," he said. "We thought we'd get some experience with office work."

"How did you find out about us?" asked Jupiter Jones, his round faced filled with curiosity.

"Last night my uncle Will hired a limousine to take us to a premiere in Hollywood," said Beefy

Tremayne. "It was a gold-plated Rolls-Royce, driven by a British chauffeur named Worthington."

"I see." Jupe laughed, for Worthington was an old friend. Some time before, Jupe had entered a contest sponsored by the Rent-'n-Ride Auto Rental Company and had won the use of the gold-plated Rolls for thirty days. Worthington had chauffeured the car for the boys, and had become fascinated with their detective work.

"Your names came up when Worthington started telling me about his regular clients," Beefy explained. "When he heard that you three had summer jobs here, he said I was in for a lively time. He said that trouble just seems to happen when you're around."

"It doesn't just seem to happen," said Pete. "Jupe stirs it up!"

"Then we all help settle it," put in Bob.

Jupiter took a card from his wallet and handed it to Beefy. It read:

THE THREE INVESTIGATORS

"We Investigate Anything"

? ? ?

First Investigator – JUPITER JONES
Second Investigator – PETER CRENSHAW
Records and Research – BOB ANDREWS

"Very professional," said Beefy. "What are the question marks for?"

The stocky First Investigator looked smug. People always asked about the question marks. "They're the universal symbol of the unknown," said Jupe. "The unknown is always intriguing."

"Yes, it is," agreed Beefy. "If I ever need a private detective firm, I might call you. Worthington says you're very clever."

"We've been able to solve a number of interesting cases," said Jupe. "We think our success is due to the fact that we believe almost anything can happen."

"You're young enough not to be prejudiced, eh?" Beefy commented. "That could be a great help in an investigation. Too bad there's nothing around here that needs investigating—besides why the coffee machine makes such lousy coffee!"

The boys heard footsteps outside the mail room. Beefy stepped back into the hall and looked towards the front of the building. "Uncle Will, what took you so long?" he called.

A second later, a tall, thin man with sandy hair and a small moustache appeared beside Beefy. He was Mr William Tremayne and, as usual, he looked very elegant. He wore beige slacks and a linen jacket the colour of cocoa. He glanced into the mail room but didn't bother to speak to the boys.

"They didn't have a spare car to lend me when I left the car at the garage," he told his nephew. "I had to call a cab. It's so tiresome. Nothing is really properly organized these days."

"I suppose not," said Beefy in his cheerful way. "Say, listen, Uncle Will, today's the day Marvin Gray's coming in with that manuscript. Do you want to see him about anything when he gets here?"

"Marvin Gray?" William Tremayne looked both bored and puzzled.

"Oh, come on, Uncle Will, you remember him," said Beefy. "He's Madeline Bainbridge's business manager. He negotiated the contract for her book."

"Ah, yes," said William Tremayne. "The chauffeur."

"He *used* to be her chauffeur." Beefy sounded irritated, but he took a deep breath and kept his voice level. "He's Bainbridge's business manager now, and that manuscript he's bringing could be terrific. Madeline Bainbridge knew everybody who was anybody in Hollywood when she was a star. Just wait till the news gets out that we're going to publish her memoirs!"

"I'm sure it will cause a sensation," said Will Tremayne disdainfully. "I do not understand this fascination with has-been actresses, but there is no reason why we shouldn't make money on it."

"Bainbridge isn't a has-been," said Beefy.

"Then what is she?" demanded his uncle. "She hasn't made a picture for thirty years."

"She's a legend," Beefy declared.

"Is there a difference?" asked William Tremayne. He turned away without waiting for an answer. A moment later the boys heard him on the stairs that led up to the first floor, where he had his office. Beefy stood looking unhappy, as he often did after an exchange with his uncle.

"Have you actually met Madeline Bainbridge?" Jupe asked.

Beefy blinked. "You know about her?"

"I'm a student of films and the theatre," Jupe explained. "I've read about her. She was beautiful, and supposedly also a fine actress. Of course, it's hard to judge today, when her films are never on release or on television."

"I haven't actually met her," said Beefy. "She's a recluse. She doesn't see anyone. She does everything through Marvin Gray. He seems a very competent business manager, even if he did start out as a chauffeur. Bainbridge bought the negatives of her films from the producers when she retired, and they're in storage in a special vault on her estate near Malibu. Marvin Gray hinted that she may sell them to television soon. If she does, her book could be the bestseller of the year."

Beefy grinned at the thought, and left the mail room. The boys heard him start up the stairs and stumble. He recovered and climbed to the first floor, whistling cheerfully.

"He's a nice guy," said Pete, "but he's got no co-ordination."

No one argued with this. The boys had been

working in the offices of Amigos Press for three weeks, and they knew that Beefy Tremayne tripped on the stairs every morning. He was as broad shouldered and muscular as any athlete, but he gave the impression of being made of slightly mismatched parts. His legs were just a bit too short to go with his barrel chest. His feet were slightly too small, and so was his nose, which he had fallen on and broken at some time in his life, so that now it was flattened and slightly crooked. His fair hair was cropped close, yet it managed to seem untidy. And although his clothes were always fresh and starched, they were also always somewhat rumpled. He was homely, and yet very pleasant looking. The boys liked him.

Pete and Bob began sorting the mail into neat stacks on the long table that ran along one side of the room. Jupe was just opening a big canvas sack stuffed with letters when a withered-looking grey-haired man came bustling in.

"Good morning, Mr Grear," said Jupiter.

"Morning, Jupe," he replied. "Morning, Bob. Pete."

Mr Grear, who was the office manager, went into the small room that adjoined the mail room and sat down at his desk. "Have you seen Mr William Tremayne this morning?" he asked.

"He went upstairs a few minutes ago," said Jupe.

"I have to see him," said Mr Grear. He sighed. Mr Grear was not fond of William Tremayne.

Indeed, no one on the staff seemed to care for him. William Tremayne was regarded as a usurper. Amigos Press had been founded by Beefy's father, and Beefy was heir to it. A tragic boating accident had made Beefy an orphan when he was nineteen, but according to the terms of the will left by Beefy's father, William Tremayne was president of Amigos Press and would control the business until Beefy was thirty.

"I guess Beefy's father only meant to protect Beefy and his inheritance," Mr Grear had said one day. "He was such a clumsy boy. No one suspected that he'd show a flair for publishing, but he did. He's got a real nose for a saleable manuscript. Now in spite of that, we're all stuck with William Tremayne—at least until next April, when Beefy turns thirty. It's a great trial. He's the only one who can make any decisions about money, so every time I need new supplies—even a box of pencils—I have to get his permission to order them!"

Mr Grear always looked outraged when he told the boys about William Tremayne. He looked outraged now, but he did not speak again. He was still in his office, staring unhappily at the papers on his desk, when Pete set out to deliver the mail to the other offices in the building.

Amigos Press was located in the Amigos Adobe, a historic two-storey structure that was sandwiched between more modern commercial buildings on busy Pacifica Avenue in Santa Monica.

The adobe dated back to the days when California was ruled by governors from Mexico. The walls were thick, as adobe walls always are, and even though the summer sun blazed outside, the rooms were cool. Decorative iron grilles on all the ground-floor windows added to the charm of the building.

Pete stopped first in the accounting department, a big room across the hall from the mail room. A dour, middle-aged man headed this department, supervising the work of two sullen women who laboured there with adding machines and heaps of invoices.

"Good morning, Mr Thomas," said Pete. He put a packet of envelopes down on the man's desk.

Thomas scowled. "Put the mail in the box on that table over there," he ordered. "What's the matter with you? Can't you remember a simple thing like that?"

"All right, Thomas," said a voice behind Pete. It was Mr Grear. He had come out into the hall and was watching Mr Thomas. "I'm sure Pete understands. Just remember, *I* supervise the mail room. If the boys get out of line, you tell me and *I'll* talk to them."

Pete scooted out of the accounting department. As he passed Mr Grear in the hall, he heard the office manager muttering to himself. "Troublemaker! He won't last a year here. I don't know how they put up with him at that pharmaceutical company for five years!"

Pete didn't comment. He had several letters for the receptionist, whose desk was in the big front room of the adobe. He delivered these, and then went up the stairs to the first floor. The editors, book designers, and production people had offices there.

Mr Grear and Mr Thomas did not speak to each other again until mid-afternoon. Then the copying machine that stood in a corner of the mail room jammed. This caused a fierce argument between Mr Thomas, who insisted that the machine be fixed immediately, and Mr Grear, who declared that the repair man couldn't come until morning.

The two men were still exchanging angry words when Jupiter went upstairs shortly before four to collect outgoing mail from the staff there. Mrs Paulson, Beefy's assistant, looked up and smiled when Jupe stopped at her desk. She was a smooth-faced, plump woman many years Beefy's senior, who had previously been assistant to Beefy's father. She handed a couple of envelopes to Jupe. Then she glanced past him at someone just coming up the stairs.

"He's waiting for you," she said, pointing to the open door of Beefy's office.

Jupe looked around. A thin, dark-haired man in a light gaberdine suit went past him and into Beefy's office.

"That's Marvin Gray," said Mrs Paulson softly. "He's delivering Madeline Bainbridge's manuscript." Mrs Paulson sighed. "He's given his whole life to looking after Madeline Bainbridge. Isn't that romantic?"

Before Jupe could comment, Beefy came out of his office with a sheaf of papers in his hands. "Oh, Jupe, I'm glad you're here," he said. "Take this manuscript down to the copying machine and make a duplicate of it right away. It's handwritten, and there's no copy. Mr Gray is concerned about its safety."

"The machine is out of order," said Jupe. "Shall I take the manuscript out and have it copied elsewhere?"

Gray appeared in the doorway beside Beefy. "No, don't do that," he said. "It would be safer just to keep it here."

"We'll take good care of it," promised Beefy.

Gray nodded. "Fine. And now that you have the manuscript, if you'll give me the cheque, I'll be on my way."

"The cheque?" Beefy echoed. "You mean the advance?"

"Why, yes," said Gray. "According to the terms of the contract, you are to pay Miss Bainbridge twenty-five thousand dollars upon delivery of the manuscript."

Beefy looked flustered. "Mr Gray, we usually read the manuscript first. The cheque hasn't even been made out yet?"

"Oh," said Marvin Gray. "I see. All right. I'll look forward to receiving the cheque in the mail."

He went off then, down the stairs.

"He's certainly in a hurry for the money," said Mrs Paulson.

"I guess he doesn't understand publishing contracts," said Beefy. "He missed the phrase about how the manuscript has to be acceptable."

Beefy went back into his office and Jupe returned to the mail room.

"Want to work overtime tonight?" Mr Grear said when Jupe came in. "The printer just sent over the brochures for the mailing on the songbird book. We can stuff the envelopes in a couple of hours, and I can take them to the post office first thing in the morning."

The boys were glad to put in the extra time, and they called their homes in Rocky Beach to report that they would be home late. They were busy folding circulars and putting them into envelopes when the rest of the staff left, singly and in groups. At a quarter to six, Mr Grear set out to take the last of the mail to the main post office. "On my way back I'll pick up some fried chicken at the shop down the street," he promised.

The boys toiled on after he left. A breeze came up and blew through the open window of the mail room. It caught the door and slammed it shut. The boys jumped at the sound, then resumed work.

It was six-fifteen when Bob stopped working and sniffed. "Do I smell smoke?" he said.

Pete looked around at the closed door. In the silence, the boys heard the hum of traffic on Pacifica Avenue. They heard another sound, too—

a low, crackling roar that came to them muffled by the thick adobe walls.

Jupe frowned. He went to the door and put his hand against it. The wood felt warm. He put his hand on the knob, which felt even warmer, and very cautiously pulled the door open.

Instantly the roar became almost deafening. A great billow of smoke gushed into the room and overwhelmed the boys.

"Good grief!" shouted Pete.

Jupe threw his weight against the door and slammed it shut. He turned to face the others. "The hall!" he said. "There's fire all over the hall!"

The smoke was seeping in around the door now, thickening the air as it wafted towards the open window, which looked out on a narrow walkway between the adobe and the building next door. He leaned on the iron grille covering the window and pushed. "Help!" he shouted. "Help! Fire!"

No one answered and the bars didn't budge.

Bob snatched up a metal chair and shoved it through the bars. He and Pete tried to prise the metal grille away from the building. The chair only bent in their hands, and one leg snapped off.

"It's no use," called Jupe from Mr Grear's office. "The telephone is dead. And there's no one around to hear us yell."

He hurried back to the door that led to the hall. "We've got to get ourselves out, and this is the only way."

He went down on his knees, and again he edged the door open. Again the smoke gushed in through the opening. Bob coughed, and Pete's eyes began streaming. The two boys knelt behind Jupe and peered out into the hall. They saw smoke that looked almost solid. It seethed and glowed red with the light of flames that danced up the walls and licked away at the old staircase.

Jupe turned his face from the fire for an instant. He took a breath that was almost a sob. Then he started forward, holding his breath. But before he could get through the doorway, a gust of hot air pushed at him like a giant hand. He flinched, drew back, and slammed the door.

"We can't," he whispered. "Nobody can go through that fire! There's no way out! We're trapped!"

2

The Bleeding Man

For a moment no one spoke. Then Pete made a choking sound. "Someone's got to see the smoke and call the fire department," he gasped. "Someone's just *got* to!"

Jupe looked around wildly. For the first time he saw something that might give them a chance. There was a trap-door under the long table that the boys used for wrapping and sorting.

Jupe pointed. "Look! There must be a cellar. The air's bound to be better down there."

The boys ran to pull the table away from the wall. Pete prised open the trap-door, and they looked down into a brick-walled cellar. Its dirt floor was more than eight feet beneath them, and they smelled air that was heavy with damp and decay. The boys didn't hesitate. Pete swung down through the trap-door opening, holding on to the edge of the floor, then let himself drop the few remaining feet. The others followed. When they were safely in the cellar, Bob stood on Pete's shoulders and pulled the trap-door shut.

The boys stood in the darkness and strained to

listen. They could still hear the fire. They were safe, but for how long? In his mind's eye Jupe pictured flames mushrooming through the first floor and eating away at the roof. What if the roof caved in? Would the floor above them hold if flaming timbers came crashing down on it? Even if it did hold, would anyone fight through the fire to find them hiding in the cellar?

"Hey!" Pete grasped Jupe's arm. "Hear that?"

There were sirens in the distance.

"It's about time!" said Bob.

"Hurry up, firemen!" pleaded Pete. "We haven't got all night!"

The sirens came closer and closer. Then there were more sirens and still more. Then, one by one, the piercing mechanical wails stopped.

"Help!" cried Pete. "Help! Hey, you guys!"

The three waited. After what seemed an age, they heard a wrenching sound and a crash above them.

"I'll bet that's the window!" said Bob. "They're yanking the grille out of the window!"

Water thundered and gushed on the planks above them. Jupe felt wetness on his face, and on his shoulders and arms. Rivulets of dirty water spattered down all around him.

"We'll drown!" Pete yelled. "Stop! We're down here!"

The sound of rushing water ceased.

"Open the trap-door!" Bob cried.

There was the protest of wood scraping on

wood. The panel above them opened and a fireman looked down.

"They're here!" he shouted. "I found the kids!"

The fireman leaped into the cellar. An instant later Bob was being boosted up through the trap-door to a second fireman, who seized him and sent him staggering towards the window. The iron grating was gone and two hose lines ran into the mail room. Bob scrambled over the sill and out on to the narrow walkway.

Bob had gone only a few steps when he heard Jupiter behind him. Pete followed, and the firemen who had pulled the boys from the cellar came after them. "Keep going!" ordered one of the men. "Move! Fast! The roof's going to cave in any second!"

The boys ran until they reached the open street. It was blocked with fire engines. Hose lines lay in tangles from kerb to kerb.

"Thank heaven! You're safe!" Mr Grear ran forward, clutching a paper sack of fried chicken.

"Hey you, get back!" shouted a fireman.

Mr Grear retreated towards the crowd that had gathered across the street. The boys went with him. "They wouldn't let me go in after you," said Grear. "I told them you were in there, but they wouldn't let me go." He seemed to be in a daze.

"It's okay, Mr Grear," said Jupiter. "We're safe." He took the sack of chicken from the old man and helped him sit down on a low wall in front of a little shopping centre.

"Mr Grear! Mr Grear!" The boys looked round to see Mr Thomas hurrying towards them. He was dodging this way and that to get through the crowd of onlookers. "Mr Grear, what happened? I saw the smoke. I was having dinner at a place near here and I saw the smoke. Mr Grear, how did it start?"

Before Mr Grear could comprehend that Thomas was questioning him, Beefy Tremayne came dashing around the corner on to Pacifica Avenue. His uncle trailed him, with Mrs Paulson bringing up the rear.

"Mr Grear!" cried Beefy. "You okay? Hey, are you boys all right?"

"We're okay," Pete assured him.

Beefy crouched beside Mr Grear.

"I would have called you," said Grear, "but I was too concerned about the boys."

"We saw the smoke from our apartment and came running," said Beefy.

A shout went up across the street. Firemen scrambled to get clear of the adobe. Then the roof of the building fell in with a roar.

Flames leaped up against the sky. The thick walls of the old building still stood, but the firemen ignored them now. Hoses played steadily on the roofs and walls of buildings up and down the street.

Jupe looked at Mrs Paulson. She was crying.

"Please don't," said Beefy. "Please, Mrs Paulson, it's only a building."

"Your father's publishing house!" sobbed Mrs Paulson. "He was so proud of it!"

"I know," said Beefy, "but it *is* just a building. As long as no one was hurt . . ."

The young publisher stopped talking and looked at the boys in a questioning way.

"We were the last ones out," said Bob. "Nobody was hurt."

Beefy managed to smile. "That's what's important," he said to Mrs Paulson. "And Amigos Press isn't wiped out—not by a long shot. Our inventory of books is safe in the warehouse and our plates are in storage. Why, we've even got the Bainbridge manuscript!"

"We have?" said Mrs Paulson.

"Yes. I put it in my briefcase and took it home. So things aren't that bad, and . . ."

Beefy broke off. A man with a hand-held camera had stepped on to the street and was walking towards the fire.

"Uh-oh," said Beefy. "The television stations are covering this. I'd better find a phone."

"Why?" asked William Tremayne.

"I want to call Marvin Gray," Beefy explained, "to tell him the Bainbridge manuscript is safe. If he watches the news and finds out that Amigos Press burned down, he'll think the manuscript went with it unless I tell him differently."

Beefy headed for the filling station on the corner, where there was a pay telephone. At that moment, Jupiter became aware that there was a man approaching from across the street—a man whose face was ghastly white. He was bleeding badly from a wound on his scalp.

"Oh, gosh!" exclaimed Pete.

The blood coursed down the man's cheek and soaked the front of his shirt.

"What on earth?" said William Tremayne.

Jupiter started forward as the man collapsed in the street. A fireman ran to bend over the fallen man, and two policemen hurried to help him. Gingerly they turned him over on his back, and one of them looked quickly at the wound on his head.

"Say, I know him!" A stout woman pushed her way out of the crowd and went to the policemen. "He works in that film place there." She pointed towards Film Craft Laboratory, a solidly built brick building which was next to the ruins of Amigos Press. "I've seen him come and go lots of times," said the woman.

One of the policemen stood up. "I'll call an ambulance," he told his partner. "Then we'd better check out that film lab. Doesn't look as if this guy's going to be able to tell us anything. He might not wake up for quite a while!"

3

The Double Disaster

THERE WAS a brief account of the fire on the late news that night. Jupiter watched it with his aunt Mathilda and uncle Titus, with whom he lived. The next morning, he was up in time to see the *Los Angeles Now* show.

"Haven't you had enough of that fire?" said Aunt Mathilda as Jupe put the portable TV on the kitchen counter. "It could have killed you!"

Jupe sat down and began to sip his orange juice. "Maybe there'll be news about that man," he said.

"The one who collapsed in the street?" Aunt Mathilda sat down to watch, and Uncle Titus poured himself a second cup of coffee.

On the television screen, newscaster Fred Stone looked grave. "There was a double disaster in Santa Monica yesterday," he said. "Fire broke out in the historic Amigos Adobe on Pacifica Avenue at approximately six o'clock. The building, which housed the offices of Amigos Press, was empty except for three young mail clerks. They were trapped by the flames, but were rescued unharmed by firemen."

The image of Stone faded from the television screen. It was replaced by scenes of the smoking ruins of Amigos Press. Stone's voice went on narrating. "The adobe building was completely destroyed. Damage is estimated at half a million dollars.

"As the fire burned, police discovered that a robbery had taken place at Film Craft Laboratory, immediately adjacent to the adobe. At some time between five and six, thieves entered the laboratory, which specializes in the restoration of old motion pictures. They made off with almost one hundred reels of film, the negatives of motion pictures made by actress Madeline Bainbridge more than thirty years ago. Miss Bainbridge, who was once a leading star, had just sold the motion pictures to Video Enterprises, which owns this station—Station KLMC—and its affiliates."

Stone appeared again on the screen. "There is a possible witness to the unusual robbery," he said. "Film technician John Hughes was working overtime at the laboratory. He was apparently beaten by the thieves in the course of the crime. He managed to make his way to the street, where he collapsed. Hughes regained consciousness briefly at Santa Monica Hospital this morning, and he is believed to have given a statement to detectives."

There were footsteps on the front porch and the doorbell chimed urgently. Jupe went to the door and admitted Pete and Bob.

"You watching the news?" said Pete. "I saw the

early show. Whoever bopped that guy on the head yesterday also swiped a whole bunch of movies from that lab in Santa Monica!"

"And they were Madeline Bainbridge's movies," said Bob. "How's that for a coincidence?"

"Much too coincidental," declared Jupiter.

The boys followed Jupe to the kitchen. On the television, Fred Stone was reporting a late development in the Bainbridge case. "This morning, a telephone call was made to Charles Davie, president of Video Enterprises," he said. "Mr Davie was told that the Bainbridge films would be returned to Video Enterprises upon payment of two hundred and fifty thousand dollars to the persons who are holding these films. Mr Davie made no statement as to whether or not Video Enterprises would ransom the pictures, which are considered irreplaceable."

"What a gimmick!" exclaimed Pete. "Swiping old movies and holding them for ransom!"

Fred Stone went on with his newscast. "Following the robbery at the Santa Monica film laboratory last evening, Station KLMC was able to arrange an interview between Jefferson Long, veteran crime reporter for the station, and Marvin Gray, who has been Madeline Bainbridge's business manager for many years. We now bring you a broadcast of that taped interview."

Fred Stone turned to look at the television monitor to his left. A second later, Jupiter and his friends saw a sun-bronzed man with wavy white hair on the screen. He sat on a straight wooden chair in front of a fireplace and held a microphone. A clock on the mantel behind him showed the time as half-past nine.

"Good evening, ladies and gentlemen," said the man. "This is Jefferson Long, your KLMC crime reporter, at the Bainbridge estate near Malibu.

"Tonight Marvin Gray, Madeline Bainbridge's long-time friend and confidant, has consented to talk with us about the films which were taken earlier this evening in the robbery of the Film Craft Laboratory. Perhaps Mr Gray will also tell us something about Miss Bainbridge and her work, which many still remember."

The camera pulled back away from Jefferson Long, and the watchers saw Marvin Gray. He appeared grubby and insignificant next to the impressive Jefferson Long. He was smiling in a superior manner, however, as if Long amused him.

"I'm sure you remember Miss Bainbridge very well, Mr Long," he said. "If I recall correctly, you were an actor once yourself. You had the role of Cotton Mather in Miss Bainbridge's last picture, *The Salem Story*. It was your first picture, wasn't it?"

"Well, yes," said Long, "but—"

"Also your last," said Marvin Gray.

"How unkind of him to put it that way," said Aunt Mathilda. "You'd think he didn't like Mr Long."

"Perhaps he doesn't," said Jupiter.

Jefferson Long looked flustered, and he hurried into his interview. "I'm sure that Miss Bainbridge was very upset when she learned that her films had been stolen," he said. "We had hoped to see her in person."

"Miss Bainbridge doesn't see reporters, ever," said Marvin Gray, "and she's resting this evening. Her doctor prescribed a sedative. As you say, she *is* upset."

"Of course," said Jefferson Long smoothly. "Mr Gray, none of Miss Bainbridge's films have been seen by the public since she retired. What influenced her to sell them to television at this time?"

Marvin Gray smiled. "Thirty years ago, studio executives didn't realize that feature motion pictures would become valuable television attractions," he said. "Madeline Bainbridge did. She had a lot of faith in the future of television—although she doesn't care for the medium."

"She doesn't watch television?" asked Long.

"No, she doesn't. But thirty years ago, she knew how important it would be, and she purchased all the rights to the pictures she had made. She decided three weeks ago that the time was right. She signed an agreement with Video Enterprises, releasing the films to them. Video Enterprises took possession of the negatives this morning and had them moved to Film Craft Laboratory for inspection and repair."

"Then it's really KLMC's loss if the films aren't recovered," said Long.

"Yes, but it's a loss to the world, too. Miss Bainbridge is a great artist. She played memorable roles—Cleopatra, Joan of Arc, Catherine the Great of Russia, Helen of Troy. The portrayals will be lost forever if the films aren't recovered."

"Certainly that would be a calamity," said Long, "and all due to a crime that is unique in a city that has seen many bizarre crimes. I am sure we all wish for the prompt apprehension of the two men who broke into the laboratory, and for the speedy recovery of the stolen films."

The camera moved in close to Jefferson Long, who looked at his audience with great sincerity. "Ladies and gentlemen, this is Jefferson Long, coming to you on videotape from the estate where Madeline Bainbridge has lived for many years as a recluse, the beauty which helped make her a star hidden from all but a few close friends. Ladies and gentlemen, I thank you."

The screen went blank. Then Fred Stone was on camera again. "And now for other news . . ." he began.

Jupiter turned off the television. "It sounds like a publicity stunt, but it can't be that," he said. "That film technician was seriously hurt. And Marvin Gray overlooked a great opportunity to mention the Bainbridge memoirs. He would have mentioned them if he were looking for publicity."

Just then there was a crash on the verandah.

"Oh, blast!" exclaimed an exasperated voice.

Jupiter went to the door. Beefy Tremayne was standing on the porch.

"I knocked over a flowerpot," said Beefy. "Sorry."

He stepped into the living-room. "Jupe, I need help," he said. Jupe saw that there were circles under his eyes. "I need The Three Investigators. Worthington says you're good, and maybe you'll help me out. Uncle Will won't pay to hire a regular detective."

Pete and Bob had come in from the kitchen. They looked at Beefy with curiosity.

"What's the matter?" Jupiter asked.

"The Bainbridge memoirs," said Beefy. "The manuscript has disappeared. Somebody stole it!"

4

A Case of Witchcraft?

"OKAY, I admit that I'm clumsy," said Beefy Tremayne. "I drop things and knock things over. However, I do pay attention to business, and I'm good at my business. I do not lose manuscripts!"

"Nonsense!" said William Tremayne.

Beefy had driven The Three Investigators from Rocky Beach to the high-rise building in West Los Angeles where he shared an apartment with his uncle. It was a modern security building; the garage doors were opened by a sonic device and the door from the lobby to the inner court was monitored by closed-circuit television. The boys had found William Tremayne lounging on a sofa in the living-room of the apartment. He was smoking a long, slender cigar and staring at the ceiling in a disinterested way.

"I refuse to waste time and effort fussing about that manuscipt," he announced. "You've misplaced it in your usual blithering fashion, and it will show up. We don't need any aspiring juveniles to snoop around with magnifying glasses and fingerprint powder."

"We left our fingerprint powder at home today, Mr Tremayne," said Jupe stiffly.

"I'm delighted to hear it," declared Tremayne. He continued to gaze at the ceiling. "Beefy, while you were out, the insurance adjustor was here. He asked a lot of idiot questions, and I didn't care for his tone. Just because I look after your financial interests, and just because the money from the insurance company will come to me for disbursement, there's no need for anyone to take the attitude that I had anything to gain from that fire."

"Uncle Will, they have to ask questions," said Beefy.

"You mean they have to make it look as if they're earning their money," snapped William Tremayne. "I only hope there's no delay in settling our claim. It's going to cost a fortune to relocate the offices and start operations again."

"I can start operating right now if I can just get my hands on that manuscript!" said Beefy.

"Then look for it!" said his uncle.

"I have looked. It isn't here!"

"Beefy, do you mind if we look?" asked Jupiter. "If you say it isn't here, I'm sure it isn't, but it won't hurt for us to double-check."

"Okay. Go ahead," said Beefy. He sat down and glared at his uncle while the boys searched the apartment. They looked behind every piece of furniture and into every cupboard and bookcase. There was no sign of a manuscript that could be the memoirs of an ageing movie star.

"All right, Beefy, it isn't here," said Jupiter at last. "Now let's begin at the beginning. When did you last have the manuscript?"

Bob sat down near Beefy, took a small pad from his pocket, and prepared to take notes.

"Last night," said Beefy, "about nine-fifteen or nine-thirty. I'd taken the manuscript out of my briefcase and started to go through it. But after the fire, and seeing that man bleeding the way he was, I was too shook up to read. I felt as if I had to do something physical. So I put the manuscript down on the coffee table, and I changed into trunks and went down to the pool for a swim."

"Were you here?" Jupiter asked William Tremayne.

The older man shook his head. "I played bridge with friends last night. I didn't get home until nearly two."

"And when you got back from the pool, the manuscript was gone?" Jupe said to Beefy.

"Yes, it was. I noticed it the minute I came in."

"Could the apartment door have been left unlocked while you were in the pool?" Jupe asked. "Do you ever go down and leave the catch off?"

"Never," said Beefy. "And I'm sure it was locked last night, because I forgot my keys when I went down to the pool. The manager had to come up and let me in with his pass-key."

Jupiter went to the apartment door, opened it, and looked closely at the door-jamb and the lock.

"There's no sign of forced entry. And the lobby door is always locked, isn't it? And this apartment is twelve storeys above the street. Someone must have a set of keys."

Beefy shook his head. "There isn't a spare set, unless you count the master key that the manager has. And that's ridiculous. We've had the same manager for years. He wouldn't take a toothpick!"

Bob looked up from his notebook. "Your set and your uncle's set are the only ones?" he asked.

"Well, there was a set in my desk at work," said Beefy. "I kept them there in case I lost mine. But they would have been destroyed in the fire."

"Hm!" said Jupe. "So it would seem." He closed the apartment door and went to stand at the open window and look down at the pool, many storeys below. "Someone came into this building, which is not easy to enter," he said. "Someone then got into this apartment, found the manuscript on the coffee table, picked it up, and took it away. How was that done?"

Pete came and stood beside Jupe. He didn't look down towards the pool. Instead he looked up towards the sky. "They flew in over the roof and came through the open window," he said, "in a very small helicopter. It's the only answer."

"How about a broomstick?" said Uncle Will sarcastically. "That would do nicely if someone wanted to come in through the window, and it narrows our field of suspects. The manuscript was taken by a witch."

Beefy started as if he had been struck. "A witch?" he exclaimed. "That's . . . that's weird!"

"Why?" said his uncle. "Do you like the helicopter theory better?"

"It's just that it's strange that you mentioned a witch. I read some of the manuscript before I went down to the pool, and it had bits of really crazy gossip about Hollywood people. Bainbridge described a dinner party given by Alexander de Champley, the director. She said he was a magician and a black witch, and he wore the pentacle of Simon Magus!"

Beefy took a pen out of his pocket and began to sketch on the back of an envelope. "There was a drawing of the pentacle in the manuscript," he said. "A five-pointed star in a circle. Bainbridge said it was gold with a circle of rubies on the outside. Now, I've heard of Simon Magus. He was a wizard back in the days of ancient Rome, and people believed that he could fly."

"Marvellous!" said Uncle Will. "This old friend of Madeline Bainbridge put on the pentacle of Simon Magus and flew in here and took the manuscript so that we wouldn't find out that he's an evil wizard."

"If anyone flew in, it wasn't Alexander de Champley," said Jupe. "He died more than ten years ago. But were there other scandalous stories in the memoirs?"

Beefy shook his head. "I don't know," he said. "I only read that one anecdote. It's certainly possible that Madeline Bainbridge knew the secrets of lots of prominent people."

"Then that could be it," said Jupiter. "That could be the reason the manuscript was taken. Some person she knows wants to prevent the publication of her story!"

"But how could that person know the manuscript was here?" asked Beefy.

"Easily!" Jupe began to pace back and forth. His eyebrows were drawn down in excited concentration. "Beefy, last night you called Marvin Gray after the fire and told him the manuscript was safe. Of course he told Madeline Bainbridge. Then Madeline Bainbridge called a friend—or perhaps Gray did—and that friend told a friend. Anyone could know."

"It wouldn't have been Bainbridge who told," said Beefy. "Marvin Gray says she doesn't use the telephone. But it's true that Gray might have passed the word on, without realizing what would happen. And Bainbridge's secretary still lives with her. Her name's Clara Adams. She might have done it."

"Of course," said Jupe. "Beefy, couldn't you arrange an interview with Miss Bainbridge? Then you could ask her whom she wrote about."

"She won't see me," said Beefy. "She doesn't see anyone at all. Marvin Gray took care of the negotiations on the contract."

"Then talk to Gray," urged Jupiter. "He must have read the manuscript."

Beefy groaned. "But I don't *want* to talk to Gray," he said. "He'll ask about the advance, and I don't want to give it to him until I've read the manuscript. And there was only one copy. If he finds out I don't have it, he'll have a stroke!"

"Then don't tell him," advised Jupe. "Tell him there might be some legal problems if you publish the manuscript, and that your lawyer has to look it over before the advance is paid. Ask him if Miss Bainbridge has proof of the stories in the manuscript. Ask him if she's still in touch with any of the people she knew, or if Clara Adams is in contact with anyone."

"I can't do it," said Beefy. "I'd blow it for sure. Gray would guess right away that something was up."

"Take Jupe with you," suggested Pete. "He's an expert at getting information from people, and they don't even know they've told him anything."

Beefy looked at Jupe. "Can you do that?" he asked.

"Usually I can," said Jupe.

"Very well." Beefy took an address book out of his pocket and headed for the telephone.

"You're not calling Marvin Gray?" said his uncle.

"I certainly am calling him," said Beefy, "and Jupe and I are going to see him this afternoon!"

5

The Haunted Grove

"WORTHINGTON TELLS ME you boys operate as a team," said Beefy Tremayne. He and Jupiter were in his car, speeding north on the Coast Highway. "He says Bob is a good researcher, and Pete's the athlete of the group, and that you're a whiz at taking a few clues and figuring out what they mean. He also says that you're a mine of miscellaneous information."

"I enjoy reading," said Jupiter, "and fortunately I remember most of what I read."

"Lucky for you," said Beefy. "You couldn't have a handier talent."

The car slowed and turned off the highway on to a side road just outside the coastal community of Malibu. Beefy was silent as he drove up into the hills above the sea. After five minutes he braked again and left the curving mountain road for a narrow gravel road. He went on for a quarter of a mile, then pulled to a stop in front of a rustic gate. A sign over the gate indicated that they had reached the Half-moon Ranch.

"I don't know what I expected," said Beefy, "but

it wasn't anything like this."

"It does look very ordinary," said Jupe. "You'd expect that a movie star who is also a recluse woud live in a palatial mansion or at least have a ten-foot wall around her estate. There isn't even a lock on that gate."

Jupe got out of the car and held the gate open while Beefy drove through. Then Jupe got in and they headed up the driveway through a grove of lemon trees.

"It's strange that Gray didn't mention the sale of Bainbridge's films to you when he brought the manuscript in yesterday," said Jupiter.

"Very strange," Beefy agreed. "It will make a big difference in sales for the book."

"Was it Gray who chose you to be Bainbridge's publisher?" Jupe asked.

"I'm not sure," said Beefy. "He called me about six weeks ago and said that Bainbridge wanted to publish her memoirs. It's common knowledge that he handles all of her affairs, and he seemed to know what he was doing. I didn't ask him why he chose Amigos Press. I wonder if he's really as sharp as he appears to be. He should have let me know about the sale of the films."

The car emerged from the lemon grove, and a white frame ranch house came into view. It was large and plain, with a verandah that stretched across the front. Marvin Gray stood on the steps, squinting in the sunlight.

"Good afternoon," said Gray as Beefy clambered

out of the car. "I saw your dust as you came through the trees."

Gray frowned slightly at Jupe. "And who might this be?" he asked.

"My cousin, Jupiter Jones," said Beefy His face flushed as he embarked on the cover story that he and Jupe had prepared. It was plain that he was not used to telling even small lies. "You saw him yesterday at Amigos Press," he went on. "He's learning the business. And he's taking a course in the history of motion pictures. I didn't think you'd mind if he came with me to see Madeline Bainbridge's home."

"I guess it's all right," said Gray. "But I'm surprised that you're here today, after the fire. I should think you'd have other things to attend to."

"If I weren't here, I'd be at home brooding about the fact that my office burned down," said Beefy.

Gray nodded. He turned and led the way up the steps. Then, instead of going into the house, he sat down in one of the wicker chairs on the porch. He motioned to his guests to take seats near him.

Beefy sat down. "Mr Gray, I'm afraid there's going to be a delay in issuing the cheque for the advance on Miss Bainbridge's memoirs," he said. "I've looked through the manuscript and found several anecdotes which might cause legal problems. In one place, for example, there's the statement that a Hollywood director was a wizard. I know that the director is dead, but his heirs could sue. So I'm asking my attorney to look at the manuscript. In the meantime, Miss Bainbridge might give us the names of people who could back up her statements. And the addresses, of course."

"We certainly can't give you any addresses," said Marvin Gray. "Miss Bainbridge doesn't keep in touch with any of the old crowd."

"Well, perhaps you'd know how we could get in touch with some of the people," said Beefy. He was looking harassed and uncomfortable. "You've read through the manuscript, I'm sure, so . . ."

"No," said Marvin Gray, "I haven't read it. Miss Bainbridge give it to me only yesterday afternoon. I couldn't help you anyway. I never was friends with any of those people. I was the chauffeur then, remember?"

"How about her secretary?" said Beefy hopefully.

"Clara Adams?" Gray looked surprised. "She hasn't left this property in years."

Beefy looked stumped, so Jupe came to his rescue. He looked around eagerly and asked, "Aren't we going to see Miss Bainbridge?" His voice was naive and somewhat brash.

"Miss Bainbridge doesn't see anyone but myself and Clara," said Marvin Gray. "Even if she was used to having visitors, she wouldn't want to see anyone today. She's upset about the theft of her films. She's upstairs resting, and Clara is with her, and I'd appreciate it if you kept your voice down."

"I'm sorry," said Jupe. He looked around curiously. "Miss Bainbridge is really a recluse, huh?" he said. "Doesn't anyone live here besides you and Clara Adams and Miss Bainbridge? Aren't there any servants?"

"We live very simply," said Gray. "Servants aren't necessary."

"I saw you on television this morning," said Jupe. "Is it true that Miss Bainbridge doesn't watch TV?"

"It's true," said Gray. "I watch, and I tell her about any news I think will interest her."

"It sounds kind of lonely," said Jupe. "Doesn't she see anybody at all? Don't you see anybody? I mean, don't you get tired of just being here all the time? And Clara Adams—doesn't she get tired of it?"

"I don't think so. I enjoy my own company pretty well, and Clara is completely devoted to Miss Bainbridge. I am, too, of course. Extremely devoted."

Jupiter turned to Beefy. "You see?" he said. "You don't have anything to worry about."

Gray looked at Beefy in a questioning way. "You were worried?" he said. "Why?"

"Well, Beefy said on the way up here he was kind of nervous," said Jupe. "He figured if anyone knew where Miss Bainbridge's manuscript was, they might try to swipe it the way they swiped her films, and hold it for ransom. If you told anyone where it is . . ."

"Now who would I tell?" said Gray.

"Sounds like you wouldn't tell anybody," said Jupe, "unless maybe somebody called . . ."

"We have an unlisted number," said Gray. "People don't call. And we only use the telephone when it's absolutely necessary."

"Gosh, the kids at school aren't going to believe this," said Jupe. The stocky boy stood up. "May I wash my hands?" he asked.

"Of course." Gray pointed to the door. "Go straight back through the hall and past the stairs. There's a lavatory next to the kitchen."

"Thanks," said Jupe, and he went into the house.

The hall seemed dim after the sunlight on the porch. The living-room on the left was sparsely furnished with straight-backed wooden chairs. The dining-room on the right had a rude wooden table and backless benches. The wide staircase was uncarpeted. Jupe found the lavatory beyond it. He went in, closed the door, turned on the water, and opened the medicine cabinet above the sink. There was nothing there but a jar which had some dried leaves in it. They smelled like mint. Jupe closed the medicine cabinet, washed his hands, and then dried them on a towel that hung from a hook on the wall. The towel seemed to be home-made.

When Jupe left the lavatory, he looked into the kitchen—and blinked in amazement at the old-fashioned appliances there. The ancient refrigerator had exposed coils on top, and the old gas range did not even have pilot lights. The taps over the sink were worn brass ones. Jupe guessed they had been installed when the house was first built many years before.

A row of glass jars was lined up on a counter near the sink. Jupe crossed to read the labels. He saw tansy and lupine, rose hips, mint leaves, and thyme. One jar puzzled him, for according to the label it contained deadly nightshade.

In a large jar at the very end of the row there were books of matches. Jupe looked at a few of them. They were all from various restaurants. Then he turned towards the window. A movement behind the house had caught his eye.

He found that he was looking out at a large grove of live oaks. The trees were old and gnarled, with twisted trunks that branched out as they stretched above the first floor of the house. The dark green, spiny leaves shut out the sky and made the day seem grey. The oaks had been planted in wide-set rows, and among them two women were walking together. They wore gowns of some dark material, gowns that were caught in tightly at the waist, and which then flowed into wide skirts that brushed the ground. Both women had long hair, which they wore twisted into knots at the back of their heads. A sleek Doberman Pinscher stalked behind them.

As Jupe stood watching, one of the women looked towards the house. Jupe gasped. He had seen pictures of Madeline Bainbridge in books about films, and it was Bainbridge he saw now under the old trees in that grey, dreary wood. Her blonde hair was now closer to white, but her lovely face was still remarkably youthful. After an instant she turned and walked on. Jupe didn't think she had noticed him.

Jupe took a step towards the window and found himself wishing for a glimpse of the sun. He felt chilled. There was an eerie sadness about the trees, and about the women who walked under the boughs dressed in dark, old-fashioned gowns.

A footstep sounded behind Jupe. "Finished washing your hands?" asked Marvin Gray.

Jupe jumped and almost cried out. Then he pointed towards the window. "Those trees make everything look so dark," he said.

"They do, don't they?" Gray agreed. "There's a rancher who used to live up the road who said the grove was haunted. It looks as if it might be, doesn't it? It was a cemetery once—a private one that belonged to the family that lived here. There were graves under the trees. They were moved when Miss Bainbridge bought the house, of course, but the woods still seem gloomy to me.

"I came to find you. Your cousin is ready to start back to town."

Jupe followed Gray back through the house. A few minutes later, he and Beefy were speeding away from Half-moon Ranch.

"Well, that visit was certainly a waste of time," complained Beefy. "We didn't get any leads on who could have stolen Bainbridge's manuscript."

"But we got plenty of food for thought," replied Jupiter.

"Such as?"

"Gray lied to us about one thing. Madeline Bainbridge wasn't upstairs. She was outside with another woman—Clara Adams, I suppose. Gray may tell lots of lies. There are matchbooks from restaurants out in the kitchen. He may get around more than he pretends."

"But why would he lie?" asked Beefy.

"To protect Madeline Bainbridge," said Jupe. "She isn't any ordinary recluse. She's a very odd lady. She and Clara Adams were wearing old-fashioned black gowns—they looked like Pilgrim ladies. And there's a jar in the kitchen that's filled with deadly nightshade."

"You're kidding!" exclaimed Beefy. "Deadly nightshade is a poison!"

"I know," Jupe said. "Madeline Bainbridge may be one of the most fascinating characters I've come across. A lady who has changed very little in thirty years. I recognized her immediately. A lady who keeps poison in her kitchen, who goes around dressed like a Pilgrim, and who owns an oak grove that was once a cemetery. According to Gray, it's supposed to be haunted. At least, that's what some people say. And from the looks of it, it wouldn't surprise me if that were true!"

6

The Magic Circle

"YOU DON'T FIND nightshade in the ordinary kitchen!" said Jupiter Jones. He was sitting behind the desk in The Three Investigators' headquarters, an ancient mobile home trailer that was hidden away behind heaps of artfully arranged junk in a far corner of The Jones Salvage Yard. Pete and Bob had returned from the library, where Jupe had sent them to do some research while he was out with Beefy. Jupe had just finished telling them of his visit to the Bainbridge ranch.

"Nightshade is a name for a whole family of plants," Jupe went on. "Many of them are narcotic poisons, and some of them were once used in magic rituals."

"Madeline Bainbridge must be a real weirdo," said Pete. "Poison in her kitchen and a private cemetery out in the back!"

"It isn't a cemetery now," Jupe pointed out. "It *used* to be one. But there *was* something eerie and unreal about the place. It gave me the creeps."

"A cemetery and strange herbs," said Bob thoughtfully. He took his notebook out of his pocket. "It fits. It fits beautifully!"

Bob began to flip through his notes. "I looked up magic and witchcraft because Bainbridge had that story about the director, Alexander de Champley, being a wizard. It must have been important to her, or she wouldn't have taken time to draw the pentacle of Simon Magus in the manuscript.

"Now there are several different kinds of witches. There's the Hallowe'en kind, who is sort of a comic-strip hag with warts on her chin. Then there are the evil ones, the sorcerers and witches who can do dreadful things because they worship the devil. He helps them out, according to the superstitious, and I guess there's no limit to what you can do if Satan is backing you."

Pete scowled. "I don't believe a word of it," he said, "but would you hurry up? I don't like hearing about stuff like that."

"Okay, then you'll like the rest better," said Bob. "There's a form of witchcraft called the Old Religion. People who practise it say that it goes back to very ancient times. It's a sort of fertility cult—it has a lot to do with growing things and harvests. It's kind of nice, really. The witches believe that they have the power to make things happen because they're in tune with the power of the universe. They're organized into groups called covens, and each coven has thirteen people in it. They meet at special places, like a crossroads. An even better place is—guess where?"

"A . . . a cemetery?" said Jupe after a second.

"Right!" said Bob. "When they meet they have regular rites. They eat freshly gathered food and they worship Selena, or Diana, the moon goddess. They perform their rites at night, not because they're wicked, but just so the neighbours won't see them and gossip. The rituals can be performed at any time, but there are four main feasts, called Sabbats, every year. An Old Religion witch always attends the Sabbats. These happen on April thirtieth, August first, October thirty-first—which is our Hallowe'en, of course—and the second eve of February."

Bob closed his notebook. "That's all I got today. There's more, and we can take some of the books out of the library if we need to. I just wonder, if someone wanted the Bainbridge manuscript suppressed, could it be because that person was a witch? It could be someone in the film colony who either was a member of the Old Religion and didn't want it known, or perhaps someone who was a Satanist."

Pete shivered. "If we do have a witch mixed up in this, I hope it's one of the Old Religion witches," he said. "I don't think I want to mess with anybody who worships the devil."

Jupiter nodded. "A Satanist could be a person who is completely without a conscience," he said. "Or he could be a person who is somewhat simple-minded. In either case, he could be dangerous. But what did you do, Pete, while Bob was reading about witches?"

"I was reading about Madeline Bainbridge," said Pete. "I went back into the microfilm files."

The Second Investigator took an untidy sheaf of papers out of his pocket and began to read his pencilled notes.

"She came here from Fort Wayne, Indiana, when she was eighteen. She'd won a beauty contest and the prize was a trip to Hollywood. Alexander de Champley spotted her while she was touring the Film Art Studio. Three weeks later she had a contract with Film Art and was set to play Mary Queen of Scots in Champley's version of the picture. That's some kind of an all-time record for getting discovered and cast in a motion picture."

Pete looked up at his friends. "All the stories said she was very, very beautiful."

"She's still beautiful," said Jupe. "I saw her today. Anything more, Pete?"

"Just general stuff," said Pete. "She seems to have been a pretty quiet person. She didn't get into scandals. She made a lot of very good pictures. Most of her roles were historical, like Cleopatra and Catherine the Great. She had the best leading men, but she never bothered with them much once a picture was finished. She didn't make lots and lots of friends. She was sort of a loner, and there was never any gossip to link her romantically with any actor until the last of her leading men—Ramon Desparto."

"What about him?" asked Bob.

"He died shortly after he finished making the picture *The Salem Story.* That was a very strange picture about the witch trials in Salem and—"

"And there we have witchcraft again," interrupted Jupe.

"Right. But this movie was very hokey. The plot was weird. Bainbridge played a Puritan maiden who is accused of witchcraft, and who saves herself by running away with an Indian brave so that she doesn't get hanged. Ramon Desparto played the Indian brave, and he also got engaged to Madeline Bainbridge just before shooting started on the picture. There was some nasty talk that the engagement was just to help his career. He got engaged a lot to his leading ladies. Not long after *The Salem Story* was finished, he was killed in a car accident. It happened after a party at Bainbridge's ranch, and Bainbridge had some kind of nervous collapse. She never worked again. She bought up all of her pictures and spent the next thirty years keeping out of sight."

"And avoiding her old friends?" said Jupiter.

"There may not have been that many old friends," said Pete. He unfolded a photocopy of a picture that he had tucked in with his notes and handed it across the desk to Jupe. "This picture was taken at the Academy Awards dinner the year *The Salem Story* was made," he said. "That group of people is called 'Madeline Bainbridge's magic circle' because they're the ones she spent her time with. There aren't so many. Marvin

Gray isn't in the picture, though."

"He wasn't a friend then," Jupiter reminded Pete. "He was still just the chauffeur."

Jupe studied the picture and read the caption. Madeline Bainbridge and the darkly handsome Ramon Desparto sat at the head of the table. On the star's other side was Jefferson Long, looking very young and handsome. The caption identified a man named Elliott Farber as Bainbridge's favourite cameraman. An actor named Charles Goodfellow sat next to an actress named Estelle DuBarry. Nicholas Fowler, a scriptwriter, was there, and so was Clara Adams, who sat next to a character actor, Ted Finley. Janet Pierce was identified as costume designer for the Salem picture, and Lurine Hazel and Marie Alexander were actresses. A very plain girl named Gloria Gibbs stared straight ahead, and was referred to as Desparto's secretary.

"How interesting!" said Jupiter Jones. "A magic circle indeed! There are thirteen people here, and thirteen at a table is considered unlucky—unless you are a witch. For a coven, thirteen is the right number!"

Jupe beamed at his fellow investigators. "Bob, your notes indicate that August first is one of the four great Sabbats of the year. This happens to be the first of August. Was Madeline Bainbridge a witch? Is she still a witch? If so, who is in her coven today? There's one way to find out! Who's game for a ride up the coast to the Malibu hills tonight?"

"Hey, that's crazy!" cried Pete. Then he grinned. "What time do we start?"

7

The Creature in the Dark

IT WAS DUSK when The Three Investigators reached the spot where the narrow gravel road to Bainbridge's ranch crossed the paved mountain road that wound up through the Malibu hills. Jupe stopped, resting on the seat of his bike. Pete and Bob drew level with him, and Jupe pointed to the left.

"The Bainbridge place is down that way," he said. "I've gone over a map of this area. There are several places where a coven could meet, if Bainbridge is going to pay attention to the rules. One is this crossroads right here. One is the grove of trees behind her house—the place that was once a cemetery. And one is about half a mile north of her house, where two footpaths meet. I suggest we spread out to make sure we don't miss Bainbridge if she leaves her property."

Jupe dug into a knapsack that was strapped to the handlebars of his bicycle. "There's a dog, so we've got to be careful," he warned. "We can't get too close to the house. I brought the walkie-talkies."

He produced three small radio sets which he himself had rigged up in his workshop at the salvage yard. Each set was a little larger than a regular transistor radio, and consisted of a combined speaker and microphone. There were also three belts with copper wire sewn to them, and each had a lead-in wire which could be plugged into a radio. The belt with the wire acted as an antenna, and the little radios operated like Citizens' Band radios, broadcasting for about half a mile. When the user wanted to speak into the microphone, he pressed a button on the side of the radio set. When he wanted to listen, he released the button.

Jupe handed a radio set to Bob, and one to Pete. "I'll watch from the hill behind that haunted-looking grove," he said. "Bob, you can hide in among the lemon trees between the road and the house. Pete, your post can be on the north side of the house—that's the left side. There's a field there with some tall grass that you can use for cover. If Madeline Bainbridge leaves the house tonight, we'll spot her no matter which way she goes. Keep an eye out for cars, and for other people walking around. They might lead us to a Sabbat."

The other two boys murmured in agreement and took the radios. The three then rode down the gravel road to the front gate of the Bainbridge ranch. There they hid their bikes in the tall grass beside the road, and separated. Bob's slim figure disappeared among the lemon trees. Pete went on down the gravel road towards the north side of the property. Jupe trudged up through the fields, skirting the house and the grove of live oaks. On the hillside behind the grove he found a clump of manzanita. He crouched behind the shrub and held his walkie-talkie to his mouth.

"This is One," he said softly. "Come in, Two."

He released the button on the radio and listened. "This is Two," said Pete's voice. "I'm in the field to the north of the house. I see lights in the house, at the back, and I see people moving around inside, but I can't tell what they're doing. Over."

"Stay put," ordered Jupiter. "How about you, Three?"

"I can see the front of the house from the lemon grove," said Bob. "It's all dark. Over."

"Now we wait," said Jupiter. "Over and out "

He leaned back against the hillside and studied the grove oaks which completely hid the ranch house from view. The trees looked even more sinister by moonlight than they had that afternoon. The moon was climbing into the sky now, casting intense black shadows under the gnarled limbs.

The radio in Jupe's hand crackled.

"This is Two," said Pete. "The lights in the house have just gone out. Now there are some little lights out in the back. Over."

A tiny light flickered in the dark woods below. Then Jupe saw a second light. Then a third.

Jupe pressed the button on his radio. "They're

moving into the live-oak grove," he said softly. "I can see candles."

He waited. The candle lights moved beneath the twisted trees. Then the movement stopped and the candles glowed steadily. And there were more lights.

"I'm going in closer," said Jupe into the walkie-talkie. "You stay just where you are for the moment."

He released the button on the radio and slipped out from behind the manzanita. He half-slid down the hillside until he reached level ground behind the Bainbridge house. Then, like a chubby shadow, he stole from bush to bush until he was at the edge of the stand of oak trees. He paused, looking towards the candle flames that burned inside the grove. There were dozens of lights now, forming a circle, and for a moment Jupe could see only the candles against the darkness that pressed in around them. Then, beyond the candles appeared a woman who stared straight ahead into the night. It was Madeline Bainbridge. Her long, white-blonde hair was loose on her shoulders, and she wore a wreath of flowers on her head. She moved slowly forward into the circle of light.

There was a movement beyond Madeline Bainbridge. A second woman appeared out of the darkness. She carried a tray that was heaped high with fruit. It was the woman Jupe had seen with Madeline Bainbridge that afternoon. Jupe knew she must be Clara Adams. She entered the circle of light and put the tray down on a table draped with a black cloth.

Another face glimmered in the dark wood. It was Marvin Gray. He, too, wore a wreath of flowers on his dark hair. Jupe realized that he could scarcely see Gray's body. The man wore a black robe. So did the two women. They were invisible in the night except for their faces and for the circlets of flowers that crowned their heads.

"I will draw the circle," intoned Marvin Gray. His hands moved, white against his black robe. The blade of a knife glinted in the candlelight.

Jupe backed away from the ghostly woods and the strange trio under the branches. When he felt it was safe to speak, he pressed the button on his walkie-talkie. "Pete? Bob? I'm in the field just behind the grove. I'm pretty sure there's a Sabbat going on here."

"Be right there," said Bob.

"Me, too," Pete said.

Pete appeared in a very few minutes, coming as quietly as a ghost. Then Bob came stealing towards them through the night.

"There are only three people, but they're getting ready for some sort of ceremony," Jupe told his friends. "Marvin Gray has a knife."

"I read about that today," said Bob. "He'll draw a circle on the ground with the knife. Witches believe that the circle increases their power."

"Let's watch," said Jupiter.

Bob and Pete silently followed Jupe in among

the trees, looking nervously ahead. What strange rites were they about to witness? They saw the three white-faced people standing in the ring of candlelight. They saw Madeline Bainbridge lift a cup high and close her eyes as if she were praying. The boys held their breath.

Then, suddenly, Pete uttered a small, wordless cry of terror. For out of the darkness, some silent-footed beast had come to stand beside him. For an instant the creature was still. Pete could feel its hot breath on him. Then it growled, low and ominously.

8

Murder by Magic?

"WHAT'S THAT?" cried Marvin Gray. "Who's there?"

The three boys froze, and the growling went on and on.

Clara Adams put her hands to her mouth and gazed out from the circle of light. Madeline Bainbridge did not move. She was like a carving in ivory and ebony. From somewhere beneath his black robe, Marvin Gray pulled out a flashlight. He charged towards The Three Investigators and the flashlight snapped on. Jupe saw that the animal standing near Pete was a dog—the sleek Doberman he had seen that afternoon. Obviously the animal had been trained to hold intruders motionless, but not to attack unless greatly provoked; it made no more to harm Pete.

"What do you boys think you're doing here?" demanded Gray.

Jupe felt Gray's gaze on him and his heart sank. How could he explain to this man that Beefy Tremayne's young cousin, who had been such a polite visitor that afternoon, had returned after dark to spy on Gray and the two women?

"Who's there, Marvin?" called Madeline Bainbridge.

"Bunch of kids. They probably came up from Malibu," said Gray. "Ought to call the sheriff and have them thrown in the clink!"

Jupe's heart began to beat wildly. Was it possible that Gray didn't recognize him?

"Hey, mister," said Jupe. "Call the dog, huh?"

"All right, Bruno," said Gray. "Here, boy!"

The dog stopped growling and went to Gray.

"Now what are you doing here?" asked Gray again. "Can't you see this is private property?"

"Not in the dark," said Jupe boldly. "We were hiking in the hills. We got off the path and we couldn't find our way back."

"Marvin!" Madeline Bainbridge sounded impatient. "Let the boys go, and come back. You're holding us up!"

Jupiter looked past Gray to Madeline Bainbridge. Then he glanced at Gray. Gray looked hesitant. He obviously couldn't decide what to do.

Jupe started towards Bainbridge. "We're really very sorry," he said. "We didn't mean to disturb you."

"The circle!" gasped Clara Adams. "He's profaning the circle!"

Jupe went on towards the table where the women stood, repeating his apologies. One hand was at his belt, unfastening the antenna of the walkie-talkie. With the other hand he held the little radio set at his side, out of sight of the women. He was quite near the table when the antenna came away from his waist. He stumbled on something in his path and fell, stretched out full length on the ground, his head and shoulders almost under the table.

"Marvin!" cried Madeline Bainbridge.

Jupe's hands disappeared for a moment under the black cloth that draped the table. Then he pulled himself to his hands and knees. "Sorry," he said again. "That was clumsy of me. We didn't mean to upset you, honest. If you could just point us in the direction of the road . . ." Jupe got to his feet.

"Marvin, show these boys how to get to the main road," said Madeline Bainbridge.

"Thank you," said Jupiter.

Gray led The Three Investigators out from under the trees. He pointed across the fields to the place where, as the boys knew, the paved road led down to the Coast Highway. "There!" said Gray. "Keep going until you hit the road. Then turn right and don't come back."

"Thanks a lot, mister," said Pete.

Gray stood watching as The Three Investigators walked away through the tall, moonlit grass.

"He isn't going to take his eyes off us until we're off this property," predicted Bob.

"I don't blame him," said Jupiter. "Would *you* want strangers at secret rites in your backyard? Let's hope that he doesn't look under the table and discover that I put my walkie-talkie there!"

"So that's why you fell!" exclaimed Pete.

"I thought it might be interesting to listen in on any conversation that occurs after we leave," said Jupe. "I wrapped part of the antenna wire around the set so that the button is pressed down. The radio won't receive, but it should send. Let's not go too far or we'll be out of range."

The boys stepped from the meadow on to the paved road. Bob looked back. Marvin Gray had disappeared. "He's probably back in the grove of oak trees," Bob said. He followed Jupe and Pete down the road to the shelter of a clump of bushes.

"Turn on your set, Bob," said Jupiter. "Let's listen in on the coven."

Bob knelt beside the bushes and turned the knob that activated his set.

". . . gone for the time being," they heard Gray say. "They won't try to come back. Not after Bruno pinned them down that way."

"I had hoped that Bruno was locked up someplace," Jupe muttered.

Gray was speaking again. "It was dumb to let them go," he declared.

"What should we have done?" said Madeline Bainbridge.

"Run them off a cliff!" growled Gray.

"Marvin!" cried a woman's voice. It was not Madeline Bainbridge, so the boys assumed that Clara Adams had been shocked at Gray's suggestion.

"Well, I don't like kids snooping around," said Gray. "They'll go home and talk about what they've seen. Next thing we know, there'll be photographers and reporters hiding behind every tree. I can see the headlines now: 'Mystery Rites at Movie Star's Ranch!' Before you know it, the cops are poking around and—"

"We hardly need to worry about the police," said Madeline Bainbridge. "We're doing nothing wrong."

"Not now!" said Gray.

"Not ever!" said the actress.

"Then you *want* the cops up here?" asked Gray. "You should have used your power on those kids, just the way you did on Desparto that night!"

"I never harmed Ramon!" cried the movie star. "Not even when he betrayed me!"

"Of course not!" Gray's voice was mocking. "You wished him long life and happiness."

"Marvin, don't!" Clara Adams pleaded.

"You keep bringing that up!" The actress's voice was rough with anger. "Over and over again. All right, I was furious with Ramon. But I didn't hurt him. I wouldn't use my power to hurt anyone, and you know it. In fact, you're counting on it, aren't you?"

"Madeline! Please!" said Clara Adams.

"Okay, okay!" grumbled Gray. "There's no use going on with the rite now. Let's get into the house." He raised his voice. "Bruno! Here, Bruno!"

"Perhaps we should leave the dog outside," said

Clara Adams, "just in case those boys come back."

"They won't come back," predicted Gray. "And if we leave him out, he'll get restless at three in the morning and set up a howl, and I'll have to get up to let him in. That's what we get for raising a guard dog who thinks he's a member of the family."

There was no more conversation from the walkie-talkie. After a few moments, Jupiter drew a deep breath. "Marvin Gray wanted Madeline Bainbridge to use her power on us, just as she used it on Ramon Desparto," he said. "What, I wonder, did she do to Desparto?"

"Nothing, according to her," answered Bob. "She said she never harmed anybody."

"Desparto died in an auto accident," said Pete. "The brakes on his car failed when he was leaving here one night after a party."

"Was it a party?" said Jupiter. "Or was it like the ritual we saw tonight? One thing we now know for sure: Madeline Bainbridge *is* a witch, or she thinks she's a witch. And she believes she has some kind of power."

"The power to . . . to kill someone?" said Pete. His voice was very low.

"Murder by magic?" Bob shook his head. "Impossible!"

"Perhaps," said Jupiter. "However, it appears that Madeline Bainbridge feels some guilt about Desparto. She wouldn't deny her responsibility so furiously if she didn't believe it was possible for her to have hurt him in some fashion."

"That Marvin Gray," said Pete. "Why'd he get her all stirred up that way? He didn't have to rake up that stuff from the past."

"Perhaps he's manipulating her," said Jupe. "He may be the real power in her household—perhaps the only power."

"I don't like him," said Pete.

"Nor do I," agreed Jupe. "Not after hearing him over the walkie-talkie. The man's a bully. I wonder if he tells lies just to protect Madeline Bainbridge's privacy. He may be even more interested in protecting his own."

"Jupe?" said Bob. "Could Gray have been involved in the theft of her manuscript?"

Jupe shrugged. "I don't see why or how. He couldn't have taken the manuscript himself—he was being interviewed by Jefferson Long when it was stolen. And he has no apparent motive for theft. Quite the opposite. As Bainbridge's business manager, it's to his advantage to have the book published and earning money. But did he talk to someone—anyone—about the book? Or did Bainbridge? After what we've heard tonight, I'm almost sure the answer to the mystery of the missing manuscript is hidden in Bainbridge's past—in that magic circle which existed long ago."

Jupe stood up. "We've done all we can do tonight. I'll go and retrieve my walkie-talkie and meet you where we left our bikes. Tomorrow . . . tomorrow we investigate the former coven."

"If that's what it was," said Bob.

"I think that's just what it was," said Jupiter, and he started across the fields towards the haunted wood.

9

The Crime Fighter

"YOU'RE KIDDING!" said Beefy Tremayne. "Madeline Bainbridge really is a witch?"

Beefy was guiding his sports car along Santa Monica Boulevard. Jupiter sat beside him, and Pete and Bob were squeezed into the back seat.

"She's a witch now," declared Jupiter, "and it seems more than likely that she was a witch back in the days when she was active in films. We think that she may have headed a coven, and that sinister things may have gone on among the people in it. Someone who was involved may well want to prevent her memoirs from being published. We plan to interview her close associates to see if we can establish some connection with Bainbridge within the last couple of days. We have to find someone who knew where the manuscript was on the night before last."

"But you can't expect anyone to admit he knew where the manuscript was," objected the young publisher. "I mean, if that person stole it."

"We don't intend to ask about the manuscript at all," answered Jupe, "at least in the beginning.

First we have to find out who in the coven is still in touch with Madeline Bainbridge, or is getting news of her. I don't think anyone will be afraid to admit a connection with her."

Beefy turned north on La Brea Avenue towards Hollywood.

"And you're going to talk to Jefferson Long for openers?" he said. "Long, the crime fighter? He's so foursquare and true-blue. I just can't imagine him being mixed up in anything weird like a coven."

"He wasn't always Jefferson Long, the crime fighter," Jupe pointed out. "He used to be an actor, and he was in Bainbridge's last picture. He had to know Ramon Desparto. Also, it's logical to begin our interviews with him, since we know where to find him. The offices of Video Enterprises, which include the studios for Station KLMC, are on Fountain Street just off Hollywood Boulevard. I called there earlier this morning, and he agreed to see me."

"Did you tell him why you wanted to talk with him?" asked Beefy.

"Not exactly. I said I was doing a report for my school paper as a summer project."

"Long must like publicity," said Pete from the back seat. "Even publicity in a school paper."

"Perhaps we all would, if we were in the public eye," said Jupiter. He glanced at Beefy. "It's really nice of you to drive us," he said. "We could have taken the bus."

"If I stayed at home, I'd only stew and worry," declared Beefy. "I'm kind of lost without an office to go to. Besides, you guys fascinate me. I don't think I'd dare just walk in on somebody like Jefferson Long."

Bob laughed. "Jupe doesn't scare easily."

"And how are you going to find the other people in the magic circle?" asked Beefy.

Pete answered, "My father works for a movie studio. He's getting us the addresses of Madeline Bainbridge's friends through the unions."

Beefy had been navigating carefully down Hollywood Boulevard. Now he turned right on to Fountain and pulled to the kerb in front of a building that looked like a huge cube of dark glass. "We'll park here and wait," he said as Jupe got out. "Take your time."

"Right," said Jupe. He turned and went into the building.

The reception room was cool, shielded from the glare outside by polarized glass. The tanned young woman at the desk directed Jupe to the elevator, and he rode up to the fourth floor.

Jefferson Long's office was filled with glass and chrome and furniture upholstered in black leather. The windows faced north, towards the Hollywood Hills. Long sat behind a teakwood desk, his back to the view, and smiled at Jupiter.

"Nice to see you," said the crime reporter. "I'm always glad to do what I can to help young people."

Jupiter had a feeling that Long had made that short speech hundreds of times before.

"Thank you very much," said Jupiter in his most humble voice. He gazed at Long, and he let his round, cheerful face take on a look of almost idiotic innocence. "I saw your telecast the other morning," he said. "The interview you did at Madeline Bainbridge's estate. I was surprised! I didn't know that you were an actor and that you knew Madeline Bainbridge."

Jefferson Long's smile vanished suddenly. "I have done more important things in my life than being an actor and knowing Madeline Bainbridge," he said. He swung around in his chair and gestured towards the shelves that lined one side of his office. "The law enforcement people would be the first to agree."

Jupiter got up and went to the shelves. There he saw plaques and medallions from cities up and down the coast. There were photographs of Long with the police chiefs of various large and small towns in California, Nevada, and Arizona. There was also a framed parchment announcing that Jefferson Long was an honorary member of a sheriff's posse.

"Golly!" said Jupe. He hoped that he sounded properly impressed.

"I have some scrapbooks, too," declared Long. "You can look through them if you're interested."

"Well, I'd sure like to," said Jupiter eagerly. "And a friend told me you're doing a series on drug abuse. That must be pretty exciting."

Jefferson Long's handsome face flushed. "It is. Can you imagine, even some people who are employed in legitimate pharmaceutical firms are involved in the illicit distribution of drugs? But I won't be able to put my series together this year. Some people not very far from here believe that it's more important to spend money on mouldy old movies than on producing a documentary series on a major problem like drug abuse."

"Oh," said Jupiter. "Oh, well. I see. That's too bad, I guess. But the Madeline Bainbridge movies must have been very expensive."

"They will be even more expensive when they have been ransomed," said Long.

"That's tough luck for you, I guess," said Jupiter. "Except maybe it could be a break, couldn't it? I mean, you're in one of the movies!"

"*The Salem Story* was an extremely bad movie," said Jefferson Long. "In fact it was such a flop that after the premiere, I never got another job as an actor. I found a much more satisfying career as a crime reporter."

"But Madeline Bainbridge retired," said Jupe. He was rambling like an artless youngster. "My aunt Mathilda remembers Madeline Bainbridge, and she says there was always some mystery about her. She said people used to say strange things about her friends. They used to talk about her and Madeline Bainbridge's coven."

"Coven?" Jefferson Long's face was suddenly wary, as if he sensed some enemy. He smiled stiffly. "Ridiculous," he said. "A coven is a group of witches."

"Yes," said Jupiter. "You worked with Miss Bainbridge. Was there a coven?"

"Certainly not!" declared Jefferson Long. "That is, so far as I know, there was no coven. Madeline Bainbridge's friends were—they were just the people she worked with, that's all."

"Did you know them?" Jupiter asked.

"Well, certainly. I was one of them."

"Well, maybe some of them knew something you didn't know," said Jupe. He gazed at Long without blinking. "Do you keep in touch with any of the others? Do you know where I could reach them? Or maybe you'd be able to put me in touch with Madeline Bainbridge herself."

"Certainly not!" exclaimed Long. "I don't have anything to do with those people any more. My friends are all in law enforcement. As for Bainbridge, I haven't seen her for thirty years—and I don't care if I don't see her for another thirty! She was a spoiled, temperamental would-be actress. Almost as bad as that Desparto character she was engaged to. Now there was a real ham!"

"He died after a party at her house, didn't he?"

"Yes." Jefferson Long looked old then, and his eyes were bleak. "After a party. Yes."

He straightened up and shook himself, as if shaking off a bad memory. "But that . . . that was a long time ago," he said. "I never think about those days now. No use dwelling in the past. And why are we talking so much about Madeline Bainbridge, anyway? I assume you've come because you're interested in my crime-fighting programmes."

"I came because of Madeline Bainbridge," said Jupe simply. "I'm doing a paper on her for my course in the history of films. If the paper's good enough, it'll get published in the school journal."

Jefferson Long looked intensely annoyed. "I wish you good luck," he said coldly. "Now you'll have to excuse me. I can't give you any more time. I have a luncheon appointment."

"I understand," said Jupe. He thanked Long and left.

"Well?" said Beefy as Jupe got into the car.

"Jefferson Long does not like Madeline Bainbridge, and he doesn't like the idea of her films being shown on television," Jupe reported. "Video Enterprises isn't going to finance a series he wants to do on drug abuse because they spent so much money on the Bainbridge pictures. Long says he hasn't seen Bainbridge for thirty years and he hasn't kept up with any of her friends. Also, he denies that there was a coven. He may be telling the truth about everything else, but I think he was lying about the coven. Actually, I think that there is something odd about Jefferson Long, but I can't quite say what it is."

Pete chuckled in the back seat. "You'll figure it

out. You always do," he said. "Anyway, here's something else to work on. I called my father at the studio while you were gone. He's got an address for us already. Elliott Farber was Bainbridge's favourite cameraman, and he was in the magic circle at that Academy Awards dinner. He isn't a cameramen any longer. He runs a television repair shop on Melrose. Let's go over there!"

10

The Witch's Curse

It was not necessary for The Three Investigators to fabricate a story about a school journal in order to see Elliott Farber. The former cameraman was not protected by a receptionist, and the three boys had only to walk into his dusty little shop in order to talk with him. Once they were in the shop—a narrow hole-in-the-wall sandwiched between a barber shop and an upholsterer—Jupe said, quite simply, "Mr Farber, you were Madeline Bainbridge's favourite cameramen, weren't you?"

Elliott Farber was a thin man with a yellowish tint to his skin. He squinted at the boys through the smoke that wafted from the cigarette between his lips. "Don't tell me," he said. "Let me guess. You're old movie buffs."

"Something like that," said Jupe.

Farber smiled and leaned back against a counter. "I worked with Bainbridge on almost every picture she ever made," he said. "She was tremendous. Great actress!"

Farber dropped his cigarette to the floor and ground it out with his foot. "She was beautiful, too. Some of the so-called glamour queens needed every bit of make-up and ever trick of lighting to look good. They had to have every break the cameraman could give them. That's why I quit the business. I got sick of taking the blame if some dame didn't look enough like Cleopatra, Queen of the Nile. But with Bainbridge, there was no sweat. She was purely and simply beautiful. I couldn't make a mistake when I was filming one of her scenes."

"Was she difficult to work with?" asked Jupe.

"Oh, she liked to get her own way, once she got established. That's how we all got involved in that horrible turkey about witches and Puritans."

"*The Salem Story?*" prompted Jupe.

"Right," said Farber. "Ramon Desparto thought that one would be great. Madeline was nuts about him, so anything he wanted, he got. Madeline saw to it. We used to worry about her—that he'd wreck her career."

"That's what he did, didn't he?" asked Pete, who had been listening quietly. "I mean, after he died, she was so heartbroken she didn't work again."

"She blamed herself," said Farber. "She and Desparto had quarrelled just before he had the car accident that killed him. She'd said some pretty nasty things to him. Not that I blame her. He was playing around with another actress, Estelle DuBarry, and Madeline was jealous. If you're organizing some fan club for Madeline, or doing an article for some kid magazine, you could just forget I told you that bit. No sense in stirring up old troubles."

"Do you ever see Madeline Bainbridge these days, Mr Farber? Or talk with her?" asked Jupiter.

"Nope. Nobody sees her. Nobody's in touch with her at all."

Bob showed Mr Farber the copy of the picture he had found at the library. "Wasn't Estelle DuBarry one of the people who were very close to Madeline Bainbridge?" he asked. "She's in this photo that was taken at an awards dinner."

"Oh, that?" Farber took the picture from Bob. "Yes. The magic circle. There they are—all thirteen of them—including yours truly."

"Isn't thirteen an odd number to have at a dinner table?" said Jupe.

Farber smiled. "Not if you're a witch," he said.

"Then there *was* a coven!" cried Bob.

Now Farber laughed out loud. "Sure. Why not? Madeline was a witch—or at least she thought she was. She called it the Old Religion. It didn't have anything to do with riding broomsticks or selling your soul to the devil, but Madeline was convinced that she had some magical powers. We all went along with the act. Madeline was the star, after all, and if she'd decided that we were all going to paint ourselves purple, we'd all have done it. We became members of the coven. Estelle DuBarry and Lurine Hazel and Janet Pierce and even poor, dull Clara Adams—witches one and all."

"And Jefferson Long?" said Jupe.

"Sure," said Farber. "I don't suppose he'd like it known today. He's got kind of a stuffy image on his television show. But he was a witch."

Jupiter smiled. "Do you keep in touch with any of those people?"

"With some of them," said Farber. "Jefferson Long speaks only to policemen these days, so nobody keeps in touch with him. Poor little Estelle, who caused all the trouble between Madeline and Desparto, never made it to the big time. She didn't really have talent and she didn't wear well. She now looks like my grandmother and she runs a little motel in Hollywood. She's not a bad sort."

"Do you think she'd consent to be interviewed?" asked Jupe.

"Sure. She'd enjoy the attention. Hey, what are you kids doing, anyway? The project of the year for a juvenile fan magazine?"

"Well, I'm taking a course on the history of films," said Jupe, "and . . ."

"I see." Farber took the photo from Bob and studied it. "I'll give you Estelle DuBarry's address," he said. "And I've got Ted Finley's telephone number. He's a great old guy. And still working in pictures even though he must be about eighty. Mention my name when you call him."

"How about the others?" asked Bob.

"Well, Ramon Desparto is dead, of course," said Farber. "I don't know how you'd get to talk to Clara Adams. She lives with Madeline and they don't see anyone. Nicholas Fowler, the script-writer, is dead, too. He had a heart attack a few years back. Forget about Janet Pierce. She married a count or a duke or somebody like that and went to Europe to live and never came back. Lurine Hazel's gone, too. She married her hometown sweetheart and went to live in Billsville, Montana. And Marie Alexander—well, it's a shame about Marie."

"She's the pretty girl with the long hair, isn't she?" said Pete. "What happened to her?"

"She went swimming off Malibu one day and got caught in a riptide and drowned."

"Good grief!" exclaimed Pete. "That's three people in the coven who are dead!"

"It's been a long time since that picture was taken," said Farber. "We haven't done too badly. Now Gloria Gibbs, the plain one who was Ramon Desparto's secretary, she works for a broker out in Century City. Every once in a while I take her out to dinner."

Jupiter took the photo and looked at it again. He pointed to the man who was identified in the caption as Charles Goodfellow. He was a very thin young fellow with dark hair that was slicked back. "He looks familiar," said Jupe. "Is he still working in films?"

Farber frowned. "Goodfellow? I'd almost forgotten about him. He did bit parts back in the old days—you know, playing taxi drivers and doormen. You've probably seen him if you watch a lot of old movies on TV. I don't know what happened to him. He's the only one I've completely lost track of. He's one of those people who are easy to forget. About the only thing I remember is that he was American, but for some reason his parents lived in Holland when he was a child. He was a strange one. Very fussy. He almost had a fit when he found out that we were all supposed to sip honey and water out of the same cup at the Sabbats. He used to do it, but he always went and gargled afterwards."

The three boys laughed. "You make a witch's coven sound as sinister as a square dance," said Jupiter.

"It was all very innocent," said Farber. "Only, after Desparto died, some of the people began to wonder whether Madeline didn't, in fact, have some power."

"She put a curse on Desparto?" asked Jupiter.

Farber sighed. "Maybe I shouldn't tell you. It was . . . well, the sort of thing people say when they're very angry. She told him to go hang himself. Now that's just an expression. I'm sure she didn't mean it. Only right after she'd said it, Ramon Desparto climbed into his car and drove away—and the brakes failed so that he drove into a tree. There were no seat belts in those days, and he was thrown clear of the car. We found him wedged in the fork of a tree part way down an embankment on the side of the road. He was just hanging there with his head to one side. His neck was broken."

"My gosh!" said Pete.

"So the coven broke up, and Madeline withdrew, and that was the end of that. Now no one talks to Madeline, and I guess not many talk about her."

"How about her manager? He used to be her chauffeur," said Jupe.

"Didn't really know him," said Farber. He took a piece of paper from a pad on the counter and wrote Estelle DuBarry's address on it. Then he added Ted Finley's telephone number and the address where Gloria Gibbs worked in Century City. He gave the paper to the boys, and when they left the shop he stood leaning on his counter, staring straight ahead in an unseeing fashion.

"Nice guy," said Pete, when they were outside, "and he sure likes to talk."

"Yes, even though I guess we stirred up some bad memories for him," said Bob. "He looks as if he's seeing Ramon Desparto again, hanging in the fork of a tree with his neck broken."

11

Friends and Enemies

THE MOTEL THAT Estelle DuBarry managed was on a side street off Hollywood Boulevard. When Bob rang the bell outside the office, an ageing woman with bleached blonde, curly hair and very black eyelashes came to the door.

"Miss DuBarry?" said Bob.

"That's right." She squinted slightly, as if she might need glasses.

"Elliott Farber told us you might be willing to talk with us," said Bob. "We're doing a paper for school. It's a summer project on the history of the motion picture."

"Why, how nice!" said the woman. "I'll be happy to talk with you." She opened the screen door and swung it wide. The boys went into a stuffy little room that was part office and part living-room. They took seats, and the faded actress immediately launched into the tale of her career in films. She had come to Hollywood as a young girl, and had taken a screen test. She told them how she had been given roles in several unimportant pictures and a few important ones. And since Estelle DuBarry's career hadn't been outstanding, she soon ran out of things to say to the boys.

Jupiter mentioned Madeline Bainbridge then, and the atmosphere in the little room changed abruptly.

"That terrible woman!" cried DuBarry. "She hated me. She always hated me! I was pretty, and not so high and mighty as she was. If it hadn't been for her, I wouldn't be running this crummy motel today. If it hadn't been for her, Ramon and I would be married and living in some big house in Bel Air!"

There was shocked silence. DuBarry glared at Jupe and he looked away. "Mr Farber mentioned a coven," he said at last. "Can you tell us anything about the coven?"

The colour left Estelle DuBarry's face, then flooded back in a crimson tide. "We . . . we were just playing games, you know," she said. "We didn't believe in it. Except for Madeline. She believed in it."

"So you didn't believe in witchcraft, and you still don't?"

"Of course not!" cried the former actress.

"You said an interesting thing a few moments ago," said Jupe. "You said that if it weren't for Madeline Bainbridge, you and Ramon Desparto would be living in Bel Air today. How could that be? Ramon Desparto died in an accident."

"That was no accident!" cried the woman. "It was . . . it was . . ."

She didn't finish the sentence.

Bob moved awkwardly in his chair. "It was very nice of you to take the time to see us," he said. "Do you know of anyone else we should see—any friend of Madeline Bainbridge who might still be in touch with her? Or with her secretary for that matter?"

"I do not," said the woman.

"There was a man named Charles Goodfellow," said Jupe. "Do you know what became of him?"

She shrugged. "He just dropped out of sight."

"I see," said Jupe.

The boys left, and walked down the drive to the car, where Beefy waited.

"She doesn't know anything that can help us," said Bob.

"She thinks Bainbridge murdered Desparto," Pete put in. "I think she's really afraid of Bainbridge."

"Elliott Farber suggested as much," said Jupe. "I wonder if Ted Finley will have any information we need."

"I wonder if Ted Finley will even talk to us," said Bob.

"I imagine he will," said Jupiter. "Madeline Bainbridge is big news today, after the theft of those films. Ted Finley won't object to being associated with her."

Jupe proved to be correct. After a quick lunch, he telephoned Ted Finley from Beefy's apartment. He gct an answering device, but Ted Finley called back almost immediately. The old character actor was cheerful and co-operative. He quickly admitted that there had been a coven, and that he had been a member. However, although he expressed great admiration for Madeline Bainbridge, he denied that he was ever in touch with her.

"Nobody keeps in touch with Madeline," he said. "That chauffeur of hers—that Gray—he took over completely once Madeline retired. He always answered the telephone, and he always said she didn't want to talk to anyone. For a while after Desparto died, I tried to keep her from being a complete hermit. It didn't do any good, and after a while I gave up. Maybe things will be better, now that her pictures have been sold to television."

"And stolen," Jupe reminded him. "They're being held for ransom."

"And they'll *be* ransomed," predicted Finley. "They're priceless. Now that you young folks will have a chance to see them, I expect I'll be getting a lot of calls about Madeline."

"Just one more thing, Mr Finley," said Jupe. "Do you know what happened to the man named Charles Goodfellow? He's the only one of Madeline Bainbridge's close friends that I haven't been able to locate."

"Goodfellow? No, can't say that I do know. He was kind of a dim young man. Maybe he went back home—wherever that might be—and got a job clerking in a hardware store or something."

Jupe thanked the actor, and Ted Finley hung up.

"Nothing," Jupe said to his friends. "He doesn't know anything and hasn't been in touch with Bainbridge for years."

"We haven't contacted Gloria Gibbs yet," Bob reminded Jupe. "You have the name of the broker she works for."

Jupiter nodded. "I'll call her, but I think we're wasting time."

In a dogged and discouraged way, Jupiter dialled the number of Gloria Gibbs's employer. The woman who answered the telephone turned out to be Gloria Gibbs herself. She was even less helpful than Madeline Bainbridge's other friends had been, and more hostile. "That was all a long time ago," she said, "and I don't feel that I'm any more important because I once knew that blonde witch."

"Yes, she was a witch," said Jupe quickly. "You were a member of her coven, weren't you?"

"Yes, and it was a big bore. I don't like staying up late just to dance around in the moonlight."

Gloria Gibbs then brusquely denied ever being in touch with Madeline Bainbridge, or with the missing coven member, Charles Goodfellow. She announced in sharp tones that Clara Adams was a poor, beaten-down creature in whom nobody would be interested, and she hung up.

"Unpleasant woman," was Jupe's comment. "However, she only confirms what others have told us. There was a coven, but if that's the sinister secret in Madeline Bainbridge's memoirs, it isn't making anyone nervous. We don't know about our missing coven member, Charles Goodfellow, but no one else is worried about witchcraft. So that's not it unless . . ." Jupe stopped and frowned. "Jefferson Long!" he said. "He's the only one who wouldn't admit to being a member of the coven. But he couldn't have stolen the manuscript. He was on camera with Marvin Gray at the time the manuscript was taken."

"He could have hired somebody," Pete suggested. "And maybe Gray did mention it to him. He could even have told him it was here, and then forgotten he did it."

"It's a bare possibility," said Jupe, "but not likely. Where would Long find the time to arrange a theft while he was busy setting up an interview? Still, for some reason Long makes me uneasy. I wonder what the law enforcement people really think about him."

"You think he's a phoney?" asked Pete.

"I had the impression he was playing a role," said Jupe. "He seems to know everybody in law enforcement in Southern California. If that's true, he's got to know Chief Reynolds in Rocky Beach. Let's see if the chief can give us some background on him. Somehow I'll believe the chief better than I'll believe a lot of plaques and scrolls."

12

The Man from Arson

"JEFFERSON LONG?" Chief Reynolds leaned back in his swivel chair. Sure, I know Jefferson Long. He shows up at every convention of law enforcement people that's held anywhere in the state."

The Chief of Police of Rocky Beach leaned forward and stared curiously at The Three Investigators. The boys sat on straight chairs across the desk from him. "Why are you interested in Long?" he wanted to know.

"I can't say exactly without betraying a confidence," Jupe told him.

"Hm!" said the chief. "That sort of talk usually means your juvenile detective firm has a client. Okay. Just so you keep out of trouble.

"I've seen Long around at meetings, and every once in a while I watch him on television. He's okay. He gives people some straight scoop on crime and criminals. Of course, he claims to be an investigative reporter. That would mean that he actually does some detective work on his own. He doesn't. In my opinion, he's just a brain-picker—he gets his information from people who have done the hard work of digging out facts. I don't even think he's all that interested in law and order. He just latched on to that as a cause; he wanted to make a name for himself and promote his crime reports on TV."

"So he's a phoney," said Pete. "But how come he gets all those awards from police departments and sheriffs' offices?"

Chief Reynolds shrugged. "He does keep the public informed about things like fraud and burglary and forged money and such things. Law enforcement people want the public to trust them, and Long does encourage people to trust the police—and to call the police if they think there's anything strange going on in their neighbourhoods. So the man does help us a lot that way."

"But he isn't the hotshot crime-fighter he pretends to be," summarized Jupiter. He nodded with satisfaction. "I had a feeling he was acting a role."

"He does it twenty-four hours a day," said the chief.

The boys thanked the chief, then left the police station and started hiking up the highway.

"Another dead end!" complained Jupiter. "We punctured Long's balloon, but now I'm sure that he had nothing to do with the theft of Madeline Bainbridge's manuscript."

"Why do you say that?" asked Bob.

"Because, from everything we've heard, I think Long really values his good relations with the police. He's built a successful career on that, and I don't think he'd jeopardize his career by stealing a manuscript that would merely embarrass him."

"Then why did he lie to you about the coven?" demanded Pete.

"It's not surprising. Why should a man in his position tell a strange kid about some silly stuff in his past? And that's all it was—silly stuff, not crimes. Anyway, even if Long knew about the manuscript and wanted to steal it, he didn't have any opportunity. The timing's all wrong."

Glumly, the Investigators separated and headed for their homes. Jupiter was moody and absent-minded during dinner with Aunt Mathilda and Uncle Titus. After the dishes were done, he went to his room to lie on his bed and stare at the ceiling. He felt utterly discouraged. It seemed that there was no way to connect any of Madeline Bainbridge's old companions to the theft of the manuscript. But if none of the actress's friends had stolen her memoirs, who had?

Jupe recalled the night of the fire. Again he seemed to hear the roar as the flames licked at the timbers of the old Amigos Adobe. After they had been hauled out of the basement, he and Bob and Pete had stood across the street watching the fire. Mr Grear had been with them, and then Beefy and his uncle had come hurrying up. Mr Thomas had been there, too, and so had Mrs Paulson. They, and only they, had known that the manuscript was in Beefy's apartment. Yet it seemed most unlikely that any of them would have taken it.

After a while, Jupe drifted off to sleep. When he woke, the sun was coming in the window. Still feeling frustrated and lethargic, Jupe got up, showered, and dressed. Then he telephoned Bob and Pete and arranged to meet them after breakfast at the bus stop on the Coast Highway.

It was almost nine when Jupe walked from The Jones Salvage Yard down to the highway. Bob and Pete were already there, waiting for him.

"You have any brainstorms overnight?" asked Pete.

"No," said Jupe. "I can't think of anything to do but go back to Beefy's and keep plodding along, checking on people."

"We're just about out of people we can check," Bob pointed out.

"We're out of people who had an obvious motive," said Jupiter. "We are not out of people who had an opportunity. In fact, we haven't even started on them!"

"The employees at Amigos Press?" asked Pete.

Jupiter nodded.

"I can't quite see any of them swiping that manuscript," said Pete, "but we've tried everybody else."

The three boys rode into West Los Angeles and arrived at the door to Beefy's apartment just as a slender man wearing gaberdine slacks and a seersucker blazer was leaving. He smiled at the boys as he passed them in the hall.

Beefy's usually ruddy face was pale when he let them in. Behind Beefy, William Tremayne paced up and down and shouted.

"It's a conspiracy!" he cried. "They hate me! They've always hated me! Bunch of idiots!"

"Take it easy, Uncle Will," pleaded Beefy.

"What do you mean, take it easy? You haven't been accused of arson!"

"Arson?" cried Jupe. "The fire was arson?"

"'Fraid so," said Beefy. "The man who just left here was from the arson squad. He wanted a list of all the employees at Amigos Press, and he wanted to know who visited the office the day the fire broke out."

"He also wanted to know to whom the insurance money would be paid," said Will Tremayne. "I know what he was *really* saying when he asked that question. He was saying that he thought I set the fire! Well, of course the insurance money will come to me. I handle all of the publishing house's financial affairs. But even if the income from my stocks *is* down . . ."

"Uncle Will, are you in trouble?" asked Beefy.

"Just a bit short of ready cash," said Will Tremayne. "Nothing important. Nothing that won't right itself in time. Now don't *you* start! It was bad enough talking to the arson investigator. I wasn't anywhere near Amigos Press when the fire started I was here at home with you."

"Whoever started the fire didn't have to be

there," said Beefy. "You heard the man. It was an incendiary device using magnesium and a battery-operated clock. It could have been put into the cupboard under the stairs anytime after six in the morning."

"You think I did it!" shouted Will Tremayne.

"I didn't say that," declared Beefy. "I only think an alibi isn't any good in this case. The arsonist was probably miles away when the fire began."

"Grear!" said Will Tremayne. "He did it! He's always hated me. Dull little mole of a man! He hates anybody who has any style. Or Thomas! What do we know about Thomas? He's only been with the firm for three months!"

"Uncle Will, *you* hired him!"

"Well, he had such good references. But that doesn't really mean anything!"

Will Tremayne went to the coffee table and snatched the lid off the box that usually contained his cigars. "Oh, blast!" he cried. "Empty!"

He glared at Beefy. "It was Grear or Mrs Paulson," he said. "They hate me! They've never forgiven me for taking your father's place! Or it was Thomas. We don't know about Thomas. Now here's what we do. You hired these three boys to find that silly manuscript by that has-been actress. We'll just have them go and watch Grear's apartment, and Mrs Paulson's house, and Thomas's place, too. They'll see what happens after the detective from arson visits them. I'm betting that after they're questioned, the one who did it will give himself away. He'll pack up and run. You'll see!"

Beefy looked helplessly at The Three Investigators.

"Why not?" said Jupiter. "Stranger crimes have been committed for stranger motives. If you'll give us the addresses, we'll go and stake out the three houses. It can't hurt."

"Okay." Beefy went into the small study off the living-room. He was back in a minute with three addresses written on three pieces of paper.

"Now," said Jupiter, "suppose I watch Mrs Paulson's. Bob, you can see what Mr Grear does when he's not working. And Pete can keep an eye on Mr Thomas."

The boys went to the door, with Beefy following them. He came out into the hall, his face grave and concerned.

"You're just doing this to humour Uncle Will, aren't you?" he said.

"Not quite," said Jupiter. "We've checked on all the members of Madeline Bainbridge's magic circle—all that we could find, that is. As far as we can tell, none had any opportunity to take the manuscript, and none of them even knew it was here. Now we had better check the people who *did* know—and who did have the means. Any one of the three could have taken your keys from your desk and had a duplicate set made. All three were at the fire and heard where the manuscript was. Perhaps the visit of the man from the arson squad *will* stir something up. Not that I think the theft of the manuscript is necessarily connected to the fire. But we can't be sure.

"There is one thing you can do for us while we're gone," Jupe added.

"What's that?" asked Beefy.

"Your uncle says he was playing bridge with friends at the time the manuscript was taken. You could talk with his hosts and make sure this is true."

Beefy looked startled. "You suspect Uncle Will?"

"I don't know," said Jupiter. "I'd just like to have his alibi confirmed."

Beefy nodded.

"We'll meet back here after the man from the arson squad has seen our three friends," said Jupiter. The Investigators went off, leaving Beefy standing in the hall, frowning to himself.

13

The Deadly Trunk

HAROLD THOMAS lived in a small apartment house not far from Beefy's building. There was a little park directly across the street, and Pete settled himself on a bench there, tried to ignore the children playing under the trees, and watched.

It was almost an hour before a plain dark sedan parked in front of Thomas's building. The man in the seersucker blazer got out of the car and went into the apartment house.

Pete didn't move, but his heart beat a little faster.

The investigator from the arson squad wasn't in the apartment more than fifteen minutes. Pete saw him come out and get into his sedan and drive away. Still Pete waited.

Half an hour after the detective had left, Harold Thomas came out and glanced up and down the street. He hesitated, looked back at the apartment, then turned south towards Wilshire and strode briskly away.

When Thomas was half a block from the apartment, Pete began to follow him, walking on the opposite side of the street. He tailed Thomas south, across Wilshire, and soon reached a dismal little area where small industrial buildings were clustered together. There were a few apartments, but these were shabby little places with peeling paint and torn screens.

Harold Thomas stopped in front of one of these run-down houses and looked up and down the street. Pete ducked out of sight behind a parked car.

After a moment, Thomas crossed the street and went in through the open gate of a car wrecking yard. He stopped briefly at a shed which stood beside the gate, then went on. Through the fence that enclosed the yard, Pete saw him threading his way past heaps of rusting car bodies and rows of mechanical parts.

Pete frowned, wondering if he should attempt to follow Thomas. Then he decided that if Jupiter had been in his place, he would keep tailing the prim accountant. If there was someone in the shed at the entrance to the yard, Pete would make up a story in grand style—just as Jupiter would. He would say that he was looking for the transmission from a 1947 Studebaker Champion.

But the shed at the gate was empty. Pete went on into the yard, moving carefully and quietly around the stripped-down car bodies and the piles of rusting used parts.

Suddenly Pete stopped still where he was. He had heard a car door open.

The tall boy listened intently. There was a tinny clanking—the sound of pieces of metal hitting together. It came from off to his left. It seemed to be just on the other side of a pile of bumpers.

Pete crept forward and peered around the bumpers. He held his breath. Harold Thomas was not five feet away. He stood next to a grey van that was parked in a clear area in the very centre of the yard. The rear doors of the van were open, and inside the vehicle were piles and piles of film cans. Pete had seen cans of motion picture film many times when he visited his father at the studio where Mr Crenshaw worked. Now Pete stared at the cans, trying to read the labels on their rims. He made out "Cleopatra—Reel I" on one label. Another was marked "Salem Story—III." The wrecking yard seemed suddenly still. There was only the roar of blood in Pete's own ears and the beating of Pete's own heart.

Then Harold Thomas slammed the doors of the van. He walked to the front of the vehicle, climbed behind the wheel, and started the engine. A moment later the van was rolling up the rutted dirt drive that led to the gate.

Pete stayed where he was for a second, stunned by what he had seen. The film cans! It seemed impossible—unbelievable—but it had to be true. Those had to be the films that had been stolen from the laboratory next to Amigos Press. And Harold Thomas had them!

Pete forced himself to move. He ran, not worrying now about caution. At the gate of the salvage yard he was in time to see the van heading north. He tried to read the licence plate, but he couldn't. Whether by accident or not, the plate was too dusty.

Pete ran to the door of the shack near the gate. He saw a desk and a couple of battered chairs—and a telephone. He took Beefy's telephone number out of his wallet with shaking fingers, and dialled.

The telephone at the other end rang once, twice.

Outside the shed, someone was walking on the hard earth that had been packed down by the passage of hundreds of cars and trucks. Pete did not look around. If the owners of the yard objected to his using the telephone, he would simply say that he had to call the police.

Beefy answered at the other end of the telephone.

"Beefy, listen," said Pete quickly. "This is Pete and I'm at a car salvage yard on Thornwall, two blocks south of Wilshire. Tell Jupe and Bob that I just saw . . ."

A shadow fell across the desk, and Pete started to turn towards the door of the shed. But something crashed into the back of his neck. Then the light was gone and the telephone clattered to the floor, and Pete was falling . . . falling . . . falling!

Pete didn't know how long he was unconscious, but when he came to his senses he was in a close, dusty place—a place that smelled of grease and old rubber. It was hot—terribly hot—and it was dark. Pete tried to move, to turn over or stretch out, but he couldn't. There was no room for him to straighten himself. His neck hurt, and there was something hard pressing down on his shoulder. His hands touched metal surfaces that were rough, as if they had been eaten away by rust and time. Pete realized that he was probably still in the wrecking yard. He was locked in the trunk of some old car, and the sun was beating down on it, turning it into an oven.

Pete tried to shout, but his throat had gone dry with heat and fear. He closed his mouth and tried to swallow. There was silence outside in the yard. No one was there. No one would come to help him. He felt a surge of panic. No one would ever come!

14

The Mysterious Second Man

BEEFY'S CAR ROARED DOWN the street, then screeched to a stop at the entrance of the wrecking yard. Bob and Jupe tumbled out and darted into the office.

Bob looked wildly around the empty shack. "Where is he?" he said. "This has got to be the place. It's the only wrecking yard near here."

Beefy stumbled through the doorway. "There's a man coming," he reported. "He looks as if he might work here."

The boys went to the door. A man with thick, curly black hair was striding up the drive, coming from some far corner of the yard. He wore overalls that were stained with grease. "Anything I can do for you folks?" he said cheerfully when he saw Beefy and the boys at the office.

"We're looking for a friend," Jupe told him. "He said he'd meet us here. Have you seen a boy about our age? A tall boy who's muscular and rugged-looking?"

"Sorry," said the man. "Haven't seen anyone like that today."

"But he must have been here!" said Jupiter. "Are you sure you didn't see him?" In spite of himself, Jupe's voice went up. It was rough now with fear and anxiety.

"I haven't seen anybody," insisted the man. "Now look, kid, I'm sorry if you missed your friend, but this is a wrecking yard, not a hangout for kids. And I can't be at this gate non-stop. Hey! Hey, where do you think you're going?"

"Pete's here!" declared Jupe. He had darted past the salvage man and stood in the drive staring at the yard—at mounds of heaped-up car parts, bumpers and doors and engine blocks and rims—and at mountains of balding tyres. "He saw something. It was something important, and he called. And somebody got to him before he could give us the message. He's here. I know it!"

Bob started suddenly and touched Jupe's shoulder. "The trunk of one of these wrecks," he said. "If I had to get rid of somebody quickly, that's where I'd put him!"

The man scowled at the two boys. "You kids are crazy!" he said, but there was an edge of doubt in his voice. "Nobody'd put your friend in one of those cars. Hey, you're kidding me, aren't you?"

"Pete!" Jupe shouted. "Pete! Where are you?"

There was no answer.

"You're not kidding, are you?" said the man, after a second. He stared about at the acres of rusting, ruined cars. "There must be about a hundred cars here that still have their trunk lids," he said. "It could take all day to find the right one."

"No," said Jupiter firmly. "If he's hidden in one of these old cars, we can get to him quickly."

Jupiter began to walk through the jumble of auto bodies. He stepped along purposefully, his eyes darting to one side and then the other. Beefy and Bob trotted after him, and the man in the overalls trailed behind, looking worried. "That kid—your pal—he could be having heat prostration if he's locked up in one of these things."

Jupe didn't answer. He had stopped beside the body of an old blue Buick. He pointed. There was a thick coat of dust over the remains of the car, but on the lid of the trunk there was a place where the dust had been disturbed and the paint showed through, clear and still fairly blue.

"Was that trunk lid open before now?" demanded Jupe.

"It . . . it could have been," said the man.

"Get a crowbar, will you?" said Jupe. "I think someone saw the open trunk lid, shoved Pete inside, then slammed the trunk shut, disturbing that dust!"

The salvage man didn't question Jupe now. He disappeared briefly, then returned with a crowbar. He jammed the tool in under the trunk lid. Then he and Beefy both leaned on the crowbar. Metal groaned as the trunk lid was forced open.

"Pete!" Bob darted forward.

Pete lay curled in the trunk. He didn't stir.

"Good grief!" The salvage man raced off towards the office. He returned in seconds with a towel which was soaked and dripping.

Pete was sitting up by this time, with Jupiter supporting him one one side and Bob on the other.

"Okay," he said. His voice was barely a whisper. "I'm okay. Just hot in there. Not enough air."

"Take it easy, kid," said the man. He dabbed at Pete's face with the towel. "I'm going to call the cops! I could have wound up with a corpse in one of my cars!"

"Pete, what happened?" said Jupiter.

Pete took the towel and held it to his face. "I saw Harold Thomas leave his apartment and come here," he reported. "I tailed him. There was a grey van parked here among the wrecks. He opened the back doors and looked in. It was full of film cans."

For an instant no one spoke. Then Bob said, "Great jumping catfish!"

"The Bainbridge films!" exclaimed Beefy. "Harold Thomas had them?"

"Sure looked like it," said Pete. "I saw a few of the labels. After he checked the films, Thomas got into the van and drove away. That's when I tried to call you and didn't quite make it."

"So Thomas stole the films," said Jupe. "He could have set the fire, too, to draw attention away from the robbery at the film laboratory."

"He must have noticed you as he drove away,"

said Bob. "He came back and bopped you while you were trying to make your telephone call."

"No." Pete frowned, remembering the incident. "It wasn't him. The guy who hit me didn't come from the street. He was walking towards the office from someplace inside the wrecking yard."

Bob's eyes went to the man in overalls.

"Oh, no!" cried the man. "It wasn't me! I don't know what all this is about, but it wasn't me. I wouldn't hit anybody. Listen, I've got kids of my own. I find kids poking around here, I just yell at them and chase them over the fence!"

"I believe you," said Jupiter. "But if Pete is sure it wasn't Harold Thomas, there had to be another man."

"Thomas's confederate," declared Bob. "Remember, there were two hold-up men who stole the films."

"Clever of them to hide the van with the films here, where there are hundreds of other vehicles," said Jupe. "But they took a terrible chance." Jupe looked at the owner of the yard. "You could have started stripping it, or . . ."

"The grey van?" said the man. "No. I wouldn't touch that grey van. A guy was paying me to let him park it here."

"Oh?" said Jupiter.

The man looked terrified. "Something stolen in it?" he said. "I didn't know there was any stolen property involved. I run a clean operation. There aren't any hot cars on my lot. Listen, are you guys going to call the police?"

"Do you want us to?" said Jupe.

"They'll never believe me," said the salvage man. "I don't know anything about stolen property, but they'll never believe me. This guy came driving in in that grey van see. He's about so tall, with dark hair slicked back."

"Thomas," said Beefy.

"That wasn't his name," declared the salvage man. "He had a funny name. Puck. Mr Puck, that's what it was. He said he didn't have any place to park his van at home. He said he couldn't park it on the street in front of his house because he's in a two-hour parking zone, and he'd get a ticket. So he wanted to know if he could leave the van here in the yard. I know that sounds kind of screwy now that I hear myself saying it, but it sounded okay then. So I figure, what the heck? It's ten extra bucks a week. Why not?"

"Because he's a crook, that's why not!" said Bob.

"Okay, okay. How was I supposed to know that?"

"Never mind," said Jupiter. "It doesn't matter now. And let's not notify the police. They wouldn't believe any of us. What we have to do now is get evidence."

"The stolen films are evidence," declared Pete. "Good solid evidence!"

"True. But Thomas has had time to hide them someplace by now. Maybe . . . maybe if we can get into his apartment, we can find something else that would be incriminating."

Pete stood up and took a step or two, as if testing his legs.

"You okay?" said Bob anxiously. "Are you going to be well enough to go with us?"

"Yes. I'm okay now."

"Then let's go," said Jupe. "Only let's be careful. Thomas could have been warned by now. He could be waiting for us."

"And there's that second man," said Bob. "We know he exists. We'd better watch out for him."

15

The Vanishing Suspects

"I'M GOING IN WITH YOU," said Beefy Tremayne after he pulled to the kerb in front of Harold Thomas's apartment building.

"Fine," said Jupiter, looking appreciatively at Beefy's broad shoulders. "We may need all the muscle we can get. Anyone who would put Pete into the trunk of that car and leave him there is bound to be dangerous."

The Three Investigators and Beefy went up the path and into the vestibule of the little apartment house. There were only four doors. One of them had a nameplate beside the doorbell that said "Harold Thomas."

Beefy rang the bell firmly. "Thomas?" he called. "Are you there?"

No one answered.

Jupiter put his hand on the doorknob and turned it. "Careful," said Bob in a low voice. "These guys are dangerous. You said it yourself."

Jupe pushed the door wide, and the boys and Beefy looked into a living-room that was quiet and orderly to the point of being bare.

"Mr Thomas?" called Jupe. He walked through the living-room and peered into an immaculate kitchen. The others followed him, and they explored the little square hall between the living-room and the bedroom, then went into the bedroom.

A closet door stood open. Except for a number of empty hangers, the closet was empty.

"Too late!" said Jupe. He went to the dresser and pulled open one drawer after another. They were all empty.

"He's gone!" said Bob.

Jupe looked at his wristwatch. "It's almost two hours since Pete saw him drive away. The second man had plenty of time to warn Thomas. Thomas and his confederate hid the films somewhere. Then Thomas came back here, packed up, and left."

Beefy stood awkwardly and watched while the boys searched the apartment. They found nothing —nothing but immaculate emptiness.

"We knew Harold Thomas was a tidy man," said Jupe at last. "He's also extremely well organized. With almost no warning, he's been able to clear out of here and not leave a trace. Well, that only makes sense. The theft of the Bainbridge films was well organized. It took place on the very day the films were delivered, and at a time when there was no one in the laboratory except one technician. Just by sitting in his office and looking across to the building next door, Thomas could have learned the routine there. But how did he know that the films were going to be sold to Video Enterprises, or that they'd be delivered to that laboratory?"

Jupiter turned to Beefy. "Did Thomas have much contact with Marvin Gray when Gray came into your office?"

"No. None that I know of."

"Hm!" Jupe's eyes were fixed on the floor next to the sofa. He bent and picked up something. "Just about the only thing in this apartment to show that Thomas was ever here," he said, and he held up a matchbook for the others to see. "The table next to the sofa is wobbly. Thomas must have jammed this matchbook under the leg to steady it."

"Just what you need!" said Bob in a mocking tone. "In the Sherlock Holmes stories, the great detective finds a collar button and immediately he can tell all about the suspect, including the fact that he was born in Ireland and that he likes kippers with his tea. You have a matchbook which is doubtless a priceless clue. Tell us about Harold Thomas!"

Jupe turned the matchbook over in his hands, and there was a strange smile on his face. "It's from the Java Isles Restaurant," he said. "From the address, I'd say that's quite near Amigos Press. In fact, Thomas could have been having dinner there the night of the fire. Except that of course he stopped first to rob the film vault."

"So?" said Pete.

"The Java Isles is an Indonesian restaurant," said Jupiter. "And suddenly it all fits together! When Harold Thomas persuaded that man at the car wrecking yard to let him park the van there, he said his name was Mr Puck. There's a character in Shakespeare called Puck. He's a sprite who goes around making trouble, and he has a second name. It's Robin Goodfellow!"

"Goodfellow?" cried Bob. "Charles Goodfellow was one of Madeline Bainbridge's magic circle!"

"Right!" said Jupiter. "The missing member of our coven. We know that Charles Goodfellow was raised in Holland, and many Dutch people are fond of Indonesian food because Indonesia was once a Dutch colony. Harold Thomas was also fond of Indonesian food, since he patronized the Java Isles Restaurant."

"Wow!" said Pete. "Harold Thomas is the same person as Charles Goodfellow! He was a member of the coven and he knew everybody."

"And how did he learn about the sale of the films? Which member of the coven told him? Or did he just happen to know someone at Video Enterprises? Jefferson Long, or someone else entirely? We can speculate on that all day without getting an answer. But we do know he stole the films."

"Maybe he swiped the manuscript, too," said Bob. "He knew where it was and he could have had a set of keys. He could have duplicated a set from the ones Beefy kept in his desk at the office."

"He could have set the fire too," said Pete.

"But why would he take the manuscript?" wondered Beefy. "How could that manuscript hurt him?"

Jupiter shrugged. "Who knows? Madeline Bainbridge may have written something that would expose him, even after all these years."

"I think we'd better call the police," said Beefy. He stood up. "It will be awkward explaining to them how we know all the things we know, but we have to call them. The Bainbridge films are involved, and they're of inestimable value. I think we'd better call them from my apartment. We don't really have any right in here, you know."

During the short drive to his home, Beefy grew more and more excited. "This will be a load off Uncle Will's mind!" said Beefy as he let himself and the three boys into the apartment. "We can definitely tie Thomas in with the theft of the films, and if the police can turn up some solid evidence to tie him in with the fire, Uncle Will is off the hook!"

Beefy went through the apartment, calling to his uncle. There was no answer.

"That's funny," said Beefy. "He left here right after you left this morning. He said he was going to play golf. He ought to be back by now."

Suddenly uneasy, Beefy went into his uncle's bedroom. The boys in the living-room heard a closet door open, and then heard a thumping and a clattering as Beefy knocked several things over.

After several minutes, Beefy appeared again in the living-room. "He's gone," he said. "He must have come back here while we were out and packed a small suitcase. There's one missing. He's . . . he's panicked and he's running. Now we can't call the police. They'll think he *did* set that fire."

"They often do think that, when suspects vanish," said Jupiter, "and are we sure—are we really sure—that he didn't?"

16

The Sleeping Beauty

"JUST BEFORE WE LEFT here this morning, I asked you to call the people who played bridge with your uncle the night the manuscript was taken," said Jupiter to Beefy.

"I did," Beefy replied. The young publisher looked haggard. "Uncle Will didn't arrive for the bridge game until almost ten-thirty. He said there'd been a minor accident on Beverly Drive and he'd been held up in traffic."

"So he could have set the fire at Amigos Press, and he also could have taken the manuscript from this apartment," said Jupe.

Beefy nodded. "I can't imagine Uncle Will as an arsonist, and yet he did have a motive. He was short of money. But why on earth would he steal the Bainbridge manuscript?"

Jupiter scowled and pulled at his lower lip—a sign that he was thinking furiously. "Could there be something damaging about *him* in that manuscript? Did he know Madeline Bainbridge when he was younger? Maybe that's why he always speaks of her so scornfully!"

Jupiter thought some more, then sighed. "No matter which way we turn, we keep coming back to the mysterious Madeline Bainbridge. Only she knows what's in her manuscript, and only she could tell us who might want it suppressed. We've just *got* to talk to her—and we have to talk to her when Marvin Gray isn't around. For whatever reason, he's too obstructive."

"But how do we reach her?" asked Beefy. "She doesn't answer the telephone. She doesn't go out. Perhaps she doesn't even open her own mail."

"You can call Gray and set up a lunch date," Jupe suggested. "Tell Gray you have something important to discuss with him and it has to be over lunch. Then pick a good restaurant and make sure the lunch lasts a couple of hours. That will give us time to get to Madeline Bainbridge."

"But . . . but what'll I discuss with Gray?" said Beefy.

"Someday you're going to have to tell him about the missing manuscript," said Bob.

"But . . . but you were going to get it back!"

Jupiter shook his head. "It's been gone for three days, and few things are easier to destroy than a manuscript. We are probably not going to get it back, and sooner or later Marvin Gray will have to be told. You can call him now and ask him to meet with you to discuss something very important."

Beefy groaned. "Okay. I'll do the best I can."

Beefy went into the den to make the telephone

call. When he came back into the living-room a few minutes later, he said, "Okay. I'm meeting Gray tomorrow at twelve-thirty at the Coral Cove in Santa Monica."

"Good," said Jupiter.

Peter was scowling. "You're so sure we're going to get in to see Madeline Bainbridge," he said. "Maybe she doesn't answer the door when Gray's not around. Or maybe that Clara Adams will block you. And don't forget there's a dog there—a big Doberman!"

"I haven't forgotten anything," said Jupiter. "I think we can see Madeline Bainbridge—if we're determined enough."

But at noon the next day, even Jupiter had some qualms. He and Pete and Bob had ridden their bicycles up the Coast Highway, and then had taken the paved mountain road to the turn-off a quarter of a mile from Madeline Bainbridge's front gate. There they took shelter with their bikes amid the oleanders that grew raggedly on the edges of Bainbridge's fields.

"We'll see Marvin Gray when he drives down to the highway," said Jupe to his friends. "Let's hope that he doesn't let the dog out on to the grounds before he goes. If he does and we meet the dog, we'll just stand still and call for Madeline Bainbridge to come and rescue us."

He looked out from behind the oleanders. A car was turning on to the road from the Bainbridge ranch.

"Here comes Gray," said Bob.

A dark grey Mercedes swept past the boys, throwing up a cloud of dust. When it had disappeared down the road towards the highway, Jupiter, Pete, and Bob pushed their bikes out on to the gravel road. They pedalled through the gate and up through the lemon grove. The dog did not appear, but when the boys reached the house and got off their bicycles a frantic barking began inside the house.

"Oh, great!' moaned Pete.

They went up the steps to the porch and Jupiter rang the bell. They heard it buzz angrily somewhere in the back of the house. They waited.

When no one came, Jupiter rang the bell again. "Miss Bainbridge!" he shouted. "Miss Adams! Please open the door!"

The dog began to leap at the door. The boys could hear him clawing at the wooden panels.

"Let's go, huh!" said Pete.

"Miss Bainbridge!" called Jupiter.

"Who is it?" cried a voice on the other side of the door. "Quiet, Bruno! Good boy!"

"Miss Adams?" said Jupiter. "Miss Adams, please open the door. My name is Jupiter Jones and I have something important to say to you."

There was a fumbling with the locks. The door opened a few inches, and a pair of faded blue eyes looked out in sleepy wonder. "Go away," said Clara Adams. "Don't you know you're not supposed to ring this doorbell? No one rings this doorbell."

"I have to see Miss Bainbridge," said Jupiter. "I'm from her publisher."

"Publisher?" echoed Clara Adams. "I didn't know that Madeline had a publisher."

Clara Adams stepped back, letting the door open wide. Her hair straggled around her face and her eyes, which looked full at Jupe, did not really seem to see him.

"Miss Adams?" said Jupe. "Are you all right?"

She blinked sleepily, and the dog growled.

"Could I ask you to shut the dog up someplace?" said Jupe. "He's . . . he's making us all nervous."

Clara Adams took the dog's collar and, walking unsteadily, led him back to the kitchen, where she shut him in. Then she came back into the hall. "Madeline?" she called. "Where are you, Madeline? Come here, please. There are some boys here to see you."

Jupe looked around. He saw the living-room, with its austere wooden chairs. He saw the dining-room, and its backless benches. He listened, but he heard no sound except the slow ticking of the clock in the living-room. "This place is like an enchanted castle," he said. "Nothing moves here, does it? No one comes or goes."

"Comes or goes?" said Clara Adams in her drowsy, rusty voice. "Who should come? We don't see anyone any more. Once we were very lively here, but no more. And when Marvin isn't here . . ." She stopped and seemed to be puzzling something out. "What happens when Marvin isn't here?" she said. "Hard to remember. He's always here. Only where is he now?"

"She acts as if she's been drugged," Pete whispered to Jupiter.

"She certainly does," agreed Jupe. He turned to Clara Adams. "Where is Madeline Bainbridge?" he demanded.

Clara Adams waved vaguely, then sat down on a chair and began to doze off.

"Something's fishy here!" exclaimed Bob.

The three boys searched then, peering into all the rooms on the ground floor. It was Pete who was the first to run up the stairs to the first storey. In a big corner bedroom with windows that looked out towards the sea, he found Madeline Bainbridge. She was lying on a homespun coverlet on a big wooden bed. She wore a long brown gown, and her hands were folded on her bosom. Her face was very quiet. It seemed for an instant that she wasn't even breathing.

Pete touched her on the shoulder. "Miss Bainbridge?" he said softly.

She didn't stir. Pete shook her, and called her name again—and again. Jupe's words went through his mind. An enchanted castle where nothing moved. And here was the sleeping beauty in the castle.

But why didn't she wake? Why didn't she answer him?

"Jupe!" shouted Pete. "Bob! Come quick! I found Madeline Bainbridge, but I'm . . . I'm not sure I found her in time!"

17

Conspiracy!

"MAYBE WE'D BETTER phone for an ambulance," said Bob.

"Hold it," said Pete. "She's coming round."

Madeline Bainbridge made a small, protesting sound. Then she opened her eyes, which were glazed and blurry with sleep.

"Miss Bainbridge, I made some coffee," said Bob. "Try to sit up and drink some."

"Madeline, dear!" Clara Adams sat down on the bed, holding her own cup of coffee. "Do wake up. These young men seem so concerned. I don't understand it, but they say Marvin gave us something to make us sleep."

The actress pulled herself up so that she was sitting on the bed. In a dazed fashion she took the cup of coffee that Bob held out to her. She sipped a little, making a wry face as she did so. "Who are you?" she said groggily to the boys. "What are you doing here?"

"Drink your coffee and we'll tell you," said Jupiter. "You need to be awake to hear our story."

When Madeline Bainbridge looked more alert,

Jupiter started explaining. "We work for Beefy Tremayne," he said. "We're trying to help him find your manuscript."

"My manuscript?" said Madeline Bainbridge. "What manuscript? I don't understand."

"Your memoirs, Miss Bainbridge," said Jupe.

"My memoirs? But I haven't finished my memoirs. Why, I know you boys! You're the ones who came down the hill the other night when we were having our . . . our . . ."

"You were celebrating the Sabbat," said Jupiter. "We know all about it, Miss Bainbridge."

Jupe then held out a pill bottle to the actress. "We found this in the bathroom off the back bedroom. It's sleeping medicine of some sort. We think Marvin Gray put it in something you ate or drank to make sure you wouldn't answer the door or the telephone while he was away."

The actress looked at the little vial. "Drank?" she said. "We drank some tea that Marvin made for us."

"Has it happened before, do you think?" asked Bob.

"Several days ago I fell sound asleep in the middle of the afternoon. It was very odd. Clara slept all afternoon, too."

"Probably the afternoon Gray brought the manuscript in to Beefy Tremayne," said Jupe.

"You keep prattling on about a manuscript, and about a person named Beefy Tremayne," said Madeline Bainbridge. Her voice was strong and assured now. "What exactly are you talking about?"

Jupiter told her then, with Bob and Pete chiming in from time to time to add details. The boys told of Gray's delivery of the memoirs to Amigos Press. They told about the fire at the publishing house, and about the theft of the manuscript from the Tremayne apartment.

"Your signature is on the contract for the publication of your memoirs," said Jupiter. "A forgery, I presume."

"Certainly," said Madeline Bainbridge. "I never signed a contract. And my memoirs are still here in this house. I worked on them only last night. Look in that big chest at the foot of the bed."

Pete opened the chest and the boys looked. There was a thick heap of papers, all handwritten.

"Marvin Gray must have copied them by hand," said Bob. "Then he delivered the copy to Beefy Tremayne. And then what? Did he arrange to have it stolen, perhaps by Charles Goodfellow?"

"Goodfellow?" said Madeline Bainbridge. "Don't tell me that little thief is still in town!"

"So you know Goodfellow is a thief," said Jupe.

"I know he was one. I caught him trying to take a diamond necklace out ot my dressing-room on the set of *Catherine the Great*. I was going to call the police, but he persuaded me he'd never do anything like that again. Then later I found out he'd been going through the women's purses while we were filming *The Salem Story*."

"A real sneak thief," said Bob. "Did you put anything about that in your memoirs?"

"I may have. I think I did mention it."

"That would have given him a motive. Even though he wasn't using the same name, he might be afraid he'd be found out. And with the theft of the films from the laboratory—"

"What films?" said Madeline Bainbridge.

"Your pictures that were sold to Video Enterprises," said Jupe. "Did you know that the negatives of all your films had been sold to television, or is that something that Marvin Gray engineered while you were asleep, too?"

"Oh, no! I knew all about the sale of the films. Marvin handled the negotiations, and I signed a contract. But you say the films were stolen?"

"They were, from a laboratory next door to Amigos Press, just before the fire started. They're being held for ransom. No doubt they're safe enough, and no doubt the ransom will be paid. Did you know that Jefferson Long came out here the night of the theft to interview you? He does a TV series on law and order."

"No!" exclaimed Madeline Bainbridge. "Is that who was here? Marvin just told me that he had some business clients coming by. I stayed out of the way, as usual. I pay Marvin to deal with the outside world."

"You were keeping out of sight the next afternoon, too, when Beefy and I came here," said Jupe. He shook his head. "Miss Bainbridge, you've put yourself into a dangerous position, having no contact at all with anyone outside this house."

The actress sighed. "I let Marvin handle everything for me. It begins to look as if he handled it too well, doesn't it?"

"He must intend to swindle you out of the advance from Amigos Press for your manuscript," said Jupiter.

"That scoundrel?" said the actress. "I can't believe it!" Then she stopped and thought for a moment. "Yes," she said, "I can believe it. He was always greedy. But to think he's been deliberately withholding information and using drugs on me! Ugh! It's horrible!"

"Wouldn't it be interesting to see how much he's swindled you, and what he plans for the future?" asked Jupe. "Why not play along with him? Pretend to be asleep when he comes home today, then watch him. I'll give you a telephone number where we can be reached—a couple of numbers, in fact."

"Oh, Madeline, let's do it!" said Clara Adams. "I've always wanted to play a joke on Marvin. He's so grumpy and serious all the time."

"It will be a marvellous joke," said Madeline Bainbridge. "I can't think of a single reason why I should trust you boys, and yet I do. I have to see exactly what Marvin is up to."

"It could be almost anything," said Bob. He held up a bright orange matchbook. "I found this in a jar with a lot of other matches when I lit the stove to make coffee. It's from the Java Isles, that restaurant where Harold Thomas ate."

"So Gray and Thomas probably were in touch," said Jupe. "Gray could have been involved in some way with the theft of the films, with the theft of the manuscript, and even with the fire at Amigos Press."

"Isn't this fun?" said Clara Adams. "Like those nice old-fashioned movies where the heroine helps the detectives. We're going to nail him!"

18

The Search

IT WAS ALMOST four when The Three Investigators rode up in the elevator to Beefy's apartment. They found the young publisher pacing and brooding.

"How was your lunch?" Bob inquired brightly.

"As lunches go, it wasn't bad," said Beefy. "But it was a lousy business conference. I bought Marvin Gray the most expensive lunch on the menu, and I also ordered a couple of martinis for him. He ate and drank everything, and when he began to glow like a neon sign I decided he was ready. I told him the bad news about the Bainbridge manuscript.

"Well, it didn't get to him right away. He'd been talking about Jefferson Long, and how tickled he was that Long was the one assigned by the television station to interview Madeline Bainbridge after her films were stolen. Then Bainbridge couldn't see him. Gray really enjoyed that. Gray doesn't like Long a bit. I guess Long was uppity to him in the old days, when Gray was just a chauffeur.

"How interesting," said Jupiter.

"It gets more interesting," said Beefy. "When Gray finally got the message that the Bainbridge memoirs were missing, he sat and blinked like a stuffed owl for a couple of seconds. Then he decided that it was all a terrible shame, but maybe not quite as terrible as I might think. He decided that maybe Madeline Bainbridge wouldn't mind writing her memoirs all over again—provided I paid her double the amount of the advance we'd agreed on when she signed the contract."

Beefy put his head in his hands and shuddered. "What a mess!" he said. "I've got to get going again on Amigos Press. I've got to rent an office and get the staff together and go to work. But it's all going to take money, and I don't have any money without Uncle Will. Maybe I don't have any money even *with* Uncle Will, because if he shows up here he may be charged with arson. And the insurance company sure isn't going to pay him for burning down his own property. And then Gray tells me I should double the advance I pay Madeline Bainbridge!"

Beefy look up at the boys. "I hope that very expensive lunch wasn't a total waste of time," he said. "Did you manage to talk with Madeline Bainbridge?"

"We sure did. Bob wrote up a report while we were coming here on the bus."

Bob grinned and took his notebook out of his pocket. He then summarized briefly the events of the day. As Beefy listened, his woebegone expression gradually disappeared. By the time Bob finished, Beefy was grinning broadly.

"I'm off the hook!" he cried. "I don't owe any advance!"

"You do not," said Jupiter. "Also, we found evidence that Gray—as well as Thomas—dined at the Java Isles restaurant. Gray could have tipped Thomas off about the films. He could have been involved in that crime."

"He could have planted the incendiary device at Amigos Press, too," said Beefy. "He had the opportunity, as did Thomas. What a relief! Of course, we'll have to prove it. Nobody will take our word for it. Is there some way we can tie the fire to Gray, so we can clear Uncle Will? Wouldn't the arsonist have to buy magnesium for his incendiary device, for example?"

"He would certainly have to get it somewhere," said Jupe cheerfully. "Suddenly a number of things have become clear to me. Beefy, may we search your apartment?"

"Search?" Beefy sat up straight. "What for?"

"For the magnesium," said Jupiter.

"Jupe, you've got to be kidding! You can't really believe that Uncle Will set that fire. Look, I know he's not the most lovable guy in the world, but he isn't a criminal. Can you picture him hiding in a corner someplace, putting together a gadget that will go off at six o'clock and destroy my office? It isn't in character."

"I know it isn't," said Jupiter. He stood still, his

head to one side as if he were listening to voices that the others couldn't hear. "There's been something that's been bothering me about this case all along—something I've been missing. I know what it is now. It's something I saw, but I didn't see. Not at the time. As a matter of fact, there were a couple of things that I missed. We can verify them when we need to. The evidence will be there. I know it will."

"Jupe's having one of his brainstorms," said Pete, who was amused by the look on Beefy's face.

"It'll be okay," Bob assured the young publisher. "Jupe has a photographic memory, and if he's just recalling something he heard or saw, you can bet he's recalling it *exactly*!"

"Now I'd like to search the apartment," said Jupe. "I'd like to start with your uncle's room."

"Well . . . well, I guess it's all right," said Beefy. "If it will help."

Beefy led the way to the big bedroom that had windows facing to the south. The boys followed him.

Jupe went directly to the closet, which had sliding doors that took up almost an entire wall of the room. He pulled back the doors. The boys saw dozens of neatly tailored jackets and racks of gleaming shoes.

Jupiter started to go through the pockets of the jackets. He worked quickly. After only a few minutes he said, "Aha!" and pulled a strip of metal from the pocket of a tan flannel jacket.

"Don't tell me that's magnesium!" said Beefy.

"I'm sure that any laboratory test would confirm it," said Jupe. "And now I am quite positive that your uncle didn't set the fire. He just panicked and ran. If he were guilty, he'd have taken the magnesium with him."

The telephone on the table beside the bed began to ring.

"Want to answer that?" said Jupiter to Beefy. Jupe looked almost joyful. "I gave this number to Madeline Bainbridge and asked her to call here or at Headquarters in Rocky Beach if Gray did anything unusual. Perhaps that's her now."

Beefy picked up the telephone and said, "Hello." He listened for a moment, then handed the telephone to Jupe. "It *is* Madeline Bainbridge," he said, "and she wants to talk with you."

19

Setting the Trap

JUPITER STOOD with the telephone to his ear, and as he listened to Madeline Bainbridge, he grinned.

"That's fine, Miss Bainbridge," he said at last. "I was hoping for something like this. Now if Gray offers you something to eat or drink tonight, just pretend to take it. And warn Miss Adams. Both of you want to be alert when Gray has his visitor. Of course, you'll pretend to be asleep.

"I think we'll be able to solve the entire series of crimes, and get proof that will satisfy the police. But there is one other person who should be there —Jefferson Long."

The telephone made muted noises which the others in the room with Jupe couldn't understand. Jupe nodded. "It won't be difficult at all," he said. "You can reach Long through Video Enterprises. He does his television series for them. Tell him that there are some things about him in your memoirs, and that you're having doubts about some of them. Say you want to go over the incidents with him because you'd hate to embarrass him in public. That will surely bring him running.

Tell him to be at the house about nine."

Jupe waited, then nodded and smiled. "Fine. We'll be there, so see that the dog isn't loose."

He hung up. "Madeline Bainbridge overheard Gray making a telephone call to someone named Charlie. He told Charlie to come tonight, and he'd have the money ready for him."

"Charles Goodfellow!" exclaimed Pete.

"It seems likely," said Jupiter. "And if Madeline Bainbridge is able to get Jefferson Long to the house, we should be able to settle everything at once. I think it will be very interesting to see Long and Gray and Goodfellow all together. Who wants to come along?"

"Are you kidding?" cried Pete. "I wouldn't miss it!"

"I hope I'm invited," said Beefy.

"Certainly," said Jupiter. "I think we should bring your uncle, too. He's had a bad time, and he might appreciate seeing the situation straightened out."

"Great," said Beefy. "How do we find Uncle Will?"

"Where does he buy his cigars?" said Jupiter.

"Huh?" said Beefy.

"Yesterday morning, just before he left here, he was out of cigars," Jupe pointed out. "From what I've seen of Mr William Tremayne, I'd guess that he smokes something expensive and unusual. Am I right?"

Beefy nodded. "He smokes special Dutch cigars.

You can't get them everywhere."

"He took his car when he left here, didn't he?"

Again Beefy nodded.

"Well, if he's driving, the cigars may not help us. But I have a feeling he isn't driving anymore than he has to. He was very frightened, and he may think the police are looking for him already. But wherever he is, he's smoking. Smokers always smoke more when they're nervous. Where does your uncle buy his cigars?"

"In a little shop on Burton Way," said Beefy. "They order the brand especially for Uncle Will."

"I'm betting they've seen him in the last twenty-four hours," declared Jupiter.

In a very few minutes, Beefy and The Three Investigators were in Beefy's car, headed towards Burton Way.

"You'd better talk to the shopkeeper," advised Jupe. "He'll think it's odd if any of us start asking questions. Tell him you and your uncle had a quarrel and your uncle walked out. Ask him if he's seen your uncle."

"That sounds like some dumb soap opera," said Beefy.

"Don't worry. The man will believe you," Jupe predicted. "It sounds more likely than the truth, which is that your uncle is hiding from the police."

Beefy laughed, and he pulled in to the kerb in front of a small shop called The Humidor. "You coming in with me?" he asked the boys.

"You go, Jupe," said Bob. "It would look weird

if all three of us went in."

Jupe and Beefy got out of the car and went into the shop, where a white-haired man in a chamois waistcoat was dusting a counter.

"Mr Tremayne, good afternoon," said the man. "Don't tell me your uncle is out of cigars already."

"No. Uh . . . not exactly." Beefy's face was redder than usual. "He bought some cigars yesterday, did he?"

"Why, yes," said the man at the counter.

"Good," said Beefy. "We . . . uh . . . we had a quarrel yesterday, you see, and he walked out and hasn't come back. I'd like to find him and . . . uh . . . apologize. Did he . . . er . . . mention where he might be going when he was here?"

"No, he didn't."

Jupiter murmured something in Beefy's ear.

"Did he have his car with him?" asked Beefy.

"Why, I don't believe he did," said the man. "He seemed to be walking. He turned towards the right when he went out, if that's any help to you."

"That's fine," said Beefy. "Thanks very much."

He fled from the shop, tripping over the door-step as he went.

"How you guys manage to do this sort of thing all the time, I can't imagine," he declared when they were back in the car. "My mind went blank about four times."

Jupiter was grinning. "The shopkeeper said your uncle was on foot, so there's a chance he's staying somewhere in the neighbourhood. Drive down that way, slowly."

Beefy started the car. They rolled along for a short distance, with Jupe scanning the fronts of the various buildings along the way. Suddenly Bob leaned forward and pointed towards a small motel on the left side of the street.

"Aha!" said Jupiter. "Exactly the sort of place Mr Tremayne would want—ultra-respectable, and the sign in front advertises locked garages. He could get his car out of sight."

"The only garage that's closed right now is the one next to room twenty-three," said Pete.

Beefy pulled into the parking place next to the room, and an instant later he and The Three Investigators were knocking on the door of number 23.

"Uncle Will!" called Beefy. "Open the door."

There was no answer.

"Mr Tremayne, we know you didn't set the fire at Amigos Press," said Jupe. "We're going to trap the real criminals and prove that they did it. If you want to come along and help us set our trap, you'll be welcome."

There was silence for a minute more. Then the door to room 23 swung open. "Very well," said William Tremayne. "You can come in if you want to, and we'll talk about it."

20

The Surprise Party

AT DUSK THAT evening, Beefy drove up from the Coast Highway to the Bainbridge ranch. The Three Investigators were with him, and so was his uncle. For once, William Tremayne did not seem bored. His eyes were eager, and from time to time he touched his pocket, where he carried a revolver.

There was a Mercedes parked near the porch of the Bainbridge house. Behind it was a light-coloured Ford. "The Ford must belong to Harold Thomas," said Jupe. "The Mercedes is Gray's. Let's make sure that neither of them leave here before we're ready for them to leave."

Pete smiled and tried the doors of the two cars. Neither vehicle was locked. "Very good," said Pete. He took a pair of pliers out of his pocket and went to work. In seconds he had disconnected the ignition wires, disabling both cars.

"I'll stay here and keep out of sight until Long arrives," he told the others. "Good luck."

Jupiter, Bob, and the Tremaynes started up the front steps. There was an outburst of barking. It sounded muffled and far away.

"Sounds like somebody locked Bruno in the cellar," said Bob.

"Thank goodness," exclaimed Jupe. "I don't want to meet him face to face. Not when he takes his orders from Marvin Gray."

Jupe then strode boldly across the porch and rang the doorbell.

After a moment, there were footsteps in the hall. "Who's there?" called Marvin Gray.

"I have something for Mr Gray," said Jupe loudly.

The front door opened and Marvin Gray looked out.

"Mr Horace Tremayne would like to talk to you," said Jupiter. "So would Mr William Tremayne."

Jupiter stood aside, and Beefy stepped forward and planted his foot squarely on the doorsill. "Sorry to be dropping in so late," he said, "but somehow this seemed like the right moment."

Gray drew back. "Mr Tremayne! What is it? I'd invite you in but . . . but the ladies have retired and I don't want to disturb them."

Beefy shoved the door wide and stepped across the threshold. His uncle and the boys were close behind him.

"You've met Jupiter Jones before," said Beefy. "Jupiter is a very curious young man. Some people might even say he's nosey. We're here tonight to help him satisfy his curiosity—and mine!"

Gray retreated as Beefy and Jupiter advanced.

He backed into the living-room, where Harold Thomas was looking around wildly, as if trying to find a place to hide the package he held.

"That's the manuscript, isn't it?" said Jupiter. "You stole it from Beefy Tremayne's apartment the same night you burned down the Amigos Adobe."

Thomas dropped the package, which broke open and spilled loose pages across the floor. He spun around and started towards the windows.

"Stay right where you are, Thomas!" shouted Uncle Will.

Thomas looked over his shoulder and saw that William Tremayne had a gun. He stopped where he was.

Beefy picked up the manuscript from the floor. He flipped through it, stopping a few times to read a paragraph or two. Then he grinned. "This is it," he said.

Jupe went back out into the hall. "Miss Bainbridge?" he called.

"She's asleep," said Marvin Gray. "She's asleep and you'd better not wake her up. I don't know anything about that bunch of papers, or the guy who brought them here, and—"

Gray stopped talking, for Madeline Bainbridge was coming down the stairs. Her white-gold hair was done up in a knot at the nape of her neck, and on her handsome face there was a smile that was both sad and triumphant.

"Marvin," she said, with a scolding note in her

voice. "You hadn't planned to see me awake, but here I am."

Her eyes went to Harold Thomas, who stood gaping. "So, Charles. It *is* you. I wish I could say that it's pleasant to see you again, but it is not."

She seated herself in the living-room. Clara Adams scampered down the stairs, her faded eyes twinkling with enjoyment. She perched on a window-sill behind Madeline Bainbridge.

"What is that?" asked the actress, pointing to the sheaf of papers which Beefy held.

Beefy smiled and handed the manuscript to the woman. "I'm Horace Tremayne, Miss Bainbrdge," he said, "and this is the manuscript that Marvin Gray delivered to my office the day your films were stolen from the laboratory in Santa Monica."

Madeline Bainbridge looked quickly at the first page. "An exact copy of the manuscript that is upstairs in my room," she said. "How tiresome of you, Marvin, to copy my manuscript and sell it. Didn't you know you couldn't possibly get away with it? Sooner or later I'd have found out."

There was a step on the front porch, and the doorbell buzzed.

"That will be Jefferson Long," said Madeline Bainbridge. "Would you let him in, Clara?"

Clara Adams darted out of the living-room. She returned in a few moments with Jefferson Long walking behind her. Long's face was stoney as he looked at the group in the room. He bowed to Madeline Bainbridge.

"I didn't know you were having a party this evening," he said.

"The first one in years," said Madeline Bainbridge. "Do sit down while our young friend here—his name is Jupiter Jones, and I think you've met—tells us why Marvin Gray copied my manuscript and sold it to Mr Tremayne. He then arranged to have it stolen. At least, I imagine that's what happened."

"That's precisely what happened," said Jupiter. "Here's the story. A certain amount of it is speculation, but I think we'll be able to verify it.

"Some time ago, Marvin Gray happened to run into Charles Goodfellow, alias Harold Thomas, in an Indonesian restaurant called the Java Isles. At this meeting, Gray learned that Goodfellow was employed by a book publishing firm. Gray has a nimble brain, and it occurred to him that he could copy the memoirs which Miss Bainbridge was writing, sell the manuscript to Goodfellow's employers, then either bribe or blackmail Goodfellow into stealing the manuscript to prevent its publication. He wanted to prevent publication because Miss Bainbridge was almost ready to find a publisher herself, and it would never do to have two publishers preparing to bring out the memoirs of the same actress.

"Gray thought he could pocket the advance that is usually paid to an author upon delivery of a manuscript. Once the counterfeit manuscript was destroyed, he could stall Beefy Tremayne for a while, and then perhaps sell the true manuscript to Beefy all over again. He was counting on the fact that Beefy would feel terribly guilty about losing the first manuscript.

"Goodfellow agreed to go along with Gray. He didn't want Gray to expose him to his employers as a person who once tried to steal a necklace from Madeline Bainbridge. First Goodfellow set Amigos Press on fire, hoping to destroy the manuscript. When he learned that he had failed, he went to Beefy's apartment and stole the manuscript. I am sure he used keys which he had duplicated from the set in Beefy's desk. I think we'll find that duplicating keys is a habit with Goodfellow, and that he had keys to the pharmaceutical firm where he used to work. That's where he got the magnesium that he used to construct the incendiary device that started the fire. Magnesium is used in pharmaceuticals. It was foolish of him to plant magnesium in William Tremayne's jacket pocket when he took the manuscript. He went too far when he did that."

Madeline Bainbridge looked up. "What about the theft of my films?" she said to Jupiter. "The counterfeit manuscript was nothing compared to that theft. They'll get a quarter of a million dollars for that one!"

"The thieves collected the ransom for the films late this afternoon, Miss Bainbridge," said Jupiter. "It was on the news at six o'clock. Video Enterprises left a package containing two hundred and fifty thousand dollars in small bills in a parking lot near the Hollywood Bowl. They were advised by telephone a short time later to recover the films from a van parked in Bronson Canyon."

Madeline Bainbridge looked surprised. "That's wonderful, but . . . but Marvin was home this afternoon!

"Marvin Gray wasn't involved in the theft of the films," said Jupe. "Charles Goodfellow was—and Jefferson Long was the mastermind."

"What?" shouted Long. "You brat! How dare you?"

"We have a witness," said Jupe. "And we can tie both Goodfellow and Long in with the missing films."

"You're crazy!" cried Long.

Jupiter didn't answer. He went out into the hall and opened the front door." Come on in," he said.

A moment later he appeared in the living-room doorway. Pete was at his side.

"Surprised?" Jupe said to Jefferson Long. "You should be. Because the last time you saw Pete, he was unconscious, and you were locking him in the trunk of a wrecked car!"

21

Crash!

"YOU'RE MAD!" said Jefferson Long. "I don't have to stay here and be insulted!"

"We would all appreciate it if you'd stay," said William Tremayne, and he waved the gun in his hand.

Long sat back and folded his arms. "Very well," he said, "if you're going to use strong-arm tactics."

Beefy grinned. "Okay, Jupe. Go ahead."

"When I was in his office the other day," said Jupiter, "Jefferson Long said that he'd researched a television series on drug abuse, and that he'd found that some people employed in legitimate drug firms were involved in the illicit distribution of drugs. My guess is that in the course of his investigation, Long happened to meet Harold Thomas, who was an employee at one of these firms. Like Marvin Gray, Long recognized Thomas. He knew he had once attempted to steal a necklace from Miss Bainbridge, and that he was once known as Charles Goodfellow. Perhaps he checked up on Goodfellow. Perhaps Goodfellow had a record. He might even be a fugitive. In any case, Long could blackmail him—or at least put considerable pressure on him."

"Is that the way it was, Long?" asked Beefy.

"I have nothing to say," announced Jefferson Long.

"Thomas, was Long blackmailing you?" the young publisher asked his former accountant.

"I'll talk to my lawyer," said Thomas. "No one else."

"All right," said Jupe, undismayed. "Now at about this time, something happened which disturbed Long very much. Video Enterprises decided to purchase Madeline Bainbridge's films, and they told Long that the series on drug abuse would be cancelled because the money originally budgeted for this series would be used for the films.

"No doubt Long was very bitter, especially since he had never liked Madeline Bainbridge. And it must have occurred to him that he could get back at Madeline Bainbridge and could also make a great deal of money if he could steal the films.

"Jefferson Long knew he could find out what day the films would be transferred to the laboratory in Santa Monica. Anyone at Video Enterprises could learn this. It wouldn't be any secret. But before that day came, while the negotiations for the films were still going on, he had Harold Thomas apply for a job at the business firm closest to the laboratory. Doubtless Thomas would have accepted a much humbler position than accountant to get into Amigos Press.

"By the time the films arrived at the laboratory, Thomas knew the routine at the film lab perfectly. He saw most of the employees leave at five that day. Then he left Amigos Press, joined Long, and they forced their way into the lab. They knocked out the technician who was there, loaded the films into a van, and drove off.

"Thomas was, of course, busier than he had planned to be, since that afternoon Marvin Gray had delivered the counterfeit memoirs from Madeline Bainbridge. Thomas had to plant his incendiary device and later, after helping to steal the films, return to Amigos Press to check on the fire. Then he had to burgle Beefy's apartment."

"You haven't a shred of evidence to back up what you're saying," declared Jefferson Long.

"But we do have evidence," said Jupiter. "I overlooked it for a long time, but when I finally remembered, everything else fell into place.

"You interviewed Marvin Gray the night the films were stolen. You said that the hold-up was perpetrated by a couple of men. It was a statement that sounded perfectly correct. But there was no way you could have known that there were two men. There could have been three or four or ten—or perhaps only one. Even the police didn't know, because the technician you knocked out to get those films did not regain consciousness until the next day—hours after the interview with Marvin Gray was taped."

Jefferson Long shrugged. "I assumed that there would be at least two men."

"You might claim that," said Jupiter, "but what are you going to say about the fingerprints?"

"Fingerprints?" said Long. "What fingerprints?"

"You saw Pete follow Harold Thomas from his apartment to that car wrecking yard in Santa Monica. No doubt Thomas was going to move the films because the arson squad was getting too close to him and making him nervous. Seeing Pete made *you* nervous. You tailed Pete, and when you realized that he had seen the van, you decided he had to be put out of the way. You didn't know who he was or what he was up to, but you couldn't take a chance. When he tried to call for help, you hit him on the head and stuffed him into the trunk of that old car. And when you slammed down the trunk lid, you left your fingerprints."

Jefferson Long opened his mouth to protest, and then closed it again.

"How could you!" said Madeline Bainbridge. "How could you do that to a mere boy?"

"And then there's the money," said Jupiter brightly. "The ransom for the films. It was only paid this afternoon. I would not be surprised if at least part of it is still in Thomas's car. And perhaps there's some in Long's car as well. There hasn't been time to put it in a secure hiding place. Shall we look and see what we can find?"

"No!" shouted Thomas. He lurched towards the door.

Beefy tackled him, bringing him crashing to the floor, and sat on him. The material of Thomas's suit ripped, and a wallet spilled out on to the floor, together with three key chains, all loaded with keys.

"Aha!" cried Beefy.

"I'll have the law on you!" shouted Thomas. "You don't have a search warrant!"

Gray had been standing in a corner of the room, quiet and almost forgotten. As Beefy held up the keys, Gray moved. He raced past Beefy, brushed Uncle Will to one side, and was out the front door and thundering down the steps before anyone could move.

"Marvin!" cried Madeline Bainbridge.

"He won't get far," Pete assured her. "I fixed his car so that it won't start. His and Thomas's and Long's, too. We'll just call the police and they can pick Gray up as he's hiking down the hill."

But then, from outside, there came the sound of a car engine starting.

"Oh, blast!" shouted Beefy. "That's my car! He's taking my car! I left the keys in the ignition!"

Peter raced for the kitchen and the telephone, and Madeline Bainbridge went to the window. "He'll be sorry," she said, as the car pulled away from the house. "He'll be very sorry."

Jupiter and Bob saw the car's headlights flash through the lemon grove. The car reached the road and skidded into the turn. It didn't slacken speed one bit.

"Oh my gosh!" yelled Bob.

The watchers in the ranch house heard tyres screech on the road, and Madeline Bainbridge screamed.

An instant later, there was a ripping of metal and a smashing of glass as the car crashed sideways into a tree. And then there was silence—a silence that seemed deadly. Madeline Bainbridge stood with her hands to her face, her blue eyes wide with horror.

"Madeline!" Clara Adams went to her and put her arms around her. "Madeline, it wasn't your fault!" she said.

"It's like the last time. It's like Ramon all over again." And Madeline Bainbridge began to weep.

"It's only a coincidence," said Jupe.

Pete had come back into the room. "The sheriff is coming," he said. "I'll call again, and I'll ask them to send an ambulance."

Jupiter nodded as he, Bob, and Beefy headed outside to see how Gray was. "It's an unfortunate way to end things," he said, "but I think we can say that this case is closed."

22

Mr Hitchcock Declines an Invitation

A WEEK AFTER THE Bainbridge films were recovered by Video Enterprises, The Three Investigators called on Alfred Hitchcock. "I assume that you have been getting your notes in order," said the famous motion-picture director as Jupiter, Pete, and Bob took seats across the desk from him.

Bob smiled and handed a file folder to Mr Hitchcock.

"Excellent," said the director. "The accounts in the press of the recovery of the money paid for the Bainbridge films were interesting enough, but I have looked forward to learning more about the part you lads played in the whole affair."

Mr Hitchcock began to read, and he did not speak again until he had perused the last sheet of paper in the folder. "Fascinating!" he said at last. "A woman victimized by her own guilt—a woman who hid herself away from the world and trusted no one."

"No one but the wrong man," said Pete. "He could have gone on swindling her, too, if we hadn't taken the bull by the horns and gone in that afternoon to find her drugged and asleep. The accountants are going through her affairs now, to see exactly how much Gray took from her. Gray's in the prison ward at the County Hospital. The district attorney will bring charges when he has more complete information."

"He's fortunate to be alive," said Mr Hitchcock. "Ramon Desparto did not survive when his brakes failed on that road. Of course I can't believe that Miss Bainbridge really caused either of those accidents. I admire mystery inordinately, but believing that a witch can cause a car accident is . . . well, a bit much, wouldn't you say?"

Jupiter smiled. "We'll never really know, I guess," he said. "Beefy Tremayne is convinced that Gray hit the tree simply because Gray took Beefy's car, and Beefy and all of his possessions are doomed to malfunction."

"That should be of some comfort to Madeline Bainbridge," said Mr Hitchcock. "She seemed distressed at the thought that she might actually have harmed both Desparto and Gray."

"She's trying to get over the idea that she's to blame," said Bob, "and she's trying to use her magical powers to help Beefy overcome his clumsiness. Actually, he doesn't seem to be tripping over so many things or knocking over so many things as he used to, so maybe the magic works."

"Also, his uncle isn't giving him such a hard time," Pete reported. "Having William Tremayne around would upset anybody and make them drop things."

"Tell me," said Mr Hitchcock, "did the police really find Jefferson Long's fingerprints on that wrecked automobile? The one in which Pete was shut up?"

The boys grinned. "That was Jupe bluffing," said Bob. "He was hoping Long would say something and give himself away. Actually, it was Thomas who cracked and ran—or tried to run. That was just as well. Thomas had all those keys in his pocket, and they included the keys to Beefy's apartment and the keys to that pharmaceutical firm where Thomas used to work. So Jupe was right when he guessed where the magnesium came from."

"Even without that bit of evidence," said Jupe, "the police have plenty on both Long and Thomas. The ransom money for the Bainbridge films was in the trunk of Long's car. He'd been so sure of himself that he hadn't even bothered to move it. He was promptly arrested. Now he's out on bail, and finding that his long friendship with law enforcement people is dead. They know now that he was just using them and they're furious.

"As for Thomas, whose real name actually *is* Goodfellow—he's served time for a number of things, including grand larceny and arson. He tried to go straight and keep an honest job, but he simply couldn't. The pharmaceutical firm where he used to work has had an audit, and there are shortages in the accounts there. Thomas simply couldn't keep from stealing, no matter what."

"How fortunate that he is no longer in circulation," said Mr Hitchcock.

"But Madeline Bainbridge *is* in circulation again," reported Bob. She's decided that it's dangerous to be a hermit, so she's giving a party next Friday evening. She's inviting the local members of her old magic circle."

"Are they coming?" asked Mr Hitchcock. "You state in your report that the ladies seemed to dislike Madeline Bainbridge."

"They do, but they're also curious," said Jupiter. "They want to see what she looks like after all these years, so they're coming. And they'll find her so unchanged that I'm sure they'll believe that she is a witch! A good witch, perhaps, but a witch all the same."

"No doubt the simple life she's led has helped to keep her young," said Mr Hitchcock.

"Wonderfully young," Jupe reported. "She says she owes it all to health foods—she's eaten nothing else for more than thirty years."

"I trust she doesn't consider deadly nightshade a health food," commented Mr Hitchcock dryly.

Jupe laughed. "No, she told us that it was reserved for use in certain Sabbat potions—in very tiny quantities, of course. By the way, you are also invited to her party if you'd like to come. We told her we were seeing you today and she said she'd always admired your work. Would you care to dine on health foods at the ranch above Malibu? Or are you nervous about eating with witches?"

Mr Hitchcock considered this, and then he shook his head. "Please convey my regrets to the lady," he said. "I am not at all nervous about witches—especially charming ones like Miss Bainbridge. However, when it comes to health foods—well, there I draw the line!"